CRIMINAL INTELLIGENCE

THE HISTORICAL FOUNDATIONS OF FORENSIC PSYCHIATRY AND PSYCHOLOGY

A DACAPO PRESS REPRINT SERIES

CRIMINAL
INTELLIGENCE

BY
CARL MURCHISON

DA CAPO PRESS • NEW YORK • 1983

Library of Congress Cataloging in Publication Data

Murchison, Carl Allanmore, 1887–
  Criminal intelligence.

  (The Historical foundations of forensic psychiatry and psychology)
  Reprint. Originally published: Worcester, Mass.: Clark University,
1926.
  1. Criminal psychology. 2. Crime and criminals — United States. I.
Title. II. Series.
HV6093.M82 1983   364.2'4   82-072285
ISBN 0-306-76183-1

Published by Da Capo Press, Inc.
A Subsidiary of Plenum Publishing Corporation
233 Spring Street, New York, N.Y. 10013

CRIMINAL INTELLIGENCE

CRIMINAL INTELLIGENCE

BY

CARL MURCHISON, Ph.D.

Professor of Psychology in Clark University

CLARK UNIVERSITY
WORCESTER, MASSACHUSETTS
1926

PRINTED IN THE UNITED STATES OF AMERICA
BY THE
HEFFERNAN PRESS, SPENCER, MASS.

PREFACE

This material is offered for the special consideration of lawyers, psychologists, sociologists, social workers, and all those who have to do with the formulation of criminal law, the treatment of criminals, and the moulding of public opinion concerning the enemies of organized society.

During the period immediately following the signing of the Armistice, while the writer was acting as Chief Psychological Examiner at Camp Sherman, Ohio, it became possible to begin the collection of data presented in this book. The writer had been asked to appear before a joint session of the Finance Committee of the Ohio General Assembly, for the purpose of presenting some data in regard to the prevalence of feeble-mindedness in the State of Ohio. At that meeting, the writer met Warden Thomas of the Ohio Penitentiary, and he suggested that a mental test be given to the prisoners in that prison. General Smith, Commanding General of Camp Sherman, generously allowed the author the necessary leave, and ordered any help needful. All the men in that prison who could be spared from their duties were marched in groups into the dining hall and given the Alpha mental test under the same conditions described for recruits in Volume 15 of the Memoirs of the National Academy of Sciences, except that no literacy requirement was used.

Shortly afterwards, the writer gave the Alpha test to the criminals in the Ohio Reformatory, the Ohio Penitentiary for Women, the Ohio Prison Farm, the Illinois Penitentiary at Joliet, the Illinois Reformatory at Pontiac, the Indiana Penitentiary, the Indiana Reformatory, and various criminal groups in and about Camp Sherman.

In the fall of 1922, Doctor E. A. Doll, during a conversation in the Princeton Psychological Laboratory, generously offered to give to the writer any data whatever that the writer might care to select from the files in Trenton, New Jersey. In that way, data on about twelve hundred cases from the New Jersey Penitentiary came into the writer's possession.

In the spring of 1923, the writer received permission from the warden of the Maryland Penitentiary, Colonel Sweezey, to give the Alpha test to his prisoners. Colonel Sweezey also very generously allowed the writer access to his files. In that way, a large amount of new and interesting data was gathered.

It seemed best, for purposes of publication and for clarity of treatment, to divide the data into four groups: white native born men, white foreign born men, negroes, and women.

No assumption is made as to whether the Alpha test measures anything that is native. For the practical purpose of this book, intelligence is whatever is expressed quantitatively as measured by the Alpha test. This makes practical comparison possible. Professional psychologists will readily understand the practical necessity for this division of discussion.

A detailed bibliography will not at present be attached to this book, since there are so many excellent bibliographies already accessible. The best bibliography devoted exclusively to the problems discussed in this book is "A Bibliography on the Relations of Crime and Feeble-Mindedness," by L. W. Crafts, in the Journal of Criminal Law and Criminology, 1916, 7, pp. 544-555. It consists of 210 references, chiefly English and German. A good and more recent bibliography is contained in "Deficiency and Delinquency," by J. B. Miner, 1918, pp. 324-343. For the general field of Criminology, probably the most complete and most important bibliography is contained in the Bulletin of the New York Public Library, Volume 15, pp. 259-317, 350-371, 379-446, 463-501, 515-557, 567-621, 635-714. This bibliography consists of 359 pages of approximately 10,000 references. It is dated 1911, and is practically complete for that date. The Index Catalogues of the Library of the Surgeon General's Office is another such bibliography. For a restricted popular bibliography along the same lines, the reader is referred to "Guide to Reading in Social Ethics and Allied Subjects," 1910, pp. 109-121, formulated by a group of teachers in Harvard University. For criminal law and criminology, the most important reference is "A Preliminary Bibliography of Modern Criminal Law and Criminology," John H. Wigmore, 1909, Bulletin No. 1 of the Gary Library of Law, Chicago.

Practically all of Part I and Part II has been published in the Journal of Criminal Law and Criminology, while much of the remainder of the text has appeared in The Pedagogical Seminary And Journal of Genetic Psychology. Thanks are extended to these two journals for permission to reprint.

Sincere thanks are extended to The Johns Hopkins University, Clark University, Professor Knight Dunlap, Doctor E. A. Doll, to the wardens of the various prisons from which the data came, and the numerous prisoners who so effectively gave their co-operation. Miss Helen Burfield assisted in compiling the tables of Chapter 21 and Chapter 22. Mr. Robert Nafe assisted in compiling the tables of Chapter 23. Mr. Ralph Gilbert assisted in compiling the tables of Chapter 25, Chapter 27, and Chapter 31. Miss Priscilla Pooler assisted in compiling the tables of Chapter 26, Chapter 29, and Chapter 30. Sincere thanks are extended to these four graduate students.

The writer wishes to express warm appreciation for the faithful and intelligent assistance of his secretary, Miss Harriet C. Marble.

CARL MURCHISON.

Clark University,
Worcester, Massachusetts.

TABLE OF CONTENTS

PART I. OPINIONS AND NORMS

Chapter   Page
1. PRE-WAR CONTEMPORARY OPINION 15
2. THE IDEA THAT CRIMINALS ARE FEEBLE-MINDED 28
3. EXTENT TO WHICH ARMY AND CRIMINAL NORMS ARE
   REPRESENTATIVE 33

PART II. WHITE NATIVE-BORN MEN CRIMINALS

4. SOME GEOGRAPHICAL CONCOMITANTS 41
5. INTELLIGENCE AND TYPES OF CRIME 58
6. INTELLIGENCE AND RECIDIVISM 70
7. LITERACY 97
8. CHRONOLOGICAL AGE 112
9. INDUSTRIAL OCCUPATIONS 124
10. SOME TECHNICAL STATISTICAL RESULTS 133
11. RELIGION 143
12. SEASONAL DISTRIBUTION 148
13. LENGTH OF INCARCERATION 150
14. HEIGHT AND WEIGHT 152
15. SOME MARITAL CONCOMITANTS 155

PART III. WHITE FOREIGN-BORN MEN CRIMINALS

16. SOME GEOGRAPHICAL CONCOMITANTS 161
17. TYPES OF CRIME 171
18. RECIDIVISM 188
19. LITERACY 192
20. CHRONOLOGICAL AGE 196

PART IV. NEGRO MEN CRIMINALS

21. SOME GEOGRAPHICAL CONCOMITANTS 201
22. TYPES OF CRIME 220
23. RECIDIVISM 228
24. LITERACY 236
25. RELIGION 243
26. LENGTH OF INCARCERATION 250
27. OCCUPATIONAL CONCOMITANTS 252
28. HEIGHT AND WEIGHT 256
29. SEASONAL DISTRIBUTION 259
30. CHRONOLOGICAL AGE 261
31. SOME MARITAL CONCOMITANTS 270

PART V. WOMEN CRIMINALS

32. SOME WHITE WOMEN CRIMINALS 277
33. SOME NEGRO WOMEN CRIMINALS 282

PART VI. LEGAL PUNISHMENT

34. THE PREVAILING FALLACY OF MATERNALISM 289

PART I

Opinions and Norms

Chapter 1

PRE-WAR CONTEMPORARY OPINION

One of the most important discussions concerning the relation of feeble-mindedness to crime is the following rather extended quotation from Doctor H. H. Goddard's "Feeble Mindedness," page 6-10, published in July, 1914.

"Society's attitude toward the criminal has gone through a decided evolution, but that evolution has been in the line of its treatment rather than of its understanding of him and of his responsibility. Almost up to the present time there has been a practically universal assumption of the responsibility of all except the very youngest children and those recognized as idiots, imbeciles or insane. The oldest method of treatment was in accordance with the idea of vengeance, an eye for an eye. The god Justice was satisfied if the offender suffered an equal amount with those whom he had made suffer. Later came the idea of punishing an offender for the sake of deterring others from similar crimes. This is the basis of much of our present penal legislation. But students of humanity have gone farther and now realize that the great function of punishment is to reform the offender.

"We have had careful studies of the offender from this standpoint. Studies have been made of his environment and of those things which have led him into crime. Attempts have been made to remove these conditions, so that criminals shall not be made, or having reformed, they shall not again be led into a criminal life. A great deal has been accomplished along these lines. But we shall soon realize, if we have not already, that on this track there is a barrier which we cannot cross. Environment will not, of itself, enable all people to escape criminality. The problem goes much deeper than environment. It is the question of responsibility. Those who are born without sufficient intelligence either to know right from wrong, or those who, if they know it, have not sufficient will-power and judgment to make themselves do the right and flee the wrong, will ever be a fertile source of criminality. This is being recognized more and more by those who have to do with criminals. We have no thought of maintaining that all criminals are irresponsible. Although we cannot determine at present just what the proportion is, probably from 25% to 50% of the people in our prisons are mentally defective and incapable of managing their affairs with ordinary prudence. A great deal has been written about the criminâl type and its various characteristics. It is interesting to see in the light of modern knowledge of the defective that these descriptions are almost without exception descriptions of the feeble-minded.

"The hereditary criminal passes out with the advent of feeble-mindedness into the problem. The criminal is not born: he is made. The so-called criminal type is merely a type of feeble-mindedness, a type misunderstood and mistreated, driven into criminality for which he is well fitted by nature. It is hereditary feeble-mindedness, not hereditary criminality, that accounts for the conditions. We have seen only the end product and failed to recognize the character of the raw material.

"Perhaps the best data on this problem come from the prisons and reformatories. It is quite surprising to see how many persons who have to do with criminals are coming forward with the statement that a greater or less percentage of the persons under their care are feeble-minded. They had always known that a certain proportion were thus affected, but since the recognition of the moron and of his characteristics, the percentage is found ever higher and higher. The highest of all come from the Institutions for Juveniles, partly because it is difficult to believe that an adult man or woman who makes a fair appearance but who lacks in certain lines, is not simply ignorant. We are more willing to admit the defect of children. The discrepancy is also due to the fact that the mental defectives are more apt to die young leaving among the older prisoners those who are really intelligent.

"The following list of reformatories and institutions for delinquents with the estimated number of defectives undoubtedly gives a fair idea of the amount of feeble-mindedness. The differences in the percentages are probably due more to the standards used in estimating the defective than to actual differences in numbers. It is the most discouraging to discover that the more expert is the examiner of these groups, the higher is the percentage of feeble-minded found. For example, Dr. Olga Bridgeman, who has made one of the most careful studies on record, finds that 89 per cent of the girls at Geneva, Illinois, are defective.

Institution	Per Cent Defective
St. Cloud, Minnesota, Reformatory	54
Rahway Reformatory, New Jersey (Binet)	46
Bedford Reformatory, New York—under 11 years	80
Lancaster, Massachusetts (girls' reformatory)	60

Lancaster, Massachusetts, 50 paroled girls _____ 82
Lyman School for Boys, Westboro, Massachusetts _____ 28
Pentonville, Illinois, Juveniles _____ 40
Massachusetts Reformatory, Concord _____ 52
Newark, New Jersey, Juvenile Court _____ 66
Elmira Reformatory _____ 70
Geneva, Illinois (Binet) _____ 89
Ohio Boys' School (Binet) _____ 70
Ohio Girls' School (Binet) _____ 70
Virginia, 3 Reformatories (Binet) _____ 79
New Jersey State Home for Girls _____ 75
Glen Mills Schools, Pennsylvania, Girls' Department _____ 72

"The percentages above given are not in all cases the official figures given out by the examiners, but are the author's interpretation based on the facts given in the reports.

"Unfortunately we cannot average the percentages because the reports from which these figures were taken do not always state the number of persons upon whom the estimate is made.

"A glance will show that an estimate of 50 per cent is well within the limit. From these studies we might conclude that at least 50 per cent of all criminals are mentally defective. Even if a much smaller percentage is defective it is sufficient for our argument that without question one point of attack for the solution of the problem of crime is the problem of feeble-mindedness.

"It is easier for us to realize that if we remember how many of the crimes that are committed seem foolish and silly. One steals something that he cannot use and cannot dispose of without getting caught. A boy is offended because the teacher will not let him choose what he will study, and therefore he sets fire to the school building. Another kills a man in cold blood in order to get two dollars. Somebody else allows himself to be persuaded to enter a house and pass out stolen goods under circumstances where even slight intelligence would have told him he was sure to be caught. Sometimes the crime itself is not so stupid but the perpetrator acts stupidly afterwards and is caught, where an intelligent person would have escaped. Many of the 'unaccountable' crimes, both large and small, are accounted for once it is recognized that the criminal may be mentally defective. Judge and jury are frequently amazed at the folly of the defendant—the lack of common sense that he displayed in his act. It has not occurred to us that the folly, the crudity, the dullness, was an indication of an intellectual trait that rendered the victim to a large extent irresponsible."

The above extended quotations constitute the text of Doctor

Goddard's entire discussion of the problem of criminality. It
has been given in order that there may be no possibility of mis-
representation. It is a typical discussion of its type, and is
probably as important as any discussion developing the same
point of view. The reader should carefully consider its errors,
the more important of which are as follows:

(1)   The majority of the institutions reported are institutions dealing wholly or in part with girls. It is not valid to
assume that the mentality of incarcerated girls is typical of
criminals in general. Relatively few girls are in prison, and
the list of their crimes differs from the catalogue of male
crimes. Also, there is always a possibility that a woman who
gets to prison is either overwhelmingly guilty or completely
unable to vamp the jury. Certainly, nothing said about the
female criminal should be applied without investigation to the
male criminal

(2)   All the cases reported are juveniles. It is not valid
to assume that the mentality of juveniles is typical of criminals in general. Most incarcerated juveniles are either friendless or helpless. Powerful men may land in prison, but the
children of powerful men do not land in juvenile institutions.

(3)   The number of cases is not given, neither is the method
of their selection described. It is not valid to assume that the
mentality of selected cases is typical of the entire group, unless the sample is large and is selected according to chance.

(4)   It is admitted that various standards were used in estimating the degree of defect. Those standards are not described, and it is thus impossible for one to be certain that the
standards were valid.

(5)   It is stated that the percentage of defectives increased
with the skill of the examiner, it being inferred that a completely perfect examiner would find that all criminals were
mentally defective.

(6)   A definition of "mental defectiveness" is not given.
The facts reported are facts of interpretation only, the interpretation getting its significance from an interpretation or a
definition that is not given.

(7)   The discussion deals with crminals in general, yet there
is not a single report from a penitentiary. The criminals that
society is greatly concerned about are the criminals that are
incarcerated or ought to be incarcerated in the state penitentiaries. It is not valid to assume that one can infer the mental
condition of penitentiary inmates.

In 1913, just one year previous to the appearance of "Feeble-Mindedness," appeared Doctor Charles Goring's monograph on "The English Convict." This monograph is in many respects the best reported investigation of the subject that has yet appeared. It is tedious, but as accurate as one could well be at that time. The following extensive quotations are taken from pages 237-263, the selections being made with great care, in order that Doctor Goring's position may be made clear.

"Our inquiry turns to the twofold problem connected with the mental differentiation of the criminal; in other words, our object is (1) to test whether, as it has been stated, the criminal is characterized by special degrees of mental characters—the so-called mental stigmata of a criminal type, and (2) to measure the extent to which criminals, committing different kinds of crime, are distinguished from each other, and to which criminals, as a class, are differentiated from the law-abiding public, by general mental capacity.

"Of these two directions now taken by our inquiry, the former leads to results of relative minor importance criminologically, and possibly, in the opinion of many, to conclusions of doubtful validity; the second path should lead us among some statistical facts of the very first significance, whose soundness should be beyond question.

"Unfortunately, mental characters, unlike physical attributes, cannot be submitted to precise measurement by calipers or tape; but we certainly would not assert on that account that all observations of mental characters are necessarily untrustworthy, and valueless as material for scientific generalization. Estimates of mental qualities can be made; and every day the world, colloquially, does make them, with a more or less broad degree of accuracy. Many judgments of the kind, truly, are quite valueless; for, in so many cases, distinctions of mental and moral characters are animated by personal feeling. Yet, because opinions, biased by feelings of generosity or malice, must be ignored, that is no reason for disregarding the judgments of a just critic on the grounds that mental characters are beyond the range of legitimate observation. Personal estimations of both mental and physical attributes, if carefully made and recorded by an unbiased and disinterested investigator, whose personal equation can be estimated and allowed for, represent evidence of substantially the same character, and of equal value scientifically, as that produced by measurement.

"For examples of the alleged mental stigmata, we might

quote from many pages of *L'homme Criminel*. The moral insensibility of the criminal and his lack of foresight, his vanity, vengefulness, and cruelty, his gambling proclivities, his lasci" vousness and laziness, and, particularly, the absence of remorse in him are asserted, not upon statistical evidence, but as general impressions, received by observation of prisoners. These impressions, indeed, are rarely supported by figures, but mainly by the citation of particular cases, and by the descriptive methods of the old psychologists.

"The criminal may be vengeful, lazy, cruel, and lascivious; but the mere assertion of these generalizations—where credence may be given to the narrative of particular cases, in support thereof—is idle in the absence of random sample statistics of criminals, and of comparative statistics, relating to the law-abiding community. Moreover, many of the stigmata quoted refer to mental and moral qualities that are either inseparable from the committing of crime, or that can hardly be investigated statistically in a law-abiding community; the criminal may be without remorse for, he may be vain-glorious of his crimes, for instance, but how are these mental states of the criminal to be tested with the corresponding conditions of the law-abiding subject who has not committed crimes for which to be remorseful? And this is why we stated that our inquiry as to the existence of mental stigmata is of minor importance criminologically, and that it may, in the opinion of many, lead to conclusions of questionable validity. On the other hand, the differentiation of the criminal in general mental capacity is a subject which should lead to fruitful results when investigated statistically, being, as it is, a matter of the greatest practical importance, and one that may prove to be very much at the root of many criminological problems.

"The following is a list of the qualities we are going to examine:

(1) Four characters referred to in the schedule of data, under the heading *Temperament,* viz.:

(a) *Suspiciousness,* recorded within the three categories of suspicious, trustful and medium: the last category registering degrees of this character, within a range intermediate between the two extremes, and corresponding to the observer's impression of what might be styled an average degree of suspiciousness.

(b) *Sanguine,* as opposed to phlegmatic, temperament; with an average category connecting these two extremes.

(c) *Contented,* opposed to *discontented,* frames of mind: neural tendencies in these respects being classified within an intermediate category.

(d) *Egotism,* recorded within the three categories of egotistic, sympathetic, and betwixt.

(2) *Temper,* recorded within a category of good or amiable or serene temper, as opposed to a category of bad temper; which latter, on one hand, is denoted by hot and violent forms, and, in another direction, includes sullen and violent forms, of temper.

(3) *Facility,* this, like temperament and temper, is a fundamental form of human personality; and convicts are classified within the three categories of facile, obstinate, and medium, according to their tendency to respond or to be resistant to the influence of other personalities and of circumstances.

"The classification of convicts, according to the degree in which they possess the above-mentioned mental attributes, was determined from general impressions received during many months' intimate acquaintanceship with their respective personalities. Their graduation, in respect of the next three attributes, was determined by objective tests corresponding more closely to measurements.

(4) *Conduct,* graduated by the average number of reports for bad behavior during one year's sojourn in prison.

(5) *Suicidal tendency,* estimated from the recorded facts of attempt to commit suicide.

(6) *Insane diathesis,* measured by the fact that a convict has, or has had, been in an asylum at some time of his life.

"...We conclude that there is no relation between the temperament of criminals and the kind of crime they commit. We see, however, that criminals are highly differentiated in general intelligence; and also that the more feeble their intellignce may be, the more marked become the average degrees of melancholic tendency, of discontentment, and especially of suspiciousness, displayed by criminals. Accordingly, to the above-stated conclusion that the criminal temperament is unrelated to crime, we would add that any apparent differentiation in this respect results solely from the fact that criminals, according to the crimes they commit, differ widely in general intelligence or mental capacity.

"...We conclude that criminals convicted of violent crimes are distinguished by hot and uncontrolled tempers, and by obstinacy of purpose, but that other differences of temper, will, and conduct, amongst convicts, depend entirely upon the grade of their general intelligence.

"...We conclude that criminals convicted of violent crimes, as well as being distinguished by hot and uncontrolled temper, and by obstinacy of will, are also differentiated from other types of convicts by increased suicidal tendency, and by an augmented proclivity to be eventually certified insane; but that in other respects—excluding a slightly increased degree of egotism displayed by offenders technically convicted of fraud,—differences of temperament, temper, will, conduct, suicidal tendency, and insane proclivity, amongst convicts, depend entirely upon their differentiation in general intelligence.

Marked unlikeness of mental characters exists between criminal groups, precisely as it abounds in great variety among different sections of the law-abiding community; but this unlikeness is associated, not with a differentiation in criminal tendency, but with the criminal's differentiation in general intelligence.

"...Our conclusion now is, not that criminals are a mentally undifferentiated class of the community, but that no mental differentiation exists in criminals beyond an extent accounted for by differences in general intelligence.

"According to estimates of their general intelligence, our criminal subjects have been distributed within the five categories called intelligent, fairly intelligent, unintelligent, weak-minded, and imbecile, respectively. Regarding this classification, we may say that it consists chiefly and originally of a two-fold division of criminals into weak-minded or imbecile, and non-weak-minded—a simple separation, based upon broad estimates of mental capacity, which we may safely state to be entirely free from the personal equation of any one observer. The conditions, in fact, determining the official description of a prisoner as weak-minded are so manifold and stereotyped, and include the exercise of, and agreement between, the judgments of so many individuals, that the actual relative weak-mindedness of the officially designated weak-minded prisoner may be regarded as an established fact, subject to no greater amount of error than attaches to any general concensus of verdict between men whose metier is it to express opinions upon technical subjects of the kind we are considering. In regard to the subsequent sub-division of the non-weak-minded class into intelligent and unintelligent, the latter category is also fairly free from the bias of personal equation, consisting mainly, as it does, of individuals concerning whose possible fitness for the weak-minded contingent the verdict of general opinion is doubtful or divided; nevertheless, since the unintelligent category also includes certain other persons who, in the opinion of only one observer, possess mental qualifications not far removed from those of the officially designated weak-minded, the unintelligent is not, on this account, so clearly defined as the mentally defective category. Finally, the division between the fairly intelligent and the unintelligent was determined solely by one individual's opinion; and, consequently, this part of the whole classification might be regarded as possibly biased by the influence of personal equation.

"It is clear, from the above description, that between criminals classified as intelligent, fairly intelligent, and unintelligent respectively, there is no definite line of demarcation, but that the several categories merge into each other. The only question is whether the original basis of the whole classification—the separation of mentally-defective criminals from the non-defective contingent—can be similarly regarded? Do the weak-minded or mentally defective form a distinct breed of criminals, naturally, as well as conventionally, separated from other offenders, in the same way as criminal lunatics are naturally distinguishable from those who are mentally sound? Or, should the term weak-minded be regarded only as conventional nomenclature, describing the notion of a class of offenders whose general intelligence has been found to be below a certain mark on the scale of common intelligence?

"We fully admit the existence of pathological imbeciles, or of persons whose natural mental development has been indisputably interfered with by morbid processes; and, while we cannot gainsay that some hidden pathological process may be at the source of the mental defectiveness of the weak-minded class of prisoner, we must, nevertheless, insist upon the fact that, apart from exceptional cases, the inherent defect in mental mechanism, postulated for individuals belonging to this class, if existent, has never yet been demonstrated as fact, and rests only upon the plausibility of an unverified hypothesis. On the other hand, if we turn to the facts, we find these harmonizing with the conclusion that the kind of mental defectiveness we are discussing is only a convenient description of the relative degree of general intelligence of persons displaying objectionable and dangerous degrees of mental qualities, which, in, some degree, are shared equally by persons of all intelligence grades.

"The Mental Capacity of the Population at Large. So far as we are aware, only one authoritative enumeration has been made of adult persons with defective intelligence in these islands; and, for particulars of it, we turn to the Report of the Royal Commission on the Care and Control of the Feeble-minded, published in the Midsummer of 1908. It will be found stated in this Report that, at the outset of their inquiry, the Commissioners were confronted with the difficult fact that no trustworthy estimate was existent, and that no statistics were available upon which to base an estimate of the proportion of mentally defective persons in the population of Great Britain. Accordingly, one of the first acts of the Commissioners was to make an enumeration of the defectives in sixteen representative districts of the British Islands; and their estimate, from the returns of the inquiry, was that .46 per cent of the whole population of England and Wales are mentally defective.

"In addition to the Inquiry in the general population already referred to, the directors of the Commission on Feeble-Minded-ness also appointed medical investigators to make an enumeration of mentally defective persons in local prisons, casual wards, shelters, etc., and the report of the investigators was to the effect that 242 such persons were found out of 2353 examined, or 10.28 per cent.

"Sir Bryan Donkin, one of the Directors of Convict Prisons, speaking at a conference in Birmingham, said that the bald statement may be accepted that the weak-minded amount to between 10 and 15 per cent of the total number of persons committed to prison; and that the true maximum is probably higher than this. And, later on, he again stated that owing to their inherited incapacities and to certain surroundings, a large number of mental defectives tend to become criminals, and the considerable proportion, even 20 per cent, of so-called criminals or law-breakers are demonstrably mentally defective.

"We see then that Sir Bryan Donkin's minimum estimate of mental defectiveness amongst prisoners generally is identical with that reached by the Feeble-Mindedness Commissioners, viz., 10 per cent; and, moreover, that it very interestingly accords with a minimum estimate of mentally defective convicts, obtained from records embodied in the yearly reports of Directors of Convict Prisons. We may take it then, that all authorities seem agreed upon an approximation of 10 per cent as a minimum estimate of the proportion of mentally defective persons in English prisons generally.

".... Accordingly, against the .46 per cent of defectives in the general population, the proportion of mentally defective criminals cannot be less than 10 per cent, and is probably not greater than 20 per cent. It is clear that criminals, as a class, are highly differentiated mentally from the law-abiding classes."

In spite of the fact that Doctor Goring's discussion is probably the best and clearest on the subject, its errors are none the less very glaring. The more important such errors are as follows:

(1) The report of the Royal Commission on the Care and Control of the Feeble-minded, published in 1908 before any reliable mental tests had been formulated, consisted of an "enumeration of defectives" in the general population. It was found that .45 per cent of the general population was defective mentally. Such report could have included only those persons that had been recognized legally as mentally defective. It could not possibly have included those persons who actually were mentally defective, but were living fairly normal lives among relatives and friends, or were living on the charity of religious and other organized and unorganized charitable organizations. The defectives in the population that actually are legally listed as defective are only the worst and most helpless cases. An estimate based upon the results of mental tests given to the entire population would, depending upon the standard arbitrarily agreed upon, probably be several times as great. It is not valid to assume that the legally listed mental defectives are the only mental defectives in the population. Unless a mental test can be given to large samples of the population, any estimate can be little more than a mere guess.

(2) The report of the same Commission on the percentage of mentally defective criminals consisted of an "enumeration of defective persons in local prisons, casual wards, shelters, etc." It is quite unlikely that representative criminals will be found in "local prisons, casual wards, shelters, etc." Mental defectives, through sheer hunger and helplessness, would eventually gravitate to such places before being sent to regular institutions for the feeble-minded. We might expect the percentage of mental defectives in such institutions to be several times as high as in regular state prisons and penitentiaries. In the light of Doctor Goring's keen insight into the problem he is discussing, it seems strange that he should commit such glaring and self-evident errors.

In 1915, Doctor William Healy published his important book,

"The Individual Delinquent." On page 447, he gives his views in the following two paragraphs: "The subject of mental defect is of great import in the study of delinquency and its causation. Just what percentage of delinquents are feeble-minded appears to be a matter of perennial interest, but well-founded statistics, even if obtained in particular places, may not be applicable to different situations. There can be no doubt that separate reformatory or prison populations if tested would show from 10 to 30 per cent or even more, to be feeble-minded. No essential purpose is subserved by exaggerated statements concerning the proportions which might be found in court work, or in various penal institutions. We might discuss at great length the numbers of mental defectives among offenders from our many notes on the subject; there has been much advance since 1910, when the author was *rapporteur* for this subject at the International Prison Congress and received astonish--ingly variant statements from different institution people, ranging from the opinion that in certain reformatories none were feeble-minded, to the assertion that 40 per cent or more were defective. But the gist of the situation is that mental defect forms the largest single cause for delinquency to be found by correlating tendency to offend with characteristics of the offender.

"Lest there be misapprehension we should here state that even with this clear-cut cause for delinquency, one rarely finds personal characteristics as a sole causative factor of criminalism. Defective offenders, in most cases, upon study prove to be individuals who easily succumb to social temptations, easily learn from vicious examples, easily are stimulated to develop criminalistic trends of thought. In morals they prove themselves wanting in resistance when neglected by their families or by society, so that they have to meet undue temptation and suggestion to immorality. In other words, in these highly representative members of the so-called criminal type one must conclude that the development of criminalism is partially the result of environment as well as of innate tendencies. If one does not believe this, let him study similar defective individuals in the conditions of a good training school for the feeble-minded, and see, under appropriate environment, how small an amount of criminalistic tendency is evolved."

It is interesting that Doctor Healy should be convinced that prison populations, "if tested," would show the traditional minimum of 10 per cent mental defectives. It should also be noticed that Doctor Healy, in the first paragraph, states that mental defect is the "largest single cause of delinquency"; while in the second paragraph he points out that mental defect is largely a concomitant of delinquency.

The extensive quotations in this chapter may seem to the reader altogether too extensive. But the quotations represent the ablest and most distinguished opinion on the problem that can be found in the pre-war literature. In no case had a prison population been tested with a standard mental test, yet all three were convinced that at least 10 per cent of all criminals are mentally defective, and that probably twice that number would be more accurate. No one of the three has suggested comparing the mental distribution of criminals with the mental distribution of the civil population. Rather, all three are discussing qualitative norms that never can be anything but an arbitrary agreement. Probably no man ever lived who was not mentally defective in some way. The large group tests of the American Army were necessary before it could become clear to psychologists that the mental distribution range of seemingly normal persons is perfectly tremendous, and that it is practically impossible to cut off a section of the distribution curve and label it "feeble-minded." It is easy to compare two or more distribution curves with each other, but it is very difficult to interpret each succeeding point on a single distribution curve.

In 1915, the classic writers on the subject were agreed that criminals are largely mentally defective, and there was agreement that 10 per cent was the minimum of defectiveness. In the absence of exact measurements, and the prevailing impossibility of making direct comparisons with large samples of the population, the question arises as to how such ideas ever got abroad in the world.

Chapter 2

THE IDEA THAT CRIMINALS ARE FEEBLE-MINDED.

When the writer visited a large penitentiary for the first time, he had the privilege of watching the inmates go marching by in silent files. He shivered as he watched the ferocious jaws, the stupid brows, the eyes of cunning and beastlike expression. He was convinced that criminals are not like other men. But the idea occurred to him that he might try an experiment on a crowded street-corner. So he went to a busy corner in the heart of the city, took his stand, and watched the passing faces while trying to imagine that he was watching the criminals march by after being released from prison. Almost immediately, the street became filled with ferocious jaws, stupid brows, and the eyes of cunning and beast-like expression.

In Havelock Ellis' book on "The Criminal," there is a comparison of a composite of 30 pen-sketches of criminals with a composite of 30 actual photographs of criminals. The result is amazing, and indicates the large part that imagination plays in the description of criminal types.

After hearing the guards in a certain penitentiary describe in condescending terms their ideas on criminals, the author had an opportunity to compare the mental test scores of the guards with the mental test scores of those same criminals. The average score of the criminals was just 75 per cent higher than the average score of the guards. The only reason the guards continued to live was because the architects of that prison had done their job well.

TRADITION. Religious tradition has undoubtedly had great influence. What perfect idiots Adam and Eve were, carrying on conversation with snakes, and doing things that they could not possibly prevent from being found out. How idiotic the behavior of Judas, even though he had been considered the most level-headed business man in the group. What a perfect ass the Devil was, with his imbecilic and foolish types of temptations—temptations which would not even appeal to the Devil himself, much less to Jesus. The author is not acquainted with any historical religion that has an intelligent and wise devil. Only the good are wise and intelligent. The devil and his followers are always foolish and idiotic. Consider the *wise* virgins and the *foolish* virgins. What a weak fool Peter was, even though he was the only man in the crowd with an ounce of courage. "Thou *fool,* this night thy soul shall be demanded of thee." *Fools,* hypocrites, etc!" It is not necessary to ring in all the phrases and stories that are so familiar to all.

Literary and dramatic tradition was certainly influential. One is familiar with the "fool" that came on the stage following the dramatic climax, or filled in between the important scenes. In some of the Miracle Plays, one finds a fool and a devil. In other Miracle Plays, the devil and the fool are one. Why was it easy for the two functions to be performed by the same personality? Because the two functions were so similar. The only other person in the Miracle Plays who could conceivably have become amalgamated with the function of the Devil was Judas himself,—yet Judas had been considered the most level-headed business man in the group.

HYPOTHESES. On pages 6-7 of De Quiro's "Modern Theories of Criminality," is the following illuminating paragraph: "Three generations after the beginnings of psychiatry, the theory of *degeneration* is set forth in France by Morel. Nevertheless, according to Dallemagne, he rather owes his ideas on degeneration to natural sciences. Morel, in his classical treatise, *Physical, Intellectual and Moral Degeneration of the Human Species,* looks upon degeneration as a kind of retrogressive natural selection, a degradation, using the word not in its ethical sense, and without any meaning of contempt. His starting point is the existence of a primitive type which the human mind reproduces in its own thought as the masterpiece and culmination of creation—a view which agrees so well with our own ideas,—and that the degeneration of our nature is due to the going astray of the primitive type, which contains in itself all the necessary elements for the preservation of the species. Intent upon making latest scientific discoveries come within the purest orthodoxy, Morel establishes as the starting point of degeneration the combination of the new conditions brought about by the original fall. Then he studies the role heredity plays—a theory already confirmed in relation to the transmission of crime by Lucas, in his *Treatise On Natural Heredity,* —in the genesis and development of the deviation of the primitive type; and, tracing through the generations the evolution of the pyschopathic process, succeeds in establishing for the first time the relation between criminality and degeneration. The strange and unknown types which people our prisons, said he, were not so strange and unknown to those who study the mor-

bid varieties of the human species from the double point of
view of the psychic and moral condition of the individuals that
compose them, for they personify the various degenerations of
the species, and the evil which produces them constitutes for
modern society a greater danger than the barbaric invasion
did for the old."

Such hypotheses are influenced in their formulation by ancient traditions, but being hypotheses, they carry greater weight
and dignity. After a generation or so, such hypotheses become
facts and are described in terms of exact percentages.

Lombroso was the type of investigator who mingled hypotheses and facts in a most ingenious way. His work determined
definitely the prevailing opinion that criminals are mentally defective. It must be remembered that Lombroso simply gave
definite form to an already established belief. His position was
not one that was arrived at after laborious research, and he did
not attempt to prove or establish more securely his position
after arriving at it. In the 1911 American edition of his "Criminal Man," on pages 135-136, he gives a typical statement of
his position: "The criminal is an atavistic being, a relic of a
vanished race. This is by no means an uncommon occurrence
in nature. Atavism, the reversion to a former state, is the first
feeble indication of the reaction opposed by nature to the per-
turbing causes which seek to alter her delicate mechanism.
Under certain unfavorable conditions, cold or poor soil, the
common oak will develop characteristics of the oak of the Qua-
ternary period. The dog left to run wild in the forest will in
a few generations revert to the type of his original wolf-like
progenitor, and the cultivated garden roses when neglected show
a tendency to reassume the form of the original dog-rose.
Under special conditions produced by alcohol, chloroform, heat,
or injuries, ants, dogs, and pigeons become irritable and savage
like their wild ancestors.

"This tendency to alter under special conditions is common to
human beings, in whom hunger, syphilis, trauma, and, still more
frequently, morbid conditions inherited from insane, criminal,
or deceased progenitors, or the abuse of nerve poisons, such as
alcohol, tobacco or morphine, cause various alterations, of which
criminality—that is, a return to the characteristics peculiar to
primitive savages—is in reality the least serious, because it rep-
resents a less advanced stage than other forms of cerebral al-
teration.

"The aetiology of crime, therefore, mingles with that of all kinds of degeneration; rickets, deafness, monstrosity, hairiness, and cretinism, of which crime is only a variation. It has, however, always been regarded as a thing apart, owing to a general instinctive repugnance to admit that a phenomenon, whose extrinsications are so extensive and penetrate every fibre of social life, derives, in fact, from the same causes as socially insignificant forms like rickets, sterility, etc. But this repugnance is really only a sensory illusion, like many others of widely diverse nature."

Many writers have pointed to Mr. Robert Dugdale's sensational book, "The Jukes," first published in 1887, as a proof that criminality is inherited and is closely related to feeble-mindedness. All such proofs are entirely invalid, as a close examination of the book will reveal. In the 1910 edition of the book, it is stated on page 16 that "lines of intermarriage between Jukes show a minimum of crime," that "crime begins in progeny where Juke crosses X blood," and that "crime preponderates in the illegitimate lines." This would indicate that criminality is not transmitted from one generation to the next directly, and so is not comparable to feeble-mindedness in that respect. Not only is criminality not inherited, but it rarely occurs where heredity is kept restricted, as in in-breeding. The Juke criminal is almost always the result of Juke blood being crossed with other blood. Recent studies in the comparative mentality of pure and mixed tribes might lead us to suppose that these Juke criminals were much more intelligent than the other Jukes.

Certainly Mr. Dugdale had no idea that his Juke criminals were feeble-minded. On page 49 he states, "Crime as compared to pauperism indicates *vigor*; criminal careers are more easily modified by environment, because crime, more especially contrived crime, is an index of capacity. ... The misfortune of one generation which throws the children into an alms-house, may lay the foundation for a criminal career for that generation if the children are of an *enterprising temperament.*" Mr. Dugdale very clearly points out that the Juke variety of criminal possessed more mental vigor on the whole than did the other Jukes.

Doctor Goddard's earlier work, "The Kallikak Family," published in 1912, shows that he believed then that criminals are largely recruited from the ranks of the mental defectives. On page 54, occurs the following statement: "The reader must remember that the type of feeble-mindedness of which we are speaking is the one to which Deborah belongs, that is, to the high grade, or moron. All the facts go to show that this type of people makes up a large percentage of our criminals."

If Doctor Goddard is right in his conviction, we should expect that the Kallikak family itself, being traced so carefully, would show a large number of criminals. But among the 480 members of the family that were investigated in detail through more than a century, only three are reported as ever having been classified as criminal. Probably no family could show any better record than that.

Doctor Goddard, perceiving this possible flaw in his argument, explains it on page 62 as follows: "We have claimed that criminality resulting from feeble-mindedness is mainly a matter of environment, yet it must be acknowledged that there are wide differences in temperament and that, while this one branch of the Kallikak family was mentally defective, there was no strong tendency in it towards that which our laws recognize as criminality. In other families there is, without doubt, a much greater tendency to crime, so that the lack of criminals in this particular case, far from detracting from our argument, really strengthens it. It must be recognized that there is much more liability of criminals resulting from mental defectiveness in certain families than in others, probably because of difference in the strength of some instincts."

Nevertheless, the "other families" have not yet been investigated, and some families that may show a greater tendency to crime may also show a much greater intelligence.

In the light of the discussion in this chapter and in the preceding one, it seems fairly obvious that the pre-war prevailing opinion that criminality and feeble-mindedness are closely related, was certainly not built upon a solid foundation of collected facts. The progenitors of the theory are not to be condemned on that account. There were no existing norms of general intelligence in the civil population. Until those norms should be formulated, no examination of criminals alone could reveal whether criminals were more or less feeble-minded than the general population. Average intelligence was greatly respected in those days. But the war has changed that too. We know now that average intelligence is nothing to be proud of. A great deal of dignity has been lost from the democratic man. Through the masses of the social group there is so much of low and mediocre mentality, that the criminal need not fear the result of direct comparison.

CHAPTER 3

THE EXTENT TO WHICH THE ARMY AND CRIMINAL NORMS ARE REPRESENTATIVE

The eventual value of this investigation depends upon the extent to which the Army norms are representative of the civil population of the country, and the extent to which the inmates of penitentiaries are representative of the criminal element in our society. It is not necessary that the degree of representativeness be known exactly, but it is necessary to know whether the two groups of norms are equally representative or not. Let us discuss the Army norms first.

The Army consisted of young men chiefly between the ages of 21 and 31. Of course there were a few younger men, and quite a number of older men. But the majority of the men were between 21 and 31. Is it valid to assume that the intelligence of the men between those age limits is representative of the adult intelligence of the country? In answering this question, it is only necessary to point out the results of testing men of various ages. In adult life, there does not seem to be a wide variation of intelligence with age. The very old men rank somewhat lower, to be sure, than young men, but such would be expected. The degeneration of intelligence follows closely upon the degeneration of the body. But among men in their physical prime, no mental tests have shown that there is a variation of score with age. So, in so far as we know anything about general intelligence, we are safe in assuming that the men between 21 and 31 years of age represented mentally the adult population of the country. We mean the last statement to refer to all men between 21 and 31, and not merely those in the Army.

It is well known that many of the men of the country were classified in preferred occupations, and were not subject to the Draft. Is it valid to assume that the men who were not so classified, and were caught by the Draft, were mentally representative of the entire adult population? The importance of this question depends upon the total numbers of men classified in preferred occupations. That number was tremendous, since it included railroads, farms, ships, and factories. But the Government was furnished with lists of preferred employees by each such employer, and it is safe to assume that the lists contained the most valuable men. That would result in the more intelligent men being placed on such lists, and exempted from military service. In this case the claim must be allowed that the Army norms are too low. It seems practically certain that the preferred occupations, in retaining their most valuable workers, retained at the same time their most intelligent workers.

Before the Draft was inaugurated, large numbers of young men voluntered for service in the various arms of the military organizations. Is it valid to assume that these men are of the same average intelligence as the draft quota? Data bearing on this question would naturally not be very extensive. The individuals concerned were very probably possessed of temperamental factors of a characteristic type. They were men who loved excitement and adventure. They were quite likely the type of men who flocked to the West half a century ago. The results of mental tests seem to indicate that the West is superior in intelligecne to the average of the entire country. It is possible to assume, consequently, that the young men who volunteered early for army service were probably more intelligent in general than the average of the country. The proof is not overwhelming, but it is fairly tangible. Probably it should be allowed, therefore, that the Army norms, being based on the Draft, are not only too low for the civil population of the country, but also are too low for the entire Army.

Many men were exempted from the Draft because they had domestic dependents. Would such men, if they had been included in the Army, have raised the average mental scores of the Army? Men who have dependents are usually men who are not afraid of responsibility, and are not afraid to assume it according to general social regulations. They are the men who determine the forms of institutions, and really represent the race in the building of civilized communities. Is their average intelligence only the average of the civil population, or is it higher? The married criminals are more intelligent than are the unmarried ones, but the same may not hold true for non-criminals. But the author is perfectly willing to admit the possibility, and concede once more that the Army norms are too low as a result.

There were many conscientious objectors and various types of slackers who were not caught by the Draft and used in the determination of the Army norms. Is it possible that those objectors and slackers were more intelligent than the willing recruits, and so can not be represented by the latter? Such objectors as were caught by the Draft and were given a mental test, did, as a matter of fact, show an average intelligence higher than that of the army in general. The most intelligent objectors probably had their religious records so accurately made out and recorded, that they escaped the Army altogether. As for the slackers, they probably had initiative and physical vigor, in order to elude the Army agents. Some of the more prominent ones are well known, and certainly possess plenty of intelligence, even if lacking in some other virtues. The author is perfectly willing to admit that the objectors and slackers were probably more intelligent than were the willing recruits, and that the Army norms are too low as a result.

On the other hand, we must remember that the physically unfit were not included in the Army. The Draft Boards in all parts of the country assisted in this elimination, and the men who were sent to the various camps were the well and sound, the choice of the communities. The physical wrecks who were left at home, nevertheless, constituted part of the adult population of the country. However, it is not known that physical deformity is accompanied by mental defectiveness. In the light of such facts as we have, it is not likely that such selection made any mental difference. The author wants to be fair here. It would be to his advantage to make much of this point. But such advantage is waived.

In so far as was possible to prevent it, no insane men were sent to the Army. Of course many mild forms found their way there. But the worst cases were detected, certainly. Such cases would constitute part of the adult civil population, and would not be represented in the Army. Are they not of lower intelligence than the average? It is not known that general intelligence varies with degree of sanity, at least not till degeneration sets in. An insane man who is due to die within a year or so probably should not be considered a member of the adult civil population. So, the elimination of the insane would probably not make any difference, so far as general intelligence is concerned.

The worst cases of the feeble-minded did not get into the Army at all. Some bad cases got there, but not the worst cases. Yet the feeble-minded are members of the adult civil population. This might make the Army norms seem too high, instead of too low. But such cases of extreme feeble-mindedness do not constitute a large percentage of the population. However, such facts must be considered.

Persons suffering from incurable diseases were not allowed to enter the Army. However, they constitute part of the population. Could they not be considered of lower intelligence than the rest of the general population, or than the Army? The author is willing not to claim this point, since there is no indication that disease reduces intelligence, except through the means of physical degeneration.

In the light of all the above arguments, it would seem reasonable to presume that the Army norms are too low to be representative of the adult civil population of the country. The author admits the reasonableness of this, and can see no reason for disputing it.

But now let us consider the criminal norms. The author, in this book, frequently assumes that the criminals here reported are representative of the criminal element of society. Are the norms here reported too high or too low, to be representative of the criminal element?

None of the data reported in this book was gathered from Federal prisons. Since the criminals in the Federal prisons are men convicted of crimes that require a large amount of care and planning, such criminals can be considered possessed of more than average criminal intelligence. Since none of them are included in this investigation, the resulting norms should be considered too low for the important types of criminal groups.

The author was unable to find any wealthy men among the inmates of the various prisons investigated. As a general rule, it requires superior intelligence, in addition to other characistics, to amass and retain considerable property. The possession of wealth would make conviction difficult, because of the amount of legal power that could be summoned. The men who get convicted are usually without wealth and without friends. As a result, it might be expected that the resulting mental norms would be too low to represent the important criminal element in society.

Many criminals are never suspected, and consequently are never caught. It requires intelligence to plan crime so cleverly that the perpetrator is not suspected. The criminals who have never been suspected are probably much more intelligent than are those who have been caught. It is impossible to have any common sense at all, and not assent to that proposition. Consequently, the men who are caught can scarcely be considered as possessing intelligence enough to furnish norms representative of the criminal element of society.

Of course, the inmates of penitentiaries are men who have actually been convicted. Many suspected men are caught and tried, but are not convicted because of the skill of legal talent and personal skill in cross-examination. Such men are probably more intelligent than are those suspected men who lack the skill and necessary wealth and influence to gain acquittal. As a result, the mental norms of convicted criminals are too low to be representative of the criminal element in society.

The mental examinations reported in this book did not exclude the physically unfit. Such were excluded from the Army, but they are not excluded from the prisons. The author does not claim that the prisons are lower as a result, but he wishes to call attention to the fact that the physically unfit contributed to the norms that are reported in this book.

The examinations reported in this book did not exclude the diseased. Men suffering from incurable diseases were excluded from the Draft, but nothing prevents their landing in prison. Their presence may make no difference in the resulting mental forms, but their presence should be remembered.

Neither did the examinations reported in this book exclude the feeble-minded, and some were present.

In the administration of the Alpha mental test in the Army, a literacy requirement of five years was usually required. This eliminated large numbers of individuals who would otherwise have increased the percentage of low scores. No such literacy requirement was demanded of the criminals who took the Alpha test. All men sent to the examiner were given the test, and every test paper that carried any possible identification mark was graded and used in the tabulation of results.

The author concludes that if the Army norms are unrepresentative because of being too low, the criminal norms are even more unrepresentative for the same reason. That is, the criminal element of society, as will be shown by the facts reported in this book, does not possess a lower average intelligence than the adult civil population; assuming the Army norms and the criminal norms here reported to be equally representative enough for the purposes of this discussion. This is well substantiated by the report in Volume 15 of the Memoirs of the National Academy of Sciences, 1921. On page 800, a comparison of 3,368 criminals at Fort Leavenworth with the 94,004 cases of the sample of the Army, shows that the criminals have the advantage in Alpha scores.

Letter Grades	Percentage of Army	Percentage of Leavenworth Prisoners
E	7.1	6.0
D	17.0	18.8
C—	23.8	20.8
C	25.0	23.8
C+	15.2	16.0
B	8.0	8.8
A	4.1	5.8

The author has no desire to play the part of the Devil's advocate in this book. He does not hold the conviction that criminals have more able minds than do the more conservative members of society. But he is convinced that great harm has been done and is being done by the propaganda which creates the impression that the criminal is feeble-minded, and an individual to be fawned over and petted. It would be of greater service, if the thinking element in society could have their minds directed to the idiotic expressions on statute books, and the imbecilic attempts to execute such idiotic expressions.

PART II

White Native-Born Men Criminals

CHAPTER 4

SOME GEOGRAPHICAL CONCOMITANTS

1. *Comparison of the Entire White Native-Born Criminal Group with the White Draft.*

According to the tables on page 690, Volume 15, Memoirs of the National Academy of Sciences, and the general discussion that accompanies the tables, the distribution of the White Draft in terms of Alpha can be accepted as approximating to the following distribution of a sample of 44,223 cases.

Alpha Score		Cases	Percentage
0- 9	___	1,774	4
10- 14	___	1,535	3.5
15- 19	___	1,855	4.2
20- 24	___	2,040	4.6
25- 34	___	4,640	10.5
35- 44	___	4,810	10.9
45- 59	___	6,754	15.3
60- 74	___	5,913	13.4
75- 89	___	4,684	10.6
90-104	___	3,609	8.2
105-119	___	2,618	5.9
120-134	___	1,703	3.8
135-149	___	1,118	2.5
150-212	___	1,170	2.6

It is assumed that the percentage column above is a close approximation to the percentage column that would result from a detailed distribution of the entire group of more than a million cases tested with Alpha. In case one has grown accustomed to thinking in terms of the Army letter grades, it is only necessary to combine the percentage figures in groups of two, in the order of the letter grades. The percentage column would then read as follows:

E	7.5
D	8.8
C—	21.4
C	28.7
C+	18.8
B	9.7
A	5.1

It is quite likely that some of my readers have accustomed themselves to thinking in terms of curves. I must plead with all such to bear with me in my method of presentation, since even they would probably never forgive me if I published the tremendous number of curves necessary for this book. So

I am using the less visually striking technique of cases and percentages for my medium of presentation.

It should be remembered that the above letter grades are supposed to approximate to certain dimensions of the Gaussian Curve. However, it is not necessary to discuss the theoretical characteristics of the Gaussian Curve, for such characteristics probably exist nowhere except in the mind of the professional mathematician. But if the above percentage column did express relatively and in order the dimensions of the Gaussian Curve, A would be the same size as E, B would be the same size as D, C would be the same size as C—, while each would bear a certain theoretical relationship to the whole curve or to any given part of it. In this case, however, it should be noted that A is less than E, that B is greater than D, while C+ is less than C—. That is, the E half of the curve contains 52 per cent of the total number of cases, while the A half of the curve contains 47.9 per cent of the total number of cases. These facts are of no significance except in so far as they may be used as norms for purposes of comparison. It would be a very simple matter to reverse the skewness, simply by changing the limitations of the letter grades. The failure to understand this has been more general than in the case of any other single element of the problem of mental testing.

Comparing the distribution of the entire white native-born criminal group with the white draft in terms of Alpha, we have the following:

Alpha Score	Criminal Cases	Percentage of Criminal Cases	Percentage of White Draft
0- 9	185	4.7	4.
10- 14	113	2.8	3.5
15- 19	124	3.2	4.2
20- 24	147	3.7	4.6
25- 34	324	8.3	10.5
35- 44	382	9.5	10.9
45- 59	553	14.	15.3
60- 74	565	14.5	13.4
75- 89	485	12.3	10.6
90-104	413	10.5	8.2
105-119	274	7.	5.9
120-134	170	4.4	3.8
135-149	106	2.7	2.5
150-212	101	2.6	2.6

It is of interest to observe in the percentage columns that the criminal group is in the minority in all cases save one in the groups below 60, and in the majority in all cases save one in the groups higher than and including 60. If a combination is made into the letter grade groups, the result is as follows:

Letter Grade	Criminal Cases	Percentage of Criminal Cases	Percentage of White Draft
E	298	7.5	7.5
D	271	6.9	8.8
C—	706	17.8	21.4
C	1,118	28.5	28.7
C+	898	22.8	18.8
B	444	11.4	9.7
A	207	5.3	5.1
Total	3,942	100.2	100.0

It is quite evident that the criminal group is superior to the white draft group. In percentage of cases, a comparison of the halves of the two curves of distribution might be made as follows:

	A Half	E Half
Criminal Group	53.8%	46.5%
White Draft	47.9%	52.0%

Interesting and significant as such comparative figures are, it would be a sad logical error to assume as a conclusion from the comparison that the criminals of America are more intelligent than was the American Army. Such an inference might be true. There is probably no proof to the contrary. Nevertheless, logical errors are just as detrimental in science as history has proven them to be in politics and in theology. The above differences can be explained in terms of geographical concomitants. Such explanations may not ultimately be the true one, yet it must be taken into consideration before any sweeping statement can logically be made either for or against the intelligence of the criminal group.

Before the entire Alpha sample of the white draft can be accepted as a norm by which to measure geographically selected groups of criminals, it will be necessary to observe the range of the group units that went to make up that sample. Let the California unit be compared with the North Carolina unit.

Alpha Score	California Cases	N. Carolina Cases	California Percentage	N. Carolina Percentage
0- 9	16	55	1.6	8.
10- 14	19	44	1.9	6.3
15- 19	24	54	2.5	7.7
20- 24	32	66	3.3	9.4
25- 34	83	100	8.5	14.3
35- 44	83	97	8.5	13.9

45- 59 _____ 137	89	14.1	12.7
60- 74 _____ 128	69	13.1	9.8
75- 89 _____ 113	50	11.6	7.1
90-104 _____ 134	38	13.7	5.4
105-119 _____ 78	21	8.	3.
120-134 _____ 55	6	5.6	.8
135-149 _____ 32	9	3.3	1.3
150-212 _____ 41	4	4.2	.6
Total _____ 975	702	99.9	100.3

The marked superiority of the California group as compared with the North Carolina group is obvious, and becomes clearer in a letter grade comparison.

Letter Grade	California Percentage	N. Carolina Percentage
E _____	3.5	14.3
D _____	5.8	17.1
C— _____	17.	28.2
C _____	27.2	22.5
C+ _____	25.3	12.5
B _____	13.6	3.8
A _____	7.5	1.9

If the members of state units in the white draft could differ so tremendously in ability to make scores in the Alpha test, is it not likely that criminal units from different states would also differ equally markedly? Certainly, in the light of the above facts, the comparison of criminal groups from a few states with the white draft from all the states is not an exhaustive process. The geographical differences in the white draft, whatever the causes of these differences might be, may be duplicated in the criminal population.

2. Comparison of the Criminal Population of a Given State with the White Draft from That State.

In such comparison the states used will be Illinois, Ohio, Indiana, New Jersey, and Maryland. In the case of each state, we will compare the criminal population examined within the state with the white draft from that state. Such comparison, to be sure, may comprise errors which will be rectified later. Let us begin with Illinois.

Alpha Grade	Illinois Criminal Population	Illinois Draft Cases	Criminal Percentage	Draft Percentage
0- 9 _____	27	75	3.1	3.5
10- 14 _____	10	62	1.1	2.9
15- 19 _____	17	78	2.	3.6
20- 24 _____	18	65	2.1	3.

25- 34 _____ 44	208	5.	9.7
35- 44 _____ 76	204	8.7	9.5
45- 59 _____ 128	347	14.5	16.2
60- 74 _____ 133	298	15.1	13.9
75- 89 _____ 130	241	14.8	11.2
90-104 _____ 112	206	12.7	9.6
105-119 _____ 79	135	9.	6.3
120-134 _____ 57	98	6.5	4.6
135-149 _____ 27	61	3.1	2.9
150-212 _____ 33	57	3.7	2.7

In terms of the letter grades, the comparison would be as follows:

	Criminal Percentage	Draft Percentage
E _____	4.2	5.4
D _____	4.1	6.6
C— _____	13.7	19.2
C _____	29.6	30.1
C+ _____	27.5	20.8
B _____	15.5	10.9
A _____	6.9	5.6

It seems evident that the Illinois criminal population group ranks higher in terms of Alpha than does the Illinois draft group, the difference being just as striking as in the comparison of the entire native-born criminal group with the entire white draft.

The comparison of the Ohio criminal population group with the Ohio white draft unit is as follows:

Alpha Grades	Ohio Criminal Population	Ohio Draft Cases	Criminal Percentage	Draft Percentage
0- 9 _____	49	33	3.4	1.4
10- 14 _____	44	40	3.1	1.7
15- 19 _____	41	79	2.9	3.4
20- 24 _____	41	63	2.9	2.7
25- 34 _____	120	197	8.5	8.5
35- 44 _____	140	240	9.9	10.4
45- 59 _____	213	358	15.	15.4
60- 74 _____	207	307	14.6	13.2
75- 89 _____	175	273	12.3	11.8
90-104 _____	154	214	10.9	9.3
105-119 _____	104	178	7.3	7.7
120-134 _____	59	139	4.2	6.
135-149 _____	40	104	2.8	4.5
150-212 _____	31	93	2.2	4.

Translating the percentage columns into letter grade percentages, we have as follows:

	Criminal Percentage	Draft Percentage
E _____	6.5	3.1

D		5.8	6.1
C—		18.4	18.9
C		29.6	28.6
C+		23.2	25.
B		11.5	13.7
A		5.	8.5

In the case of Ohio, the comparison shows a decided advantage on the side of the draft group. Nevertheless, the Ohio criminal group, in terms of Alpha, is far superior to the North Carolina draft group. Let us proceed to a comparison of the Indiana groups.

Indiana Alpha Grades	Criminal Population	Indiana Draft	Criminal Percentage	Draft Percentage
0- 9	36	1	5.6	0
10- 14	20	0	3.1	0
15- 19	21	52	3.3	4.4
20- 24	36	68	5.6	5.8
25- 34	60	151	9.3	12.9
35- 44	57	147	8.9	12.5
45- 59	87	217	13.6	18.5
60- 74	83	175	12.9	15.
75- 89	89	119	13.9	10.1
90-104	69	100	10.8	8.5
105-119	41	74	6.4	6.3
120-134	25	37	3.9	3.1
135-149	12	21	1.8	1.8
150-212	5	9	.8	.8

In letter grades, the comparison is as follows:

	Indiana Criminals	Indiana Draft
E	8.7	0.0
D	8.9	10.2
C—	18.2	25.4
C	26.5	23.5
C+	24.7	18.6
B	10.3	9.4
A	2.6	2.6

In spite of the fact that the Indiana draft shows no cases in the E group, the criminal group shows a marked superiority. The lack of E cases in the Indiana draft is purely the result of the method of selecting the Indiana sample, as the writer remembers distinctly some of the atrocious Alpha grades made by certain Indiana units. Let us consider next the comparison of the New Jersey groups.

Alpha Scores	N.J. Criminal Population	N.J. Draft	Criminal Percentage	Draft Percentage
0- 9	63	164	8.5	17.5
10- 14	31	45	4.2	4.8

15- 19	40	42	5.4	4.5
20- 24	39	59	5.3	6.3
25- 34	80	77	10.8	8.2
35- 44	86	79	11.7	8.4
45- 59	87	134	11.8	14.2
60- 74	101	79	13.7	8.5
75- 89	62	79	8.4	8.5
90-104	55	47	7.5	5.
105-119	37	50	5.	5.3
120-134	19	35	2.6	3.7
135-149	15	16	2.	1.7
150-212	23	31	3.1	3.3

Translating the percentage columns into letter grades, we have :

	Criminal Percentage	Draft Percentage
E	12.7	22.3
D	10.7	10.8
C—	22.5	16.6
C	25.5	22.7
C+	15.9	13.5
B	7.6	9.
A	5.1	5.

There is nothing in either of the New Jersey groups to be proud of. Nevertheless, such differences as are evident are to the advantage of the criminal group. Let us compare the Maryland groups.

Maryland Alpha Scores	Criminal Population	Maryland Draft	Criminal Percentage	Draft Percentage
0- 9	10	18	3.9	2.9
10- 14	8	19	3.1	3.1
15- 19	7	33	2.7	5.4
20- 24	13	34	5.1	5.5
25- 34	20	72	7.8	11.7
35- 44	22	60	8.6	9.7
45- 59	38	102	14.9	16.6
60- 74	31	95	12.2	15.4
75- 89	29	59	11.4	9.6
90-104	23	55	9.	8.9
105-119	23	28	9.	4.5
120-134	10	16	3.9	2.6
135-149	12	15	4.7	2.4
150-212	9	10	3.5	1.6

Translating the percentage columns into letter grades, there results :

	Criminal Percentage	Draft Percentage
E	7.	6.
D	7.7	10.9

C—	16.4	21.4
C	27.1	32.
C+	20.4	18.5
B	12.9	7.1
A	8.2	4.

Here again it is evident that such differences as exist are to the advantage of the criminal group.

In short, the above comparisons of criminal populations with state draft units show, with but one exception, a superiority in terms of Alpha on the part of the criminal groups. The one exception is the case of Ohio. This discrepancy on the part of Ohio can be explained. On page 554 of the Memoirs referred to above, it is stated that the records from Camp Sherman were not included in the sample from which the state draft units were drawn. That means that the Ohio draft unit is composed of Ohio men examined in other camps. In the light of evidence that will be presented later, the result of such selection of Ohio cases will cause the Ohio draft unit to rank too high. A little work on the adding machine will reveal the fact that the Ohio draft unit, as reported on page 690 of the Memoirs, averages more than 10 per cent higher than the draft unit from any other state in the Middle West. Such fact is no compliment to Ohio, but is simply the result of the method of selection used in drawing for the sample. That is, the Ohio draft unit reported on page 690 of the Memoirs should actually have been reported from six to ten per cent lower, and would have been, if the Camp Sherman records had been used in the drawing for the sample. That statement will become accepted by the reader later in this chapter. Under no circumstances should this paragraph be construed as a criticism of the psychologists who compiled the Memoirs. Nevertheless, it is a pity that a drawing was not made from the Camp Sherman group examination records, such drawing made under the same conditions that obtained for the other drawings. The results could have been published in separate tables in the Memoirs.

For purposes of accuracy, let us compare the total white native-born criminal group with the total white draft and with the white draft from the five combined states of Illinois, Ohio, Indiana, New Jersey, and Maryland.

Alpha Scores	Percentage of Criminal Cases	Percentage of White Draft	Percentage of Illinois, Ohio, Indiana New Jersey and Maryland Draft
0- 9	4.7	4.	4.
10- 14	2.8	3.5	2.3

15- 19	3.2	4.2	3.9
20- 24	3.7	4.6	4.
25- 34	8.3	10.5	9.8
35- 44	9.5	10.9	10.2
45- 59	14.	15.3	16.1
60- 74	14.5	13.4	13.2
75- 89	12.3	10.6	10.7
90-104	10.5	8.2	8.7
105-119	7.	5.9	6.5
120-134	4.4	3.8	4.5
135-149	2.7	2.5	3.
150-212	2.6	2.6	2.8

Translating into letter grades, we have the following:

	Percentage of Criminal Cases	Percentage of White Draft	Percentage of Illinois, Ohio, Indiana, New Jersey and Maryland Draft
E	7.5	7.5	6.3
D	6.9	8.8	7.9
C—	17.8	21.4	20.
C	28.5	28.7	29.3
C+	22.8	18.8	19.4
B	11.4	9.7	11.
A	5.3	5.1	5.8

It would be interesting to have some of the experts on criminal problems take the above three percentage columns and the three titles that go with them, and assign to each column its appropriate title. Close scrutiny indicates that the Illinois, Ohio, Indiana, New Jersey, and Maryland combined draft is superior to the total white draft but still inferior to the criminal group. The differences are slight, but slight differences are not necessarily insignificant. And it should be remembered that the differences would be greater if the Camp Sherman records had been used. The proof for that statement is to be offered later.

3. *Possible Factors of Distance, Industrial Attractiveness, and the Frontier.*

The total criminal population of any given state comprises a large percentage of men who were born outside of that state. These men have come from varying distances, and from communities of varying industrial attractiveness and degree of social development. Do these different experienced influences make any difference in the mentality of the criminal population of any given state? Let us compare the criminals born west of the Mississippi River with those born east of the Mississippi, not including any born in Illinois, Ohio, Indiana, New Jersey, or Maryland. It must not be assumed that the writer is making any assumptions concerning the differences in industrial attractiveness, social development, and general degree of civilization, between the western and the eastern halves of the United States. The differences which will be indicated may be the result of other factors altogether. But distance and the frontier are probably real factors, not in a causative, but in a selective sense. Other things being equal, a moving population is probably more intelligent than a stationary one. It is not the movement that makes the difference, but rather the reverse.

Alpha Grades	Cases West of Mississippi	Cases East of Mississippi	Percentage West	Percentage East
0- 9	7	35	2.9	3.3
10- 14	2	34	.9	3.2
15- 19	6	36	2.5	3.4
20- 24	7	40	2.9	3.7
25- 34	15	102	6.3	9.3
35- 44	14	91	5.9	8.6
45- 59	30	139	12.6	13.1
60- 74	34	174	14.3	16.3
75- 89	28	109	11.8	10.2
90-104	34	110	14.3	10.3
105-119	19	80	8.	7.5
120-134	17	45	7.1	4.2
135-149	12	30	5.	2.8
150-212	13	38	5.5	3.6

Translating into letter grades, we have the following:

	Percentage West	Percentage East
E	3.8	6.5
D	5.4	7.1
C—	12.2	17.9
C	26.9	29.4
C+	26.1	20.5
B	15.1	11.7
A	10.5	6.4

Not a single state in America sent a draft quota into the army that could compare mentally with the criminals born west of the Mississippi and confined in Eastern prisons.

Now let us compare the criminals born in Illinois, Ohio, Indiana, New Jersey, and Maryland, and confined within their home state, with the criminals born in those same states but confined outside their home state.

Alpha Scores	Cases Confined in Home State	Cases Confined Outside Home State	Percentage of Former	Percentage of Latter
0- 9	137	6	5.8	2.3
10- 14	72	5	3.	2.
15- 19	74	9	3.1	3.5
20- 24	94	4	4.	1.5
25- 34	188	18	8.	6.9
35- 44	256	19	10.8	7.3
45- 59	350	36	14.6	14.
60- 74	322	35	13.8	13.5
75- 89	312	32	13.1	12.3
90-104	235	34	9.9	13.1
105-119	155	21	6.5	8.1
120-134	87	23	3.8	9.
135-149	54	8	2.3	3.1
150-212	40	10	1.7	4.

Translating into letter grades, we have the following:

	Percentage Confined in Home State	Percentage from Same States, But Confined Outside Home State
E	8.8	4.3
D	7.1	5.
C—	18.8	14.2
C	28.4	27.5
C+	23.	25.4
B	10.3	17.3
A	4.	7.1

It is obvious that the criminals who migrate to other states to commit their crimes are superior in Alpha grades to their fellow citizens who commit their crimes at home.

Now let us compare the criminals incarcerated in their home state with all the native-born white criminals examined in prisons outside their home state.

Alpha Grades	Cases Confined Outside of Home State	Percentage Confined Outside Home State	Percentage in Home State
0- 9	48	3.	5.8
10- 14	41	2.6	3.
15- 19	50	3.2	3.1
20- 24	53	3.4	4.
25- 34	136	8.7	‹
35- 44	126	8.	10.8
45- 59	203	13.	14.6
60- 74	243	15.5	13.8
75- 89	173	11.	13.1
90-104	178	11.3	9.9

105-119	119	7.6	6.5
120-134	83	5.3	3.8
135-149	52	3.3	2.3
150-212	61	3.9	1.7

Translating into letter grades, we have the following:

	Percentage Outside Home State	Percentage in Home State
E	5.6	8.8
D	6.6	7.1
C—	16.7	18.8
C	28.5	28.4
C+	22.3	23.
B	12.9	10.3
A	7.2	4.

The differences here are marked, though not so clear cut as in the case of the comparison of home incarcerated criminals with fellow citizens imprisoned outside their native state. But the reason is obvious. The criminal group contains a large number of relatively low grade men from Kentucky. This pulls down the average of the men confined outside their home state, while the average of men confined within their home state is not at the same time lowered by the inclusion of the still lower grade men confined in the prisons of Kentucky. In this study the Illinois, Ohio, and Indiana prisons alone have contributed 126 criminals from Kentucky. It might be interesting to compare the Kentucky groups.

Alpha Grades	Cases of Kentucky Criminals	Cases of Kentucky Draft	Percentage Kentucky Criminals	Percentage Kentucky Draft
0- 9	4	62	3.	7.4
10- 14	7	51	5.3	6.1
15- 19	6	62	4.5	7.4
20- 24	5	63	3.8	7.5
25- 34	19	114	14.4	13.6
35- 44	11	102	8.3	12.2
45- 59	19	125	14.4	14.8
60- 74	21	103	15.9	12.3
75- 89	16	46	12.1	5.5
90-104	12	52	9.1	6.2
105-119	5	23	3.8	2.7
120-134	3	15	2.3	1.8
135-149	3	11	2.3	1.3
150-212	1	8	.7	.9

Translating into letter grades, we have the following:

	Percentage of Kentucky Criminals	Percentage of Kentucky Draft
E	8.3	13.5

D	8.3	14.9
C—	22.7	25.8
C	30.3	27.1
C+	21.2	11.7
B	6.1	4.5
A	3.	2.2

It is difficult to study the influence of single factors in the behavior of such complex organisms as human beings. And it is true that, psychologically, such terms as distance, degree of social development, industrial attractiveness, and the frontier are vague at best. But, eliminating the five states in which criminals were examined, let us divide the United States into three traditional sections. There are certain connotations that accompany the terms the South, the North and the West. The South is noted for its conservatism, its small communities, its lack of frontier life, its inbreeding, and, till recently, its industrial apathy and educational indifference. The North has ever been washed with migrating hordes from Europe, and has experienced a perpetual renewing of social frontiers. However, the North has retained its small communities, has developed educational and social conservatism, but still offers large industrial and professional rewards. The West has been the country of frontier, of large communities in terms of space, of outbreeding, of liberalism, of education for the masses, of indifference to great distances. Of the three, the South is most ancient in its civilization, the West most recent. How will the criminals from these three sections of the country compare? The southern criminals are bound to be either the most intelligent or the least. The same can be said of the western criminals. The northern criminals will be between the other two. Let us compare them.

Alpha Grades	Cases South	Cases North	Cases West	Percentage in Order of		
				South	North	West
0- 9	12	26	8	4.6	3.5	2.6
10- 14	9	25	2	3.5	3.4	.6
15- 19	14	22	7	5.4	3.	2.3
20- 24	8	30	8	3.1	4.	2.6
25- 34	32	63	20	12.4	8.5	6.6
35- 44	23	61	18	8.9	8.2	6.
45- 59	35	103	34	13.6	13.9	11.3
60- 74	43	120	42	16.6	16.2	14.
75- 89	29	75	36	11.3	10.1	12.
90-104	18	76	46	7.	10.3	15.3
105-119	12	55	30	4.6	7.4	10.
120-134	11	33	17	4.2	4.5	5.6
135-149	6	21	16	2.3	2.8	5.3
150-212	6	29	15	2.3	3.9	5.

Translating into letter grades, we have the following:

| | Percentage in Order of | | |
	South	North	West
E	8.1	6.9	3.2
D	8.5	7.	4.9
C—	21.3	16.7	12.6
C	30.2	30.1	25.3
C+	18.3	20.4	27.3
B	8.8	11.9	15.6
A	4.6	6.7	10.3

In tabulating data for the above three sections, it was assumed that the South consisted of Virginia, North Carolina, South Carolina, Kentucky, Tennessee, Georgia, Florida, Alabama, Mississippi, Arkansas, and Louisiana; that the North consisted of Maine, New Hampshire, Vermont, Massachusetts, Rhode Island, Connecticut, New York, Pennsylvania, Delaware and West Virginia; while the West consisted of Michigan, Wisconsin, and all states west of the Mississippi river except Arkansas and Louisiana.

It is characteristic of high intelligence to resent conservatism, conformity and social suppression. That is one of the possible explanations of the uniformly high intelligence of the criminal group. Liberal political theory in this country has ever been the product of the frontier. In Revolutionary times, it was the frontier that ran close to the Atlantic. In more recent times, it has been the frontier west of the Mississippi. It is necessary to go to the West to find the cradle of the Republican Party, the Populist Party, the Progressive Party, the Farm Bloc Party and the I. W. W. Liberalism and certain forms of socialism and individualism flourish on the frontier. And from such sections come the criminals of high intelligence. Both of the old political parties are viewing with alarm the growing power of those western non-conformist groups in politics. The occasion for such alarm in the North and South will increase for at least fifty years yet.

The factor of distance alone, without great regard to the frontier, can best be demonstrated by comparing the inmates of home-state prisons with prisoners who have come great distances from all directions. Let us select for this purpose the men from Maine, Massachusetts, Florida, Louisiana, Alabama, Mississippi, Texas, Arizona, California, Oregon, North Dakota, Minnesota, Nebraska and Colorado. These men compare with the men from Illinois, Ohio, Indiana, New Jersey and Maryland, imprisoned in their home state as follows:

Alpha Scores	Cases of Home Prisoners	Cases of Distant Prisoners	Percentage of Former	Percentage of Latter
0- 9	137	1	5.8	.6
10- 14	72	1	3.0	.6
15- 19	74	3	3.1	1.9
20- 24	94	4	4.	2.5
25- 34	188	9	8.	5.7
35- 44	256	7	10.8	4.5
45- 59	350	15	14.6	9.6
60- 74	322	24	13.8	15.3
75- 89	312	15	13.1	9.6
90-104	235	23	9.9	14.7
105-119	155	14	6.5	8.9
120-134	87	20	3.8	12.7
135-149	54	11	2.3	7.
150-212	40	10	1.7	6.4

Translating into letter grades, we have the following:

	Percentage of Home Prisoners	Percentage of Criminals from Great Distances
E	8.8	1.2
D	7.1	4.4
C—	18.8	10.2
C	28.4	24.9
C+	23.	24.3
B	10.	21.6
A	4.	13.4

The superiority of the criminals from great distances is marked, and is of significance in social and historical science.

A further indication of the above factors can be obtained by comparing the New York criminals in the New Jersey prisons with the New York criminals in the prisons of Maryland, Illinois, Ohio, and Indiana. New Jersey is very near New York, while the other states are much further away.

Alpha Grades	New York Cases in New Jersey	New York Cases in Illinois, Ohio, Indiana and Maryland	Percentage New York Cases in New Jersey	Percentage in Four States Farther Away
0- 9	7	4	4.	3.2
10- 14	6	3	3.4	2.4
15- 19	6	2	3.4	1.6
20- 24	5	3	2.9	2.4
25- 34	20	6	11.4	4.8
35- 44	20	7	11.4	5.6
45- 59	28	18	16.	14.3
60- 74	26	24	14.8	19.1
75- 89	12	16	6.8	12.7
90-104	15	20	8.6	15.9

105-119 _____	11	13	6.3	10.3
120-134 _____	7	2	4.	1.6
135-149 _____	6	3	3.4	2.4
150-212 _____	6	7	3.4	5.6

Translating into letter grades, we have the following:

	Percentage New York Cases in New Jersey	New York Cases Illinois, Ohio in Maryland, and Indiana
E _____	7.4	5.6
D _____	6.3	4.
C— _____	22.8	10.4
C _____	30.8	33.4
C+ _____	15.4	28.6
B _____	10.3	11.9
A _____	6.8	8.

In this regard also, the Pennsylvania criminals in the prisons of New Jersey and Maryland might be compared with the Pennsylvania criminals in the prisons of Illinois, Ohio and Indiana. Pennsylvania borders on New Jersey and Maryland, but in the case of the other three states, on a small section of Ohio only. It might be expected that the Pennsylvania criminals in Illinois, Ohio and Indiana, will be superior to the Pennsylvania criminals in New Jersey and Maryland. The comparison will be as follows:

Alpha Grades	Cases in New Jersey and Maryland	Cases in Ohio, Illinois and Illinois	Percentage of Former	Percentage of Latter
0- 9 _____	7	3	5.6	1.9
10- 14 _____	4__	5	3.2	3.2
10 -15 _____	9	1	7.3	.6
20- 24 _____	10	4	8.	2.6
25- 34 _____	15	9	12.1	5.8
35- 44 _____	13	14	10.5	9.
45- 59 _____	16	25	12.9	16.
60- 74 _____	17	26	13.7	16 6
75- 89 _____	9	22	7.3	14.1
90-104 _____	8	13	6.4	8.3
105-119 _____	6	10	4.8	6.4
120-134 _____	1	15	.8	9.6
135-149 _____	6	3	4.8	1.9
150-212 _____	3	6	2.4	3.9

Translating into letter grades, we have the following:

	Percentage of Pennsylvania Cases in New Jersey and Maryland	Percentage of Pennsylvania Cases in Illinois, Ohio and Indiana
E _____	8.8	5.1

D	15.3	3.2
C—	22.6	14.8
C	26.6	32.6
C+	13.7	22.4
B	5.6	16.
A	7.2	5.8

No further comment is necessary concerning the significance of the above figures. At this point it might be well to add that it is greatly to be regretted that the criminal population has not been tested in the states of California, Texas, Nebraska, Iowa and Missouri. Comparative data from those states would be of tremendous interest for the discussion of this problem. But enough data has been presented to the serious reader to make quite clear to him that the problem of criminal intelligence can no longer be discussed adequately without due reference to geographical concomitants. This is no isolated problem. We are dealing here with factors that influence social behavior in general, and a solution of the problem will contribute not only to a more adequate understanding of the behavior of the obscure inmate of the prison cell, but also will contribute something toward an understanding of historical migratory success.

Tentative Conclusions:

1. In terms of Alpha scores the criminal group seems superior to the white draft group. Not only is this true of a general comparison, but it is true if we make the comparison in separate units according to the states from which the draft quotas and criminal groups were drawn.

2. However, the criminals from some states are much more intelligent than are the criminals from some other states. This may be explained in terms of distance and in terms of the degree to which the frontier exerts its influence. A moving population is probably more intelligent than is a stationary one. The men from west of the Mississippi River seem much more intelligent than are the men from east of the same river.

3. Men who are incarcerated outside their home state seem more intelligent than are the men incarcerated within their home state. The results indicate that geographical concomitants must not be ignored in the discussion of criminal intelligence.

CHAPTER 5

INTELLIGENCE AND TYPES OF CRIME

Criminal offenses change in number and variety almost as frequently as do social customs. The criminal offenses in one age of history may be largely civil offenses in the succeeding age, while the civil offenses of one age may be largely criminal offenses in the succeeding age. In addition to this interchange, there is an accretion from and a loss to the purely individual and personal interests. Murder, for example, came into the category of criminal behavior after being borrowed from the category of purely personal affairs. This interchange between the criminal group and the civil population will bring about a similarity between the two as far as intelligence is concerned, unless there are other factors not necessarily criminal alone. A careful study of the history of types of crime would itself lead to the conclusion that criminal intelligence can not differ very widely from the intelligence of the civil population. But economic, geographical and emotional factors may bring about a real difference. It is a most stupid fallacy to assume that the criminal, per se, must be feeble-minded. It takes high intelligence to perceive in the changing social order, just what constitutes criminal behavior. To imagine that the criminal in all ages will perceive and elect such behavior, being feeble-minded, is sheer nonsense. The inmates of a certain prison in this country averaged nearly a hundred per cent higher in the Alpha test than did the guards of that same prison. Which group was feeble-minded?

The white native-born criminal intelligence that is being discussed here landed behind prison bars because of the commission of approximately seventy-two different crimes. Some of these crimes were committed by hundreds of individuals, while others were committed by only one or two. The law of probability prevents a small group of two or three from being comparable to a group of several hundred. The writer suggests that the seventy-two crimes, for purposes of comparison, be classified into seven groups as follows: (1) Obtaining property through deception and fraud, known legally as forgery, embezzlement, false pretenses, conspiracy, confidence games, receiving stolen property, blackmail, counterfeiting, and uttering of fraudulent checks. (2) Obtaining property through force, known legally as robbery, burglary, assault to rob, breaking and entering, entering to commit felony, burglary and larceny, safe blowing, attempted burglary, kidnapping, child stealing, housebreaking, attempt to rob, and burglary of inhabited dwelling. (3). Obtaining property through common thievery, known legally as larceny, pocket picking, vehicle taking, horse stealing and automobile stealing. (4) Statutory offenses, known legally as unlawful use of motor vehicle, illegal sale of drugs, illegal sale or possession of intoxicating beverages, carrying concealed weapons, unlawful use of explosives, operating motor vehicle without owner's consent, violating automobile law, having burglar tools, concealing weapons to aid escape, escaping prison and removing railroad property. (5) Crimes of physical injury, known legally as murder, maiming, manslaughter, assault to murder, accessory to murder, cutting, shooting or stabbing to kill or wound; arson and malicious destruction of property. (6)Crimes of social dereliction, known legally as abandonment, desertion, vagrancy, begging, non-support, neglect of minor child, child abandonment, bigamy, lewdness, seduction, perjury, publishing of obscene writing, abduction, and receiving earnings of prostitute. (7) Sex crimes, known legally as rape, sodomy, indecent liberty with child, incest, assault to rape, crime against nature, assault to commit crime against nature, crime against child, adultery, and carnal abuse.

The first group consisting of 331 cases, is distributed as follows:

Alpha Scores	Cases	Percentage	Alpha Scores	Cases	Percentage
0- 9	3	.9	60- 74	49	14.8
10- 14	5	1.5	75- 89	44	13.3
15- 19	13	4.	90-104	38	11.5
20- 24	14	4.2	105-119	34	10.3
25- 34	16	4.8	120-134	18	5.5
35- 44	22	6.6	135-149	17	5.1
45- 59	34	10.3	150-212	24	7.2

Translating these percentage figures into the traditional letlet grades, we have the following:

Letter Grade	Percentage of Cases	Letter Grade	Percentage of Cases
E	2.4	C+	24.8
D	8.2	B	15.8
C—	11.4	A	12.3
C	25.1		

It is obvious that crimes of deception and fraud are committed by men of no mean ability. Only 22% are inferior to a grade of C, while 52.9% are superior to a grade of C.

The second group, consisting of 1542 cases, is distributed as follows:

Alpha Scores	Cases	Percentage	Alpha Scores	Cases	Percentage
0- 9	58	3.7	60- 74	220	14.3
10- 14	40	2.6	75- 89	191	12.4
15- 19	44	2.8	90-104	176	11.4
20- 24	45	2.9	105-119	108	7.
25- 34	127	8.2	120-134	74	4.9
35- 44	160	10.4	135-149	41	2.7
45- 59	236	15.3	150-212	32	2.1

Translating the above percentage figures into the letter grades, we have the following:

Letter Grade	Percentage of Cases	Letter Grade	Percentage of Cases
E	6.3	C+	23.8
D	5.7	B	11.9
C—	18.6	A	4.8
C	29.6		

The third group, consisting of 992 cases, is distributed as follows:

Alpha Scores	Cases	Percentage	Alpha Scores	Cases	Percentage
0- 9	46	4.7	60- 74	140	14.2
10-14	26	2.6	75- 89	128	13.
15-19	30	3.	90-104	120	12.1
20-24	43	4.3	105-119	70	7.
25-34	80	8.1	120-134	43	4.3
35-44	90	9.1	135-149	22	2.2
45-59	133	13.4	150-212	21	2.1

Translating the above percentage figures into the letter grades, we have the following:

Letter Grade	Percentage of Cases	Letter Grade	Percentage of Cases
E	7.3	C+	25.1
D	7.3	B	11.3
C—	17.2	A	4.3
C	27.6		

The fourth group, consisting of 187 cases, is distributed as follows:

Alpha Scores	Cases	Percentage	Alpha Scores	Cases	Percentage
0- 9	7	3.7	60- 74	31	16.6
10-14	5	2.7	75- 89	22	11.8
15-19	8	4.3	90-104	16	8.5
20-24	6	3.2	105-119	12	6.4
25-34	15	8.	120-134	9	4.8
35-44	17	9.1	135-149	2	1.1
45-59	33	17.6	150-212	4	2.1

Translating into letter grades, we have:

Letter Grade	Percentage of Cases	Letter Grade	Percentage of Cases
E	6.4	C+	20.3
D	7.5	B	11.2
C—	17.1	A	3.2
C	34.2		

The fifth group, consisting of 521 cases, is distributed as follows:

Alpha Scores	Cases	Percentage	Alpha Scores	Cases	Percentage
0- 9	36	7.	60- 74	70	13.3
10-14	17	3.3	75- 89	67	12.8
15-19	16	3.1	90-104	45	8.7
20-24	20	3.9	105-119	31	6.
25-34	52	10.	120-134	14	2.7
35-44	50	9.6	135-149	15	2.9
45-59	78	15.	150-212	10	1.9

Translating into the letter grades, we have:

Letter Grade	Percentage of Cases	Letter Grade	Percentage of Cases
E	10.3	C+	21.5
D	7.	B	8.7
C—	19.6	A	4.8
C	28.3		

The sixth group, consisting of 119 cases, is distributed as follows:

Alpha Scores	Cases	Percentage	Alpha Scores	Cases	Percentage
0- 9	11	9.3	60- 74	14	11.8
10-14	7	5.9	75- 89	10	8.5
15-19	8	6.8	90-104	12	10.
20-24	1	.8	105-119	10	8.4
25-34	13	11.	120-134	5	4.2
35-44	11	9.3	135-149	2	1.7
45-59	12	10.	150-212	3	2.5

Translating into the traditional letter grades, we have the following:

Letter Grade	Percentage of Cases	Letter Grade	Percentage of Cases
E	15.2	C+	18.5
D	7.6	B	12.6
C—	20.3	A	4.2
C	21.8		

The seventh group, consisting of 253 cases, is distributed as follows:

Alpha Scores	Cases	Percentage	Alpha Scores	Cases	Percentage
0- 9	2¹	9.5	60- 74	35	13.9
10-14	12	4.8	75- 89	20	7.9
15-19	12	4.8	90-104	15	6.
20-24	15	5.9	105-119	15	6.
25-34	24	9.5	120-134	6	2.4
35-44	33	13.1	135-149	4	1.6
45-59	32	12.7	150-212	6	2.4

Translating into the traditional letter grades, we have the following:

Letter Grade	Percentage of Cases	Letter Grade	Percentage of Cases
E	14.3	C+	13.9
D	10.7	B	8.4
C—	22.6	A	4.
C	26.6		

If we now asemble the letter grades of the seven groups of types, we have the following:

Letter Grade	Fraud	Force	Thievery	Statutory	Physical Injury	Dereliction	Sex
E	2.4	6.3	7.3	6.4	10.3	15.2	14.3
D	8.2	5.7	7.3	7.5	7.	7.6	10.7
C—	11.4	18.6	17.2	17.1	19.6	20.3	22.6
C	25.1	29.6	27.6	34.2	28.3	21.8	26.6
C+	24.8	23.8	25.1	20.3	21.5	18.5	13.9
B	15.8	11.9	11.3	11.2	8.7	12.6	8.4
A	12.3	4.8	4.3	3.2	4.8	4.2	4.

Grouping the letter grades inferior to C, and doing the same for the letter grades superior to C, we have:

Type	Superior	Inferior
Fraud	52.9	22.
Force	40.5	30.6
Thievery	40.7	31.8
Statutory	34.7	31.
Physical Injury	35.	36.9
Dereliction	35.3	43.1
Sex	26.3	47.6

It would seem that statutory crimes and crimes of physical injury are causally related very slightly to intelligence, in so far as intelligence can be measured by mental tests. But more than half of the individuals who commit crimes of fraud are superior individuals, according to the Army norms. At the same time, about half of the individuals who commit crimes against sex are inferior individuals according to the same standards. Crimes of social dereliction are committed by a large percentage of unusually superior individuals and also by a large percentage of unusually inferior individuals. Temperament must play a much larger role than intelligence in the commission of statutory crimes, crimes of physical injury, and crimes of social dereliction. Of course, it is quite possible that temperament, meaning by temperament the emotional complex, plays the chief role in the commission of all crime.

In discussing the high intelligence of men who commit fraud, it might be well to point out certain similarities in our general social life. One remembers the large amount of news that has appeared lately in the daily press concerning the failure of certain brokerage and promotional firms. These men are the type we are discussing. One remembers also the sensational exposure of certain prohibition leaders. These men also are the type we are discussing. One remembers the ignominious flight of a certain minister. Here also is the type. War contractors and prominent politicians furnish examples of the same type. Certain would-be religious leaders are the same type, but their genius, through the force of circumstances, has been confined to religious fraud.

There are important geographical concomitants to be considered in a discussion of types of crime. Let us compare, in the case of each type group, the criminals imprisoned in their home state with the criminals imprisoned outside their home state. Let us consider the fraud group first.

Alpha Scores	Cases at Home	Cases Away From Home	Percentage of Former	Percentage of Latter
0- 9	1	2	.5	1.3
10- 14	4	1	2.2	.6
15- 19	9	4	5.	2.6
20- 24	9	5	5.	3.3
25- 34	9	7	5.	4.6
35- 44	17	5	9.4	3.3
45- 59	23	11	12.7	7.3
60- 74	26	23	14.4	15.3
75- 89	23	21	12.7	14.
90-104	20	18	11.	12.
105-119	18	16	10.	10.6
120-134	9	9	5.	6.
135-149	7	10	3.9	6.6
150-212	6	18	3.3	12.

In letter grades, the percentage distribution of the above group is as follows:

Letter Grades	Percentage at Home	Percentage Away from Home
E	2.7	1.9
D	10.	5.9
C—	14.	7.9

C _____ 27.1   22.6
C+ _____ 23.7   26.
B _____ 15.   16.6
A _____ 7.2   18.6

It is clearly to be seen that the criminals who are imprisoned away from their home state are almost as numerous as and far superior to the home grown variety. Slightly more than 45% of this group was born outside the state in which it is now incarcerated.

Let us consider in the same way the second group, the "property by force" group.

Alpha Scores	Cases at Home	Cases Away From Home	Percentage of Former	Percentage of Latter
0- 9	42	16	4.4	2.7
10- 14	26	14	2.7	2.4
15- 19	28	16	3.	2.7
20- 24	26	19	2.7	3.3
25- 34	69	58	7.2	10.
35- 44	100	60	10.4	10.3
45- 59	147	89	15.3	15.3
60- 74	129	91	13.4	15.6
75- 89	125	66	13.	11.3
90-104	112	64	11.7	11.
105-119	68	40	7.1	6.9
120-134	47	27	4.9	4.6
135-149	24	17	2.5	2.9
150-212	17	15	1.8	2.6

Translating into the letter grades:

Letter Grades	Percentage at Home	Percentage Away from Home
E	7.1	5.1
D	5.7	6.
C—	17.6	20.3
C	28.7	30.9
C+	24.7	22.3
B	12.	11.5
A	4.3	5.5

In this group, the influence of nativity is not so marked. However 38% of the group is incarcerated outside its home state. Robbery and burglary are the two chief crimes in this group. In burglary, the geographical factors are fairly clear, but such factors are practically lacking in robbery. It might be well to compare the two crimes. Let us take robbery:

Alpha Scores	Cases at Home	Cases Away From Home	Percentage of Former	Percentage of Latter
0- 9	12	7	3.4	3.3
10- 14	7	5	2.	2.3

15- 19	10	1	2.8	.5
20- 24	7	7	2.	3.3
25- 34	28	15	8.	7.
35- 44	41	25	11.6	11.7
45- 59	46	34	13.1	15.9
60- 74	45	29	12.8	13.5
75- 89	46	23	13.1	10.7
90-104	39	31	11.1	14.5
105-119	27	18	7.7	8.4
120-134	22	11	6.2	5.1
135-149	13	3	3.7	1.4
150-212	9	5	2.6	2.3

Translating into letter grades:

Letter Grades	Percentage at Home	Percentage Away from Home
E	5.4	5.6
D	4.8	3.8
C—	19.6	18.7
C	25.9	29.4
C+	24.2	25.2
B	13.9	13.5
A	6.3	3.7

Let us now consider the group of burglars, and compare them with the robbers. The burglars are distributed as follows:

Alpha Scores	Cases at Home	Cases Away From Home	Percentage of Former	Percentage of Latter
0- 9	17	5	5.4	3.1
10- 14	8	5	2.5	3.1
15- 19	5	5	1.6	3.1
20- 24	9	6	2.8	3.8
25- 34	23	8	7.2	5.
35- 44	30	9	9.5	5.7
45- 59	53	22	16.8	13.8
60- 74	40	31	12.6	19.5
75- 89	45	21	14.2	13.2
90-104	45	13	14.2	8.2
105-119	19	11	6.	6.9
120-134	15	9	4.7	5.7
135-149	2	7	.6	4.4
150-212	5	7	1.6	4.4

Translating into letter grades, we have:

Letter Grades	Percentage at Home	Percentage Away from Home
E	7.9	6.2
D	4.4	6.9
C—	16.7	10.7
C	29.4	33.2

C+	28.4	21.4
B	10.7	12.6
A	2.2	8.8

It would seem from the comparison that the robbers are the criminals least influenced by geographical factors, and data concerning them influence the entire second group of criminal types. It may be possible to reconsider this peculiarity later.

We shall now consider the distribution of the third group, the "common thievery" group, consisting of 992 cases.

Alpha Scores	Cases at Home	Cases Away From Home	Percentage of Former	Percentage of Latter
0- 9	35	11	6.2	2.6
10- 14	18	8	3.2	1.7
15- 19	21	9	3.7	2.1
20- 24	27	16	4.7	3.8
25- 34	52	28	9.1	6.6
35- 44	66	24	11.5	5.7
45- 59	72	61	12.6	14.5
60- 74	68	72	11.8	17.1
75- 89	78	50	13.6	11.9
90-104	64	56	11.2	13.3
105-119	43	27	7.5	6.4
120-134	13	30	2.3	7.1
135-149	9	13	1.6	3.1
150-212	6	15	1.1	3.6

Translating into letter grades, we have the following:

Letter Grades	Percentage at Home	Percentage Away from Home
E	9.4	4.3
D	8.4	5.9
C—	20.6	12.3
C	24.4	31.6
C+	24.8	25.2
B	9.8	11.5
A	2.7	6.7

In this group also, the geographical factor is seen to be a very distinct consideration.

Let us proceed next with a distribution of the fourth group, the group of statutory offenses, consisting of 187 cases.

Alpha Scores	Cases at Home	Cases Away From Home	Percentage of Former	Percentage of Latter
0- 9	6	1	5.4	1.3
10- 14	4	1	3.6	1.3
15- 19	5	3	4.5	3.9
20- 24	4	2	3.6	2.6
25- 34	6	9	5.4	11.7
35- 44	11	6	10.	7.8
45- 59	23	10	20.9	13.

60- 74	17	14	15.4	18.2
75- 89	13	9	12.7	11.7
90-104	9	7	8.2	9.1
105-119	5	7	4.5	9.1
120-134	5	4	4.5	5.2
135-149	1	1	.9	1.3
150-212	1	3	.9	3.9

Translating into letter grades, we have:

Letter Grades	Percentage at Home	Percentage Away from Home
E	9.	2.6
D	8.1	6.5
C—	15.4	19.5
C	36.3	31.2
C+	20.9	20.8
B	9.	14.3
A	1.8	5.2

So, in this group also, we find the geographical factor. Let us continue with the distribution of the fifth group, the group of crimes involving physical injury. This group will consist of 521 cases.

Alpha Scores	Cases at Home	Cases Away From Home	Percentage of Former	Percentage of Latter
0- 9	28	7	8.5	4.2
10- 14	6	11	1.8	5.8
15- 19	9	7	2.7	3.7
20- 24	16	4	4.8	2.1
25- 34	31	21	9.3	11.2
35- 44	35	15	10.5	8.
45- 59	60	18	18.	9.6
60- 74	42	28	12.6	14.9
75- 89	49	18	14.7	9.6
90-104	21	24	6.3	12.2
105-119	15	16	4.5	8.5
120-134	7	7	2.1	3.7
135-149	9	6	2.7	3.2
150-212	5	5	1.5	2.7

Translating into letter grades, we have:

Letter Grades	Percentage at Home	Percentage Away from Home
E	10.3	10.
D	7.5	5.8
C—	19.8	19.2
C	30.6	24.5
C+	21.	21.8
B	6.6	12.2
A	4.2	5.9

The geographical concomitants are clear, except that there is a larger percentage than should be expected of the E men among those incarcerated away from home. Foreign-born parentage may explain this, and will be discussed later.

Let us proceed now to the distribution of the sixth group, the group of social dereliction, consisting of 119 cases.

Alpha Scores	Cases at Home	Cases Away From Home	Percentage of Former	Percentage of Latter
0- 9	7	4	13.2	6.1
10- 14	4	3	7.5	4.5
15- 19	2	6	3.8	9.1
20- 24	1	0	1.9	---.
25- 34	7	6	13.2	9.1
35- 44	3	8	5.7	12.1
45- 59	5	7	9.4	10.6
60- 74	7	7	13.2	10.6
75- 89	6	4	11.3	6.1
90-104	6	6	11.3	9.1
105-119	3	7	5.7	10.6
120-134	1	4	1.9	6.1
135-149	0	2	... .	3.
150-212	1	2	1.9	3.

Translating into letter grades, we have the following:

Letter Grades	Percentage at Home	Percentage Away from Home
E	20.7	10.6
D	5.7	9.1
C—	18.9	21.2
C	22.6	21.2
C+	22.6	15.2
B	7.6	16.7
A	1.9	6.

The presence of a geographical factor is very clear, and needs no further comment just yet. Let us proceed with the distribution of the seventh group, a group consisting of sex crimes and comprising 253 cases.

Alpha Scores	Cases at Home	Cases Away From Home	Percentage of Former	Percentage of Latter
0- 9	18	6	10.6	7.2
10- 14	10	2	5.9	2.4
15- 19	5	7	2.9	8.4
20- 24	13	2	7.6	2.4
25- 34	16	8	9.4	9.6
35- 44	21	12	12.3	14.4
45- 59	22	10	13.	12.
60- 74	20	15	11.8	18.
75- 89	15	5	8.8	6.
90-104	12	3	7.1	3.6
105-119	8	7	4.1	8.4
120-134	3	3	1.8	3.6
135-149	3	1	1.8	1.2
150-212	4	2	2.3	2.4

Translating into letter grades, we have the following:

Letter Grades	Percentage at Home	Percentage Away from Home
E	16.5	9.6
D	10.5	10.8
C—	21.7	24.
C	24.8	30.
C+	15.9	9.6
B	5.9	12.
A	4.1	3.6

With the exception of group two, the geographical concomitants bring about distinctions within each group that are just as clear as the differences between the groups themselves. This merely shows how highly co-ordinated with intelligence the geographical concomitants are. Either that, or the differences between types of crimes are not differences that can be expressed in terms of intelligence with much accuracy.

The percentages of men from different sections of the country committing certain types of crime might be compared with the percentages of men imprisoned at home who have committed the same types of crime. Let us take the traditional sections of the North, West and South, and compare the percentages from these sections with the percentages incarcerated at home. This comparison will not consider the Alpha scores, but merely the number of cases committing each type of crime.

Types of Crime	Percentage of Men from Each Section of Country Committing Given Type of Crime, the Percentages Being in the Order			
	West	North	South	Home
Fraud	9.	10.5	10.7	7.6
Force	39.3	41.9	35.3	40.7
Thievery	25.6	30.9	26.1	24.2
Statutory	5.6	5.1	5.9	4.7
Physical Injuries	11.3	11.1	15.	13.3
Dereliction	5.3	4.8	4.8	2.2
Sex	3.6	7.4	2.4	7.2

The general criminal type disappears in the classification of types of crime and the discovery that the types differ greatly in intelligence. Seven such type groups are suggested. However, it is found that, in each type group, the men incarcerated outside their home state seem more intelligent than are the men incarcerated within their home state, with but one exception.

CHAPTER 6

INTELLIGENCE AND RECIDIVISM

1. *Gross Comparison of Recidivists with First Offenders.*

The data on recidivism are confined to the states of Indiana, New Jersey and Maryland. For various reasons, such data were not obtainable in Ohio and Illinois. In this chapter the discussion will be confined to data from Indiana, New Jersey and Maryland. The two groups compare grossly as follows:

Alpha Scores	Cases First Offenders	Cases of Recidivists	Percentage of Former	Percentage of Latter
0- 9	67	42	6.8	6.4
10- 14	39	28	4.	4.3
15- 19	48	20	5.	3.
20- 24	57	30	5.8	4.5
25- 34	112	48	11.4	7.3
35- 44	95	68	9.6	10.3
45- 59	112	100	11.4	15.
60- 74	111	103	11.3	15.6
75- 89	112	69	11.4	10.4
90-104	76	71	7.7	10.8
105-119	67	34	6.8	5.2
120-134	34	19	3.5	2.9
135-149	24	16	2.4	2.5
150-212	25	12	2.5	1.8

Translating into the traditional letter grades, we have the following:

Letter Grades	Percentage of First Offenders	Percentage of Recidivists
E	10.8	10.7
D	10.8	7.5
C—	21.	17.6
C	22.7	30.5
C+	19.1	21.2
B	10.3	8.1
A	4.9	4.3

As can be seen, the recidivists have 33.6% superior to a grade of C, and 35.8% inferior to a grade of C. On the other hand, the first offenders have 34.3% superior to a grade of C, and 42.6% inferior to a grade of C. In percentage of individuals superior to a grade of C, the two groups are approximately equal. But in individuals inferior to a grade of C, the first offenders are more numerous. In addition, the recidivists possess a much larger percentage of C individuals. It seems fairly obvious that the first offenders, as a group, are not so intelligent as the recidivists.

To many, it will seem astounding that recidivists should be found more intelligent than are first offenders. Such a conclusion will be found to be exactly the opposite of the traditional beliefs on the subject, that is, of those beliefs that are founded on hearsay and on illegal generalizations from limited observation. But traditional beliefs, like the traditional methods of treating disease, are usually fallacious. It should be remembered that no attempt is made in this book to define the term intelligence. Intelligence and Alpha score are assumed to be synonomous for the purposes of this book.

2. First, Second and Habitual Offenders.

The gross comparison of first offenders and recidivists is probably not exact enough for scientific requirements though such has been the general practice. Let us compare the first offenders with second offenders and with habitual offenders.

Alpha Scores	Cases of Each in the Order First	Second	Habitual	Percentages in the Order of First	Second	Habitual
0- 9	67	24	18	6.8	5.4	8.5
10- 14	39	13	15	4.	2.9	7.
15- 19	48	11	9	5.	2.5	4.3
20- 24	57	22	8	5.8	5.	3.8
25- 34	112	34	14	11.4	7.7	6.6
35- 44	95	52	16	9.6	11.6	7.5
45- 59	112	78	22	11.4	17.4	10.4
60- 74	111	74	29	11.3	16.6	13.7
75- 89	112	43	26	11.4	9.6	12.2
90-104	76	44	27	7.7	9.8	12.8
105-119	67	22	12	6.8	5.	5.6
120-134	34	15	4	3.5	3.4	1.9
135-149	24	8	8	2.4	1.8	3.8
150-212	25	8	4	2.5	1.8	1.9

Translating into letter grades, we have the following:

Letter Grades	Percentages in the Order of First	Second	Habitual
E	10.8	8.3	15.5
D	10.8	7.5	8.1
C—	21.	19.3	14.1
C	22.7	34.	24.1
C+	19.1	19.4	25.
B	10.3	8.4	7.5
A	4.9	3.6	5.7

Let us consider the three groups in terms of percentages superior to a grade of C, percentages inferior to a grade of C, and percentages of C.

	Inferior To C	C	Superior To C
First _____	42.6	22.7	34.3
Second _____	35.1	34.	31.4
Habitual _____	37.7	24.1	38.2

Approximately half of all first offenders become second offenders, and approximately half of all second offenders become habitual offenders. If it is true, as some have claimed, that feeble-mindedness is an important factor in recidivism, it is equally true that high intelligence is just as important a factor. It behooves the serious worker in this field to discontinue the paternal and mightier-than-thou attitude towards the criminal, and at least attempt a closer relationship with the facts. And it is possible that the facts may not be as palatable as one might wish. But most of our guiding ideas concerning the criminal have drifted in from Italy, where graft and corruption in the administration of justice is of notorious and common practice, and where only the friendless, the feeble-minded and the boobs ever get to prison. Even in this country, the daily stories in the press concerning the shortcomings of the mighty and influential citizens are not very often followed by stories of conviction.

3. Gross Geographical Concomitants of Recidivism.

Let us compare the recidivists imprisoned in their home state with the recidivists imprisoned outside their home state.

Alpha Scores	Cases at Home	Cases Away from Home	Percentage of Former	Percentage of Latter
0- 9 _____	28	14	7.6	5.
10- 14 _____	16	5	4.4	1.7
15- 19 _____	11	9	3.	3.2
20- 24 _____	25	5	6.8	1.7
25- 34 _____	28	20	7.6	7.
35- 44 _____	44	24	11.9	8.4
45- 59 _____	58	42	15.8	14.7
60- 74 _____	52	52	14.1	17.9
75- 89 _____	47	22	12.8	7.7
90-104 _____	34	37	9.2	13.
105-119 _____	14	20	3.8	7.
120-134 _____	3	16	.8	5.6
135-149 _____	7	9	1.9	3.2
150-212 _____	1	11	.3	3.9

In letter grades, the comparison becomes clearer.

Letter Grades	Percentage at Home	Away from Home
E _____	12.	6.7
D _____	9.8	4.9
C— _____	19.5	15.4
C _____	29.9	32.6

C+ ---	22.	20.7
B ---	4.6	12.6
A ---	2.2	7.1

It is obvious that the recidivists from other states seem a more intelliegnt group than are the home-grown variety. Let us compare also the first offenders imprisoned at home with the first offenders from other states.

Alpha Scores	Cases at Home	Cases Away from Home	Percentage of Former	Percentage of Latter
0- 9	46	21	9.2	4.4
10- 14	22	17	4.4	3.6
15- 19	26	22	5.2	4.6
20- 24	30	26	6.	5.4
25- 34	52	60	10.4	12.5
35- 44	50	45	10.	9.4
45- 59	64	48	12.8	10.
60- 74	41	70	8.2	14.6
75- 89	67	45	13.4	9.4
90-104	40	36	8.	7.5
105-119	31	36	6.2	7.5
120-134	12	22	2.4	4.6
135-149	7	17	1.4	3.6
150-212	11	14	2.2	2.9

In letter grades, the comparison becomes:

Letter Grades	Percentage at Home	Away from Home
E	13.6	8.
D	11.2	10.
C—	20.4	21.9
C	21.	24.6
C+	21.4	16.9
B	8.8	12.1
A	3.6	6.5

Let us arrange the letter grades of the home-grown recidivists parallel to the letter grades of the home-grown first offenders.

Letter Grade	Percentage of Recidivists	Percentage of First Offenders
E	12.	13.8
D	9.8	11.4
C—	19.5	20.6
C	29.9	20.9
C+	22.	21.3
B	4.6	8.5
A	2.2	3.5

Let us also compare the letter grades of recidivists and first offenders born outside the state in which incarcerated.

Letter Grade	Percentage of Recidivists	Percentage of First Offenders
E	6.7	8.
D	4.9	10.
C—	15.4	21.9
C	32.6	24.6
C+	20.7	16.9
B	12.6	12.1
A	7.1	6.5

The relatively large number of average or C men in both groups of recidivists should be noticed. The transient recidivists seem more intelligent than the home grown variety, and are more superior to the transient first offenders than are the home grown recidivists to the home grown first offenders.

4. *Geographical Concomitants of First, Second and Habitual Offenders.*

Let us consider first, from among those incarcerated in their home state, the first, second and habitual offenders.

Alpha Scores	Cases of First	Cases of Second	Cases of Habitual	Percentages in Order of First	Second	Habitual
0- 9	46	18	10	9.2	6.6	10.4
10- 14	22	11	5	4.4	4.	5.2
15- 19	26	8	3	5.2	2.9	3.1
20- 24	30	19	6	6.	7.	6.3
25- 34	52	21	7	10.4	7.7	7.3
35- 44	50	34	10	10.	12.5	10.4
45- 59	64	46	12	12.8	16.9	11.5
60- 74	41	43	9	8.2	15.8	9.4
75- 89	67	31	16	13.4	11.4	16.6
90-104	40	23	11	8.	8.5	11.4
105-119	31	11	3	6.2	4.	3.1
120-134	12	1	2	2.4	.4	2.1
135-149	7	5	2	1.4	1.9	2.1
150-212	11	1	0	2.2	.4	---

Translating the percentages into letter grades, we have the following:

Letter Grades	Percentages in the Order of First	Second	Habitual
E	13.6	10.6	15.6
D	11.2	9.9	9.4
C—	20.4	20.2	17.7
C	21.	32.7	21.9
C+	21.4	19.9	28.
B	8.6	4.4	5.2
A	3.6	2.3	2.1

The outstanding features are the large number of average or C men among the second offenders, and the large number of C+ men among the habitual offenders.

Now let us compare the first, second and habitual offenders among those incarcerated outside their home state.

Alpha Scores	Cases of First	Cases of Second	Cases of Habitual	Percentage in Order of First	Second	Habitual
0- 9	21	6	8	4.4	3.2	7.3
10- 14	17	2	3	3.6	1.	2.7
15- 19	22	3	6	4.6	1.6	5.5
20- 24	26	3	2	5.4	1.6	1.8
25- 34	60	13	7	12.5	6.8	6.4
35- 44	45	18	6	9.4	9.4	5.5
45- 59	48	32	10	10.	16.7	9.2
60- 74	70	31	20	14.6	16.2	18.3
75- 89	45	12	10	9.4	6.3	9.2
90-104	36	21	16	7.5	11.	14.7
105-119	36	11	9	7.5	5.8	8.3
120-134	22	14	2	4.6	7.3	1.8
135-149	17	3	6	3.6	1.6	5.5
150-212	14	7	4	2.9	3.7	3.7

Making the transition into letter grades, we have:

Letter Grades	Percentage in the Order of First	Second	Habitual
E	8.	4.2	10.
D	10.	3.2	7.3
C—	21.9	16.2	11.9
C	24.6	32.9	27.5
C+	16.9	17.3	23.9
B	12.1	13.1	10.1
A	6.5	5.3	9.2

The habitual offenders are distinguished both by the large number of low grade men and by the number of high grade men.

Using the percentages given above, let us compare the first offenders imprisoned at home with the first offenders imprisoned away from home.

Letter Grades	First Offenders in Order of Home and Away	
E	13.6	8.
D	11.2	10.
C—	20.4	21.9
C	21.	24.6
C+	21.4	16.9
B	8.6	12.1
A	3.6	6.5

The geographical concomitants are marked. Let us make the same comparison in the case of the second offenders imprisoned at home and imprisoned away from home.

Letter Grades	Percentage of Second Offenders Home	Away
E	10.6	4.2

D	9.9	3.2
C—	20.2	16.2
C	32.7	32.9
C+	19.9	17.3
B	4.4	13.1
A	2.3	5.3

The geographical concomitants are exceedingly marked in the above comparison. The usually high yet similar percentages of average or C men should be noted. Now let us make the same comparison for the habitual offenders.

	Percentage of Habitual Offenders	
Letter Grades	Home	Away
E	15.6	10.
D	9.4	7.3
C—	17.7	11.9
C	21.9	27.5
C+	28.	23.9
B	5.2	10.1
A	2.1	9.2

The geographical concomitants are more marked than ever in the case of the habitual offenders.

5. *First Offenders, Recidivists and Types of Crime*

In this respect we shall use the seven types of crime that we have previously agreed upon, and in each type shall compare the recidivists with the first offenders. Some of the types, to be sure, are represented by too few cases to be considered seriously in this respect.

From the three states of Indiana, New Jersey and Maryland, data on the 146 cases of fraud was obtained. Of these, 58 were recidivists and 88 were first offenders. The distribution of the two groups compares as follows:

Alpha Scores	Cases First Offenders	Cases of Recidivists	Percentage of Former	Percentage of Latter
0- 9	0	2	----	3.4
10- 14	3	1	3.4	1.7
15- 19	3	1	3.4	1.7
20- 24	3	7	3.4	12.1
25- 34	5	2	5.7	3.4
35- 44	5	4	5.7	6.9
45- 59	6	6	6.8	10.3
60- 74	7	11	8.	19.
75- 89	14	9	16.	15.5
90-104	8	5	9.1	8.6
105-119	10	1	11.3	1.7
120-134	6	4	6.8	6.9
135-149	6	2	6.8	3.4
150-212	12	3	13.6	5.2

Translating into letter grades, we have:

Letter Grades	Percentage First	Percentage of Recidivists
E	3.4	5.1
D	6.8	13.8
C—	11.4	10.3
C	14.8	29.3
C+	25.1	24.1
B	18.1	8.6
A	20.4	8.6

In this group of crimes, the first offenders seem more intelligent than are the recidivists. Certainly, the relatively high intelligence of recidivists in general is not brought about by the recidivists in crimes of fraud. But the high intelligence of the first offenders in this group should be noticed. Such men are not the type who get caught very frequently. Let us continue with the distribution of 474 cases in the second of the seven types, the "force" group.

Alpha Scores	Cases First Offenders	Cases of Recidivists	Percentage of Former	Percentage of Latter
0- 9	14	13	5.2	6.5
10- 14	12	5	4.4	2.5
15- 19	10	7	3.7	3.5
20- 24	15	5	5.5	2.5
25- 34	42	16	15.3	8.
35- 44	23	23	8.4	11.5
45- 59	35	33	12.8	16.5
60- 74	39	33	14.2	16.5
75- 89	32	21	11.7	10.5
90-104	18	23	6.5	11.5
105-118	19	11	6.9	5.5
120-134	9	3	3.3	1.5
135-149	4	6	1.5	3.
150-212	2	1	.7	.5

Translating into the letter grades, we have:

Letter Grades	Percentage First	Percentage of Recidivists
E	9.6	9.
D	9.2	6.
C—	23.7	19.5
C	27.	33.
C+	18.2	22.
B	10.2	7.
A	2.2	3.5

In the above comparison, we have a fine example of the tendency of recidivists to be grouped about the average. In this group, however, there is not so large a percentage of superior men among the recidivists or the first offenders, and the recidivists and the first offenders are more nearly alike in all respects except in the case of the C men.

Let us observe a comparison of the recidivists and the first offenders in the third group, the "common thievery" group.

Alpha Scores	Cases First Offenders	Cases of Recidivists	Percentage of Former	Percentage of Latter
0- 9	15	19	5.8	7.6
10- 14	9	10	3.5	4.
15- 19	11	7	4.3	2.8
20- 24	18	12	7.	4.8
25- 34	18	19	7.	7.6
35- 44	26	25	10.1	10.
45- 59	34	36	13.2	14.3
60- 74	30	35	11.7	14.
75- 89	34	24	13.2	9.6
90-104	26	29	10.1	11.6
105-119	12	17	4.7	6.8
120-134	11	9	4.3	3.6
135-149	7	4	2.7	1.6
150-212	6	5	2.3	2.

Translating into letter grades for convenience, we have:

Letter Grades	Percentage First	Percentage of Recidivists
E	9.3	11.6
D	11.3	7.6
C—	17.1	17.6
C	24.9	28.3
C+	23.3	21.2
B	9.	10.4
A	5.	3.6

Here again, the recidivists and the first offenders do not differ so much in the percentages of superior men or of inferior men, but rather in the percentage of average men.

In the case of the statutory offenses, there are only 69 cases of which 18 are first offenders and 51 are recidivists. This in itself is the most important fact that can be pointed out concerning this group. The cases are too few for a comparative distribution, but we shall make such a distribution for purposes of completion.

Alpha Scores	Cases First Offenders	Cases of Recidivists	Percentage of Former	Percentage of Latter
0- 9	3	2	16.6	4.
10- 14	2	1	11.1	2.
15- 19	2	2	11.1	4.
20- 24	1	4	5.5	8.
25- 34	3	5	16.6	10.
35- 44	0	2	----	4.

45- 59 _____	3	11	16.6	22.
60- 74 _____	2	9	11.1	18.
75- 89 _____	2	5	11.1	10.
90-104 _____	0	6	____	12.
105-119 _____	0	3	____	6.
120-134 _____	0	0	____	____
135-149 _____	0	1	____	2.
150-212 _____	0	0	____	____

Translating into the letter grades:

Letter Grades	Percentage First	Percentage of Recidivists
E _____	27.7	6.
D _____	16.6	12.
C— _____	16.3	14.
C _____	27.7	40.
C+ _____	11.1	22.
B _____	____	6.
A _____	____	2.

In the above group, the recidivists seem superior to the first offenders. In spite of that fact, the recidivists are far more numerous than the first offenders through the C range of the Alpha scale.

Let us now observe the distribution of the first offenders and the recidivists in the fifth group, the group of "physical injury" crimes. In this group there are 187 first offenders and 66 recidivists.

Alpha Scores	Cases First Offenders	Cases of Recidivists	Percentage of Former	Percentage of Latter
0- 9 _____	19	3	10.2	4.5
10- 14 _____	6	0	3.2	____
15- 19 _____	13	0	7.	____
20- 24 _____	14	0	7.5	____
25- 34 _____	24	5	12.8	7.6
35- 44 _____	21	12	11.2	18.2
45- 59 _____	24	12	12.8	18.2
60- 74 _____	12	12	6.4	18.2
75- 89 _____	22	8	11.8	12.1
90-104 _____	11	6	5.9	9.1
105-119 _____	13	1	7.	1.5
120-134 _____	4	2	2.1	3.
135-149 _____	2	3	1.1	4.5
150-212 _____	2	2	1.1	3.

Translating into the letter grades, we have:

Letter Grades	Percentage First	Percentage of Recidivists
E _____	13.4	4.5
D _____	14.5	____
C— _____	24.	25.8

C		19.2	36.4
C+		17.7	21.2
B		9.1	4.5
A		2.2	7.5

In the above group, the percentages of superior men are about equal in the case of recidivists and first offenders. However, there are very few low grade recidivists and relatively a large number of average recidivists.

In the case of the sixth group, the group of "social dereliction," there are 50 first offenders and only 6 recidivists. This makes it impossible to compare the letter grades of the recidivists and the first offenders, but their distribution on the Alpha scale can be observed.

Alpha Scores	Cases First Offenders	Cases of Recidivists	Percentage of Former	Percentage of Latter
0- 9	4	0	8.	----
10- 14	3	0	6.	----
15- 19	4	1	8.	Omitted
20- 24	0	0	----	----
25- 34	6	1	12.	Omitted
35- 44	4	0	8.	----
45- 59	5	0	10.	----
60- 74	8	1	16.	Omitted
75- 89	1	0	2.	----
90-104	4	0	8.	----
105-119	5	1	10.	Omitted
120-134	2	1	4.	----
135-149	2	0	4.	Omitted
150-212	2	1	4.	Omitted

The fact of so few recidivists in the above group renders it impossible to discuss the group in this book to much advantage. That problem must lie over till the writer issues his monograph on psychology and the criminal law.

Let us consider next the distribution of first offenders and recidivists in the seventh group, the "sex" group. In this group there are 105 first offenders and 21 recidivists. The number of cases is not large enough for exact comparison, but the distribution on the Alpha scale will be interesting.

Alpha Scores	Cases First Offenders	Cases of Recidivists	Percentage of Former	Percentage of Latter
0- 9	12	3	11.4	14.3
10- 14	4	4	3.8	19.
15- 19	5	2	4.8	9.5
20- 24	5	2	4.8	9.5
25- 34	14	0	13.3	---
35- 44	16	2	15.2	9.5
45- 59	5	2	4.8	9.5
60- 74	13	2	12.4	9.5

75- 89 _____	7	2	6.6	9.5
90-104 _____	8	2	7.6	9.5
105-119 _____	8	0	7.6	---
120-134 _____	2	0	1.9	---
135-149 _____	3	0	2.9	---
150-212 _____	3	0	2.9	---

Translating into the letter grades, we have:

Letter Grades	Percentage First	Percentage of Recidivists
E _____	15.2	33.3
D _____	9.6	19.
C— _____	28.5	9.5
C _____	17.2	19.
C+ _____	14.2	19.
B _____	9.5	---
A _____	5.8	---

The recidivists who commit sex crimes seem inferior to the first offenders in these crimes.

6. Geographical Concomitants and Types of Crime of First Offenders and Recidivists

In this discussion also, it must be remembered that in some instances the number of cases is not large enough to merit serious consideration. In all respects, however, the distributions will be given for the sake of future additions and comparisons.

We shall consider the "fraud" group first, in the order of first offenders and of recidivists. The first offenders are distributed as follows:

Alpha Scores	Cases at Home	Cases Away	Percentage of Former	Percentage of Latter
0- 9 _____	0	0	---	---
10- 14 _____	2	1	6.6	1.8
15- 19 _____	2	1	6.6	1.8
20- 24 _____	1	2	3.3	3.6
25- 34 _____	0	5	---	9.
35- 44 _____	2	3	6.6	5.4
45- 59 _____	1	5	3.3	9.
60- 74 _____	2	5	6.6	9.
75- 89 _____	5	9	16.6	16.1
90-104 _____	2	6	6.6	10.7
105-119 _____	5	5	16.6	9.
120-134 _____	2	4	6.6	7.1
135-149 _____	3	3	10.	5.4
150-212 _____	3	7	10.	12.5

Translating into the letter grades, we have:

Letter Grades	Percentage at Home	Percentage Away
E	6.6	1.8
D	9.9	5.4
C—	6.6	14.4
C	9.9	18.
C+	23.2	26.8
B	23.2	16.1
A	20.	17.9

Let us compare the above distribution of first offenders with the recidivists of the same group. Following is the distribution of the recidivists:

Alpha Scores	Cases at Home	Cases Away	Percentage of Former	Percentage of Latter
0- 9	1	1	3.	4.2
10- 14	1	0	3.	---
15- 19	0	1	---	4.2
20- 24	6	1	17.6	4.2
25- 34	1	1	3.	4.2
35- 44	3	1	8.8	4.2
45- 59	5	1	14.7	4.2
60- 74	8	3	23.5	12.5
75- 89	6	3	17.6	12.5
90-104	1	4	3.	16.6
105-119	0	1	---	4.2
120-134	1	3	3.	12.5
135-149	0	2	---	8.3
150-212	1	2	3.	8.3

Translating into the letter grades, we have:

Letter Grades	Percentage at Home	Percentage Away
E	6.	4.2
D	17.6	8.4
C—	11.8	8.4
C	38.2	16.6
C+	20.6	29.1
B	3.	16.7
A	3.	16.6

It appears that in crimes of fraud, the home-grown first offenders are about as intelligent as the other first offenders, but the home-grown recidivists are quite inferior to the other recidivists. Also, the home-grown recidivists contribute quite largely to the phenomenon previously noticed of unusually high percentage of C men among second offenders.

Let us consider next the distributions of the second group, the "property by force" group, taking the first offenders first.

Alpha Scores	Cases at Home	Cases Away	Percentage of Former	Percentage of Latter
0- 9	8	6	6.1	4.2
10- 14	6	6	4.6	4.2

15- 19 _____	6	4	4.6	2.8
20- 24 _____	6	9	4.6	6.3
25- 34 _____	21	21	16.1	13.9
35- 44 _____	8	15	6.1	10.4
45- 59 _____	20	15	15.4	10.4
60- 74 _____	14	25	10.8	17.4
75- 89 _____	19	13	14.6	9.
90-104 _____	10	8	7.7	5.5
105-119 _____	8	11	6.1	7.6
120-134 _____	4	5	3.1	3.5
135-149 _____	0	4	---	2.8
150-212 _____	0	2	---	1.4

Translating into the letter grades, we have:

Letter Grades	Percentage at Home	Percentage Away
E _____	10.7	8.4
D _____	9.2	9.1
C— _____	22.2	24.3
C _____	26.2	27.8
C+ _____	22.3	14.5
B _____	9.2	11.1
A _____	---	4.2

Treating the recidivists in the same way, we have:

Alpha Scores	Cases at Home	Cases Away	Percentage of Former	Percentage of Latter
0- 9 _____	9	4	8.4	4.3
10- 14 _____	3	2	2.8	2.1
15- 19 _____	4	3	3.7	3.2
20- 24 _____	5	0	4.7	---
25- 34 _____	8	8	7.5	8.6
35- 44 _____	8	15	7.5	16.1
45- 59 _____	18	15	16.8	16.1
60- 74 _____	16	17	15.	18.3
75- 89 _____	14	7	13.1	7.5
90-104 _____	12	11	11.2	11.8
105-119 _____	5	6	4.7	6.5
120-134 _____	1	2	.9	2.1
135-149 _____	4	2	3.7	2.1
150-212 _____	0	1	---	1.1

Translating into the letter grades, we have:

Letter Grades	Percentage at Home	Percentage Away
E _____	11.2	6.4
D _____	8.4	3.2
C— _____	15.	24.7
C _____	31.8	34.4
C+ _____	24.3	19.3
B _____	5.6	8.6
A _____	3.7	3.2

It is interesting that the home-grown first offenders and recidivists in this group show a large percentage of men in the C range, a phenomenon that is just the reverse among the first offenders and recidivists in the "fraud" group. There are probably some common factors in the wandering forger and the individual who is a burglar in his own community. Otherwise, the geographical factors are not so keenly in evidence in this group.

Let us consider next similar distributions of the third group, the "common thievery" group, taking the first offenders and then the recidivists.

Alpha Scores	Cases at Home	Cases Away	Percentage of Former	Percentage of Latter
0- 9	12	3	8.7	2.5
10- 14	6	3	4.3	2.5
15- 19	8	3	5.8	2.5
20- 24	7	10	5.1	8.5
25- 34	7	11	5.1	9.3
35- 44	17	9	12.3	7.6
45- 59	17	17	12.3	14.4
60- 74	13	17	9.4	14.4
75- 89	23	11	16.6	9.3
90-104	14	12	10.1	10.1
105-119	7	5	5.1	4.2
120-134	3	8	2.2	6.8
135-149	1	6	.7	5.1
150-212	3	3	2.2	2.5

Translating into the letter grades, we have:

Letter Grades	Percentage at Home	Percentage Away
E	13.	5.
D	10.9	11.
C—	17.4	16.9
C	21.7	28.8
C+	26.7	19.4
B	7.3	11.
A	2.9	7.6

Making the same distribution for the recidivists, we have the following:

Alpha Scores	Cases at Home	Cases Away	Percentage of Former	Percentage of Latter
0- 9	13	6	9.4	5.3
10- 14	7	3	5.1	2.7
15- 19	3	4	2.2	3.5
20- 24	9	3	6.5	2.7
25- 34	14	5	10.1	4.4
35- 44	19	6	13.8	5.3
45- 59	18	18	13.	15.9
60- 74	12	23	8.7	20.4

75- 89 _____	19	5	13.8	4.4
90-104 _____	14	15	10.1	13.3
105-119 _____	8	9	5.8	8.
120-134 _____	0	9	---	8.
135-149 _____	2	2	1.4	1.8
150-212 _____	0	5	---	4.4

Translating into the letter grades, we have:

Letter Grades	Percentage at Home	Percentage Away
E _____	14.5	8.
D _____	8.7	6.2
C— _____	23.9	9.7
C _____	21.7	36.3
C+ _____	23.9	17.7
B _____	5.8	16.
A _____	1.4	6.2

The home-grown offenders and recidivists show a high percentage of C cases, just as in the case of the second type group. The home-grown recidivists show a relatively low percentage of average or C cases, while the other recidivists show an unusually high percentage of such C cases. In fact, the distributions of the two groups of recidivists are markedly different.

In the case of the fourth group, the "statutory group," the number of cases is not large enough for accurate comparison. However, for the sake of future additions, the distributions will be given. In the case of the first offenders, the percentages will not be given, but the percentages will be given in the case of the recidivists. There are only 18 of the first offenders and 51 of the recidivists. Even in the case of the recidivists, the number is too small for accurate comparison. The distribution of the first offenders is as follows:

Alpha Scores	Cases at Home	Cases Away	Percentages Are Omitted
0- 9 _____	2	1	
10- 14 _____	2	0	
15- 19 _____	1	1	
20- 24 _____	0	1	
25- 34 _____	0	3	
35- 44 _____	0	0	
45- 59 _____	2	1	
60- 74 _____	0	2	
75- 89 _____	0	2	
90-104 _____	0	0	
105-119 _____	0	0	
120-134 _____	0	0	
135-149 _____	0	0	
150-212 _____	0	0	

Making a similar distribution for the recidivists, but also giving the percentages for purposes of gross comparison, we have the following:

Alpha Scores	Cases at Home	Cases Away	Percentage of Former	Percentage of Latter
0- 9	2	0	8.	---
10- 14	1	0	4.	---
15- 19	1	1	4.	3.8
20- 24	3	1	12.	3.8
25- 34	2	3	8.	11.5
35- 44	1	1	4.	3.8
45- 59	6	5	24.	19.3
60- 74	5	4	20.	15.4
75- 89	2	3	8.	11.5
90-104	2	4	8.	15.4
105-119	0	3	---	11.5
120-134	0	0	---	---
135-149	0	1	---	3.8
150-212	0	0	---	---

Translating into the letter grades, we have:

Letter Grades	Percentage at Home	Percentage Away
E	12.	---
D	16.	7.6
C—	12.	15.3
C	44.	34.7
C+	16.	26.9
B	---	11.5
A	---	3.8

Among the recidivists above, the number of C men is unusually high, while the number of C among those born outside the state in which incarcerated is unusually high as in the case of the "fraudulent group." In general, statutory crimes seem to be committed by recidivists. The first offenders who do commit such crimes seem of low average intelligence.

The distributions of the fifth group, the physical injury group, will now be considered. The first offenders give the following distribution:

Alpha Scores	Cases at Home	Cases Away	Percentage of Former	Percentage of Latter
0- 9	14	5	11.9	7.2
10- 14	2	4	1.7	5.8
15- 19	7	6	5.9	8.7
20- 24	10	4	8.5	5.8
25- 34	14	10	11.9	14.5
35- 44	13	8	11.	11.6
45- 59	19	5	16.1	7.2
60- 74	7	5	5.9	7.2

75- 89	15	7	12.7	10.1
90-104	5	6	4.2	8.7
105-119	7	6	5.9	8.7
120-134	2	2	1.7	2.9
135-149	1	1	.8	1.4
150-212	2	0	1.7	---

Translating into the letter grades, we have:

Letter Grades	Percentage at Home	Percentage Away
E	13.6	13.
D	14.4	14.5
C—	22.9	26.1
C	22.	14.4
C+	16.9	18.8
B	7.6	11.6
A	2.5	1.4

The low percentage of C men among those incarcerated outside their home state should be noted. Making the same distribution for the recidivists, we have the following.

Alpha Scores	Cases at Home	Cases Away	Percentage of Former	Percentage of Latter
0- 9	1	2	2.3	8.7
10- 14	0	0	---	---
15- 19	0	0	---	---
20- 24	0	0	---	---
25- 34	3	2	7.	8.7
35- 44	12	0	27.9	---
45- 59	9	3	20.9	13.
60- 74	8	4	18.6	17.4
75- 89	4	4	9.3	17.4
90-104	3	3	7.	13.
105-119	1	0	2.3	---
120-134	1	1	2.3	4.3
135-149	1	2	2.3	8.7
150-212	0	2	---	8.7

Translating into the letter grades, we have:

Letter Grades	Percentage at Home	Percentage Away
E	2.3	8.7
D	---	---
C—	34.9	8.7
C	39.5	30.4
C+	16.3	30.4
B	4.6	4.3
A	2.3	17.4

The high percentage of C men among home-grown recidivists should be noted, equally with the high percentage of C men among the recidivists incarcerated outside their home state. It also is of significance that recidivists of very low intelligence are not likely to commit crimes of this nature.

The opposite has usually been taken for granted. This type of criminal does not vary widely from average intelligence. The recidivists have an unusually small standard deviation.

Let us consider now the sixth group, the social dereliction group. Such crimes are rarely committed by any but first offenders, and these first offenders are usually far from their home state. Crimes of social dereliction are closely related to the breaking of community ties. Of the 57 cases in this type group, there are only 6 recidivists. Of the first offenders, 16 are home-grown and 35 are from other states. Of the six recidivists, only two are home-grown. For the convenience of future additions, the distribution of the six recidivists is given as follows:

Alpha Scores	Cases at Home	Cases Away	Alpha Scores	Cases at Home	Cases Away
0- 9	0	0	60- 74	1	0
10-14	0	0	75- 89	0	0
15-19	1	0	90-104	0	0
20-24	0	0	105-119	0	1
25-34	0	1	120-134	0	1
35-44	0	0	135-149	0	0
45-59	0	0	150-212	0	1

The 51 first offenders give the following distribution:

Alpha Scores	Cases at Home	Cases Away	Percentage of Former	Percentage of Latter
0- 9	2	2	12.5	5.7
10- 14	1	2	6.2	5.7
15- 19	1	3	6.2	8.6
20- 24	0	0	---	----
25- 34	1	5	6.2	14.3
35- 44	1	3	6.2	8.6
45- 59	2	3	12.5	8.6
60- 74	2	6	12.5	17.1
75- 89	1	0	6.2	---
90-104	3	2	18.7	5.7
105-119	1	4	6.2	11.4
120-134	0	2	---	5.7
135-149	0	2	---	5.7
150-212	1	1	6.2	2.9

Translating into the letter grades, we have:

Letter Grades	Percentage at Home	Percentage Away
E	18.7	11.4
D	6.2	8.6
C—	12.4	22.9
C	25.	25.7
C+	24.9	5.7
B	6.2	17.1
A	6.2	8.6

Perhaps, in the light of the small number of cases, it will be better not to point out the characteristics of the above distributions. The distributions will be valuable for future additions.

In the group of sex crimes, there are only 21 recidivists. But 19 of these 21 recidivists are home-grown, which is an important fact to note. The distribution of the 21 recidivists is as follows:

Alpha Scores	Cases at Home	Cases Away	Alpha Scores	Cases at Home	Cases Away
0- 9	2	1	60- 74	2	0
10-14	4	0	75- 89	2	0
15-19	2	0	90-104	2	0
20-24	2	0	105-119	0	0
25-34	0	0	120-134	0	0
35-44	1	1	135-149	0	0
45-59	2	0	150-212	0	0

The lack of high grade intelligence in the above recidivists is the most outstanding characteristic. The more intelligent professional criminals simply are not convicted of these crimes. This is certainly not because intelligent men do not desire such behavior, for some of the first offenders in such crimes are very intelligent men and highly educated. There is a logical inconsistency in the social degradation that is heaped upon these men. They are much better citizens than are the forgers and embezzlers.

Alpha Scores	Cases at Home	Cases Away	Percentage of Former	Percentage of Latter
0- 9	8	4	13.3	9.5
10- 14	3	1	5.	2.4
15- 19	1	4	1.7	9.5
20- 24	6	0	10.	---
25- 34	9	5	15.	11.9
35- 44	9	7	15.	16.6
45- 59	3	2	5.	4.8
60- 74	3	10	5.	23.8
75- 89	4	3	6.6	7.1
90-104	6	2	10.	4.8
105-119	3	5	5.	11.9
120-134	1	1	1.7	2.4
135-149	2	1	3.3	2.4
150-212	2	1	3.3	2.4

Translating into the letter grades, we have:

Letter Grade	Percentage at Home	Percentage Away
E	18.3	11.9
D	11.7	9.5
C—	30.	28.5

C ---	10.	28.6
C+ --	16.6	11.9
B ---	6.7	14.3
A ---	6.6	4.8

The usually small number of average or C men among the home grown first offenders is especially to be noted. The two distributions of first offenders are both tri-modal in form. Future additions and analyses will be necessary for an interpretation.

7. *Recidivism in Relation to West, South and North*

It might be well, since we have referred to the three traditional sections of the country in relation to crime, to give the distributions of first offenders and recidivists in each of those traditional sections.

Let us consider first the cases from the "West."

Alpha Scores	Cases First Offenders	Cases of Recidivists	Percentage of Former	Percentage of Latter
0- 9 ------------	2	2	3.1	7.1
10- 14 ------------	1	1	1.6	3.6
15- 19 ------------	0	0	--	--
20- 24 ------------	3	2	4.7	7.1
25- 34 ------------	9	1	14.	3.6
35- 44 ------------	5	1	7.8	3.6
45- 59 ------------	6	1	9.4	3.6
60- 74 ------------	9	5	14.	17.8
75- 89 ------------	8	4	12.5	14.3
90-104 ------------	7	5	11.	17.8
105-119 ------------	6	5	9.4	17.8
120-134 ------------	2	0	3.1	---
135-149 ------------	4	0	6.2	---
150-212 ------------	2	1	3.1	3.6

Translating into the letter grades, we have:

Letter Grades	Percentage of First	Percentage of Recidivists
E --	4.7	10.7
D --	4.7	7.1
C— ---	21.8	7.2
C --	23.4	21.4
C+ ---	23.5	32.1
B --	12.5	17.8
A --	9.3	3.6

Approximately one-third of the recidivists are in the C range, while a very small percentage are located in the C— range.

Let us consider in the same way the first offenders and recidivists from the "South."

Alpha Scores		Cases First Offenders	Cases of Recidivists	Percentage of Former	Percentage of Latter
0- 9	------------	8	3	9.2	6.7
10- 14	------------	3	2	3.4	4.4
15- 19	------------	5	1	5.7	2.2
20- 24	------------	2	1	2.3	2.2
25- 34	------------	12	4	13.8	8.9
35- 44	------------	9	6	10.3	13.3
45- 59	------------	7	8	8.1	17.8
60- 74	------------	16	9	18.4	20.
75- 89	------------	11	4	12.7	8.9
90-104	------------	2	4	2.3	8.9
105-119	------------	4	2	4.6	4.4
120-134	------------	5	1	5.7	2.2
135-149	------------	0	0	--	--
150-212	------------	3	0	3.4	--

Translating into the letter grades, we have:

Letter Grades		Percentage of First	Percentage of Recidivists
E	--------------------------------------	12.6	11.1
D	--------------------------------------	8.	4.4
C—	--------------------------------------	24.1	22.2
C	--------------------------------------	26.5	37.8
C+	--------------------------------------	15.	17.8
B	--------------------------------------	10.3	6.6
A	--------------------------------------	3.4	---

The criminals from the "South" are of an average much lower than from the other two traditional sections. As a result, the relative position of the unusually high percentage of C men among the recidivists is about the same as the C range among the recidivists of the other sections. But, as in the case of the western group, there is a high percentage of C— men among the first offenders.

Let us consider next the groups from the "North."

Alpha Scores		Cases First Offenders	Cases of Recidivists	Percentage of Former	Percentage of Latter
0- 9	------------	13	7	4.9	4.4
10- 14	------------	10	1	3.8	.6
15- 19	------------	13	6	4.9	3.8
20- 24	------------	18	2	6.8	1.3
25- 34	------------	29	12	11.	7.6
35- 44	------------	27	13	10.2	8.2
45- 59	------------	30	30	11.4	19.
60- 74	------------	38	24	14.4	15.2
75- 89	------------	19	9	7.2	5.7
90-104	------------	23	20	8.7	12.7
105-119	------------	18	8	6.8	5.1
120-134	------------	7	10	2.7	6.3
135-149	------------	10	7	3.8	4.4
150-212	------------	9	9	3.4	5.7

Translating into the letter grades, we have:

Letter Grades	Percentage of First	Percentage of Recidivists
E	8.7	5.
D	11.7	5.1
C—	21.2	15.8
C	25.8	34.2
C+	15.9	18.4
B	9.5	11.4
A	7.2	10.1

In the northern group also, we find an unusually high percentage of C men among the recidivists. But the point of especial significance is the fact that the northern recidivists as a group are unusually intelligent as compared to the first offenders. Such is not the case with the southern and western groups. And it is also important to notice that a much larger percentage of northern criminals are recidivists than in the case of the southern and western criminals.

8. *Uniformity and Variety in Recidivistic Behavior*

Much has been published by the police and other newspaper writers concerning the individual uniformity of criminal behavior. For example, it has been claimed that burglars specialize on particular methods of breaking into houses, some being known as bath-room specialists, others as basement-window specialists, etc. It has been claimed by some that notorious burglars have been traced by their known peculiar and unvarying methods of behavior. No one claims that all criminals can be thus classified. But, in the light of such reports, it might be interesting to compare the recidivists who commit the same crime time after time with the recidivists who vary their criminal behavior. Will the Alpha test indicate any difference between the forger who commits forgery time after time and the individual who deviates from forgery into larceny and rape?

In this discussion, the Maryland data will have to be omitted since the Maryland records do not indicate the cause of the previous conviction. So the discussion will be based on the Indiana and New Jersey data. We shall consider the type-groups in order, then the total. Let us consider the "fraud group" first.

Alpha Scores	Cases of Variation	Cases of Uniformity	Percentage of Former	Percentage of Latter
0- 9	2	0	7.7	---
10- 14	1	0	3.8	---
15- 19	1	0	3.8	---

20- 24 ------------	3	3	11.5	11.5
25- 34 ------------	0	1	---	3.8
35- 44 ------------	4	0	15.4	---
45- 59 ------------	3	3	11.5	11.5
60- 74 ------------	5	4	19.2	15.4
75- 89 ------------	2	6	7.7	23.1
90-104 ------------	2	2	7.7	7.7
105-119 ------------	1	0	3.8	---
120-134 ------------	1	3	3.8	11.5
120-134 ------------	1	1	3.8	3.8
150-212 ------------	0	3	---	11.5

Translating into the letter grades, we have:

Letter Grades	Percentage Variation	Percentage Uniformity
E -----------------------------------	11.5	---
D -----------------------------------	15.3	11.5
C— -----------------------------------	15.4	3.8
C -----------------------------------	30.7	26.9
C+ -----------------------------------	15.4	30.8
B -----------------------------------	7.6	11.5
A -----------------------------------	3.8	15.3

It is seen that the individuals who persist in the commission of the same crime are more intelligent as a group than are the individuals who have varied their criminal behavior by the commission of dissimilar crimes.

Let us continue with the second type-group, the "force" group."

Alpha Scores	Cases of Variants	Cases of Constants	Percentage of Former	Percentage of Latter
0- 9 ------------	8	5	7.	6.8
10- 14 ------------	1	2	.8	2.7
15- 19 ------------	5	4	4.3	5.5
20- 24 ------------	4	0	3.5	---
25- 34 ------------	12	3	10.4	4.1
35- 44 ------------	13	11	11.3	15.1
45- 59 ------------	16	14	13.9	19.2
60- 74 ------------	21	12	18.2	16.4
75- 89 ------------	9	8	7.8	11.
90-104 ------------	15	5	13.	6.8
105-119 ------------	7	4	6.1	5.5
120-134 ------------	2	2	1.7	2.7
135-149 ------------	2	3	1.7	4.1
150-212 ------------	0	0	---	---

Translating into the letter grades, we have:

Letter Grades	Percentage of Variants	Percentage of Constants
E -----------------------------------	7.8	9.5
D -----------------------------------	7.8	5.5
C— -----------------------------------	21.7	19.2
C -----------------------------------	32.1	35.6

C+	20.8	17.8
B	7.8	8.2
A	1.7	4.1

Here, the differences are not marked, but are slightly to the advantage of the constants.

Let us proceed to the third group, the "thievery" group.

Alpha Scores	Case of Variants	Case of Constants	Percentage of Former	Percentage of Latter
0- 9	8	10	8.9	6.8
10- 14	4	6	4.4	4.1
15- 19	3	3	3.3	2.1
20- 24	4	7	4.4	4.8
25- 34	5	11	5.5	7.5
35- 44	15	11	16.6	7.5
45- 59	14	16	15.5	10.0
60- 74	14	21	15.5	14.4
75- 89	4	18	4.4	12.3
90-104	10	19	11.1	13.
105-119	5	11	5.5	7.5
120-134	4	6	4.4	4.1
135-149	0	3	---	2.1
150-212	1	4	1.1	2.7

Translating into the letter grades, we have:

Letter Grades	Percentage of Variants	Percentage of Constants
E	13.3	10.9
D	7.7	6.9
C—	22.1	15.
C	31.	25.3
C+	15.5	25.3
B	9.9	11.6
A	1.1	4.8

Here also, the differences are in favor of the constants.

In the "statutory group," there are 50 variants and only 2 constants. In the "physical injury group," there are 47 variants and 9 constants. In the group of "social dereliction," there are 4 variants and only 1 constant. In the "sex group," there are 18 variants and 2 constants. As a result, the distributions of the last four groups will not be worth giving. Therefore, we shall next give the distributions of the total variants and constants.

Alpha Scores	Cases of Variants	Cases of Constants	Percentage of Former	Percentage of Latter
0- 9	23	18	6.6	6.6
10- 14	11	8	3.1	3.
15- 19	14	7	4.	2.6
20- 24	17	10	4.9	3.7
25- 34	27	17	7.7	6.3
35- 44	45	23	12.9	8.5

45- 59 _____	54	34	15.4	12.6
60- 74 _____	60	40	17.1	14.8
75- 89 _____	27	34	7.7	12.6
90-104 _____	41	36	11.7	13.3
105-119 _____	18	15	5.1	5.5
120-134 _____	9	12	2.6	4.4
135-149 _____	4	7	1.1	2.6
150-212 _____	1	8	.3	3.

Translating into the letter groups, we have:

Letter Grades	Percentage of Variants	Percentage of Constants
E _____	9.7	9.6
D _____	8.9	6.3
C— _____	20.6	14.8
C _____	32.5	27.4
C+ _____	19.4	25.9
B _____	7.7	9.9
A _____	1.4	5.6

It is possible that the above facts might tend to contradict certain previous explanations used in this book. But, of course, it is possible that constancy of criminal behavior may not be interpreted as being conservatism on the part of the criminal! It is significant that uniformity in recidivistic behavior is confined almost entirely to crimes involving the possession of property—the first three of the type-groups. Crimes of physical violence are almost never committed by individuals who have committed such crimes before. That in itself indicates the emotional complexes connected with such behavior may be causative factors. Certainly, it would be interesting to analyze the theory and practice of criminal law in the light of the psychological and other factors concomitant with recidivism.

Tentative Conclusions:

1. Recidivists seem more intelligent than are first offenders, in so far as differences exist. Intelligence is just as serious a problem for criminology as is feeble-mindedness.

2. The migratory recidivists are more intelligent than are the home-grown ones—a distinction that is duplicated among the first offenders.

3. The recidivists are not more intelligent than are the first offenders in all the type groups. In fraud, the first offenders are much more intelligent than are the recidivists. The recidivists and first offenders are nearly alike in the force and thievery groups. In the statutory group the recidivists are

superior to the first offenders.   In the case of the sex crimes, the first offenders are much superior to the recidivists.   However, the geographical concomitants are marked, both in the case of the recidivists and the first offenders.

4.   The more intelligent recidivists also persist in repeating the same crime while the less intelligent ones deviate into other crimes—in the case of crimes against property.   The reverse is true in the case of crimes of physical and sex violence.

CHAPTER 7

LITERACY

As is well known, the standards of school instruction vary widely in different communities. Seven years in some schools is worth much more than eight years in some other schools. It is also true that some high school graduates are better educated at the end of their high school course than are some individuals at the completion of two years in college. Such known variations in instruction make it unnecessary that criminal literacy be reported in detail year by year. The sixteen years of school life can better be reported in unit groups of two or more years each. In this chapter the following division will be used:

Group	Grade or Years
1	0- 2
2	3- 4
3	5- 6
4	7- 8
5	9-11
6	12-14
7	15-16

There may be some objections to this classification, but it is the one that seems to be most acceptable for reporting the Army data. Of course, it is the Army data that must serve as norms in the discussion of problems of this character. In the remainder of this chapter the literacy groups will be referred to by number.

1. *Gross Comparison of Army and Criminal Data*

In reporting the Army data all cases of more than sixteen years' schooling will be reported as having had sixteen years—will be reported in Group 7. This plan will be followed in the case of the criminal data also. On page 750, volume 15, of the Memoirs, 1921, is given the Army data from which the following classification of Army literacy is made:

Literacy Group Years in School	Army Cases	Percentage
1	530	1.
2	3,723	7.2
3	10,346	20.
4	23,078	44.7

5	8,278	16.
6	4,331	8.4
7	1,334	2.6

It is seen that the above classification gives a fairly "normal" distribution of the 51,620 Army cases of the sample. It is seen that 11% of the Army cases are high school graduates and college men. However, the curve is not skewed towards the upper end, there being 27% superior to the mode and 28.2% inferior to the mode. This is as good a norm distribution of the Army cases as the writer could make. The eighth grade in school is the great literacy watershed, and determines the numerical superiority of Group 4 above. The Army data are taken at their face value as the Army data, and no attempt is made to interpret the extent to which such data are represenaive of the rest of the country. Even thus restricted, the problem is quite large enough.

Let us now observe the literacy distribution of the entire group of criminal cases being treated in this book.

Literacy Group	Criminal Cases	Percentage
1	113	2.9
2	653	16.6
3	1,095	27.8
4	1,433	36.4
5	455	11.6
6	150	3.8
7	33	.8

For easy comparison and personal convenience let us place together the Army and the criminal percentages.

Literacy Group	Percentage of Army	Percentage of-Criminals
1	1.	2.9
2	7.2	16.6
3	20.	27.8
4	44.7	36.4
5	16.	11.6
6	8.4	3.8
7	2.6	.8

A still more startling comparison is as follows:

Percentage Inferior to Group 4		Percentage Superior to Group 4
28.2	Army	27.
47.3	Criminals	16.2

The criminal group is skewed very decidedly towards the lower end of the scale. This is all the more remarkable when we remember that the criminals are superior in intelligence to the same Army group. However, the difference in educational attainments is far greater than is the difference in Alpha scores. It is greatly to be regretted that we do not have the literacy distribution of the Army Group in terms of states or geographical divisions. It is the belief of the writer that the differences would be still greater in that case.

2. *The Literacy of the Home-Grown Criminal As Compared with the Criminal Incarcerated Outside His Home State.*

It may occur to the more thoughtful reader that the fundamental difference between the criminal and the law abiding citizen can be expressed in terms of literacy. If the reader is of the reformer type, there occurs to him at once a vision of the possibility of driving crime from the world. Higher education for the masses will become for him a challenge to duty. But there never has been a simple panacea for any ill, and there probably never will be. America holds a larger percentage of criminals than any other civilized nation, and America has made popular the growing custom of higher education for the masses.

Let us now compare the home-grown criminal with the other kind in terms of literacy:

Literacy Group	Cases of Home	Cases Away	Percentage of Former	Percentage of Latter
1 -------------	81	32	3.4	2.
2 -------------	394	259	16.6	16.5
3 -------------	722	373	30.5	23.8
4 -------------	854	579	36.	37.
5 -------------	242	213	10.2	13.6
6 -------------	63	87	2.6	5.5
7 -------------	11	22	.5	1.4

To make the comparison more easy:

Percentage Inferior to Group 4		Percentage Superior to Group 4
50.5 --------------	Home -------------	13.3
42.3 --------------	Away -------------	20.5

The above comparison shows clearly that the geographical concomitants are not to be ignored, and are just as important in the problem of literacy as in the problem of intelligence itself. Higher education for the masses would not eliminate this geographical difference. Certainly it is not merely a coincidence that the criminals incarcerated outside their home state have more than twice as large a percentage of high school graduates and college trained men among them than have the home-grown criminals. It would seem that the problem grows more complex instead of more simple. There may be literacy differences in the type groups, which would still more complicate the problem.

3. *The Literacy of Type Groups.* Let us now consider the distribution into literacy groups of the seven type crime groups. We shall begin with the "fraud group."

Literacy Group	Cases of Fraud	Percentage
1	2	.6
2	28	8.4
3	66	20.
4	116	34.6
5	62	18.5
6	41	12.2
7	20	6.3

The "fraud group" seems superior to the Army group in literacy. Let us make it clear in this way:

Percentage Inferior to Group 4		Percentage Superior to Group 4
28.2	Army	27.
29.	Fraud Group	37.

The glittering generalities concerning the relative literacy of criminals and the population in general seem to disappear when we contemplate the relative literacy of the "fraud group" and the Army group. Once more it may be remarked that perhaps there is no such thing as a general criminal class.

Let us continue with the second type group, the "force" group. This group, we will remember, is more like group one in intelligence than are any of the other groups. Yet there is a decided difference in literacy. In fact, this group is one of the least literate.

Literacy Group	Cases of "Force"	Percentage
1	37	2.4
2	241	15.8
3	455	29.8
4	579	38.
5	179	11.7
6	30	1.9
7	4	.3

In this group, 48% are inferior to group 4, while 13.9% are superior to the mode. This makes a most decided skew towards the left end of the curve—in marked contrast to the "fraud group."

Following is the distribution of the third group, the
"thievery group:"

Literacy Group	Cases of "Thievery"	Percentage
1	27	2.7
2	168	16.8
3	257	25.7
4	379	37.9
5	128	12.8
6	44	4.4
7	2	.2

It is noticed that high school graduates and college trained
men are more likely to steal than they are to commit robbery or
burglary.

The fourth group, or "statutory group," will be considered
next:

Literacy Group	Cases of the "Statutory Group"	Percentage
1	4	2.1
2	31	16.6
3	59	31.5
4	67	35.8
5	18	9.6
6	8	4.3
7	0	0.0

The small number of cases might account for the lack of
college graduates, but it does not account for the small percentage of men trained even slightly in high school.

Let us continue with the fifth group, the "physical injury"
group.

Literacy Group	Cases of "Physical Injury"	Percentage
1	26	5.1
2	102	20.1
3	151	29.8
4	173	34.2
5	37	7.3
6	15	3.
7	2	.4

The lack of high literates in this group is even more marked
than in the previous group. Statutory crimes and crimes of
physical injury rarely lead to any great profit. And modern
education trains men to look primarily for profit in worldly behavior.

Let us continue with the sixth group, the "social dereliction
group"

Literacy Group	Cases of Dereliction	Percentage
1	5	4.1
2	25	20.5
3	25	20.5
4	42	34.4
5	19	15.6
6	5	4.1
7	1	.8

The high percentage of men with some high school training is rather remarkable in the light of the presence of so many low literates and so few college trained men. But it is probable that crimes of social dereliction and sex crimes are not crimes, properly speaking, but diseases of rather vague classification. Nevertheless, it is interesting and probably significant that the literacy of the "dereliction" group should be so restricted.

Let us continue with the seventh group, the "sex group."

Literacy Group	Cases	Percentage
1	12	4.8
2	58	23.
3	82	32.5
4	77	30.5
5	12	4.8
6	7	2.8
7	4	1.6

In this group we reach the low ebb of literacy for all the criminal groups. It might make more clear the differences in the literacy of the criminal groups if we make the following rough comparison of the sex and fraud groups in terms of percentages inferior to and superior to the mode of literacy group 4. Of course, the mode of the sex group is group 3, but the comparison will make the differences clearer.

Percentage Inferior to Group 4		Percentage Superior to Group 4
60.3	Sex	9.2
29.	Fraud	37.

Certainly, the two type groups differ more widely in literacy than do the entire Army and criminal groups. And it must not be forgotten that recidivism is much more likely to occur in the fraud group than in the sex group. It may be still more likely to occur in the highly trained promoter or politician who has never been shamed by a public conviction.

Let us bring together for easy observation the percentages inferior and superior to group 4 of the literary groups.

Percentage Inferior to Group 4				Percentage Superior to Group 4
29.	----------	(331)	Fraud ----------	37.
48.	----------	(1542)	Force ----------	13.9
45.2	----------	(992)	Thievery ------	17.4
50.2	----------	(187)	Statutory ------	13.9
55.	----------	(521)	Physical Injury	10.7
45.1	----------	(119)	Dereliction ----	20.5
60.3	----------	(253)	Sex -----------	9.2

Let us now compare the literacy of the home grown type groups with the literacy of the type groups that are incarcerated outside their home state. We shall proceed in the regular order, taking the fraud group first.

Literacy Group	Home Percentage (181 cases)	Percentage Away (150 cases)
1	1.1	---
2	8.7	7.9
3	23.3	15.2
4	39.1	29.1
5	16.3	21.2
6	8.7	16.5
7	2.7	10.

The influence of education, or at least its concomitance, is rather remarkable. We have omitted giving the number of cases, as they have been given in other places. Whatever the value of the Alpha test may ultimately be considered, these literacy differences will remain.

Let us consider the force group in the same way.

Literacy Group	Home Percentage (950 cases)	Percentage Away (592 cases)
1	2.9	1.5
2	14.6	17.7
3	33.1	24.6
4	35.6	41.7
5	11.8	11.7
6	1.6	2.6
7	.3	.2

The differences are not marked in this group.

Let us proceed with the thievery group in the same way.

Literacy Group	Home Percentage (572 cases)	Percentage Away (420 cases)
1	3.3	1.9
2	18.4	14.4
3	27.2	23.3
4	38.7	36.3

5	9.4	17.2
6	3.	6.3
7	---	.5

In this group the literary differences are again in evidence. This, of course, emphasizes the geographical concomitants further.

Let us now consider the statutory group.

Literacy Group	Home Percentage (110 cases)	Percentage Away (77 cases)
1	2.7	1.3
2	13.6	20.8
3	34.5	27.3
4	36.3	35.1
5	10.9	7.7
6	1.8	7.7
7	---	---

It is remarkable that there should be none of the high literates at all in this group, and the geographical concomitants so slight at the same time.

Let us proceed with the physical injury group.

Literacy Group	Home Percentage (334 cases)	Percentage Away (187 cases)
1	5.1	5.3
2	20.5	19.4
3	31.8	25.9
4	35.1	32.3
5	5.3	11.2
6	1.8	5.3
7	.3	.6

The small percentage of high literates and the fairly marked geographical differences should be noticed.

Let us consider the social dereliction group.

Literacy Group	Home Percentage (53 cases)	Percentage Away (66 cases)
1	5.4	3.
2	20.	20.9
3	21.8	19.4
4	34.5	34.3
5	14.5	16.4
6	3.6	4.5
7	---	1.5

The almost complete lack of geographical differences should be noticed. The small differences that exist are to the advantage of the "away" group, but they are not important.

Let us continue with the sex group in the same way.

Literacy Group	Home Percentage (170 cases)	Percentage Away (83 cases)
1	5.5	3.3
2	23.9	21.3
3	32.4	32.6
4	28.2	34.8
5	5.5	3.3
6	3.1	2.2
7	1.2	2.2

In this group also the geographical differences are not very evident.

Considering all the type groups, the geographical differences are marked in only three—the fraud group, the thievery group, and the physical injury group. Of these the greatest differences are to be found in the fraud group.

4. *The Literacy of First Offenders and Recidivists.*

We shall compare the home-grown first offenders and recidivists with the first offenders and recidivists incarcerated outside their home state. The fraud group compares as follows:

Literacy Group	Home First (30 Cases)	Home Recidivists (34 Cases)	First Away (56 Cases)	Recidivists Away (24 Cases)
1	---	3.1	---	---
2	---	9.4	10.7	8.3
3	28.1	15.6	14.3	12.5
4	31.2	59.4	23.2	33.3
5	12.5	9.4	26.6	12.5
6	21.9	3.1	16.1	25.
7	6.2	---	8.9	8.3

The home-grown recidivists rather cluster about the eighth grade, or the fourth literacy group, while the other recidivists are also prominently recruited from the sixth literacy group. Combining the first offenders together and the recidivists together, we have the following:

Literacy Group	Percentage First (86 Cases)	Percentage Recidivists (58 Cases)
1	---	1.8
2	6.8	8.9
3	19.3	14.3
4	26.1	48.3
5	21.6	10.7
6	18.2	12.5
7	7.8	3.6

It is seen that the first offenders are much more literate than are the recidivists, and that the geographical concomitants are smoothed out. This merely emphasizes the importance of making as many comparisons as possible.

Now let us consider the force group.

Literacy Group	Home First (130 Cases)	Home Recidivists (107 Cases)	First Away (144 Cases)	Recidivists Away (93 Cases)
1	5.3	6.5	2.1	1.1
2	16.	18.7	22.2	21.5
3	37.4	30.8	20.8	24.7
4	32.1	32.7	38.2	45.2
5	9.2	9.3	13.2	7.5
6	---	1.9	2.8	---
7	---	---	.7	---

The recidivists seem to lose ground, especially among those imprisoned outside their home state. Let us combine the first offenders together and the recidivists together.

Literacy Group	Percentage First (274 Cases)	Percentage Recidivists (200 Cases)
1	3.7	4.
2	19.3	20.
3	28.5	28.
4	35.3	38.5
5	11.3	8.5
6	1.5	1.
7	.4	---

The similarity of the first offenders and the recidivists is so marked, as far as literacy is concerned, that it is the chief characteristic to be pointed out here.

Let us now proceed with the thievery group.

Literacy Group	Home First (138 Cases)	Home Recidivists (138 Cases)	First Away (118 Cases)	Recidivists Away (113 Cases)
1	3.5	3.	.8	2.8
2	21.1	21.3	13.6	14.1
3	26.8	28.	21.2	27.4
4	38.7	40.	39.	32.7
5	6.3	7.3	15.3	17.7
6	3.5	.7	10.2	5.5
7	---	---	---	---

The first offenders seem to have the advantage over the recidivists as far as literacy is concerned. It may be more evident if we combine the first offenders together and the recidivists together. Following is the combination:

Literacy Group	Percentage First (256 Cases)	Percentage Recidivists (251 Cases)
1	2.3	2.8
2	17.7	18.

3	----------------------------------	24.2	27.6
4	----------------------------------	38.8	36.4
5	----------------------------------	10.4	12.
6	----------------------------------	6.5	2.8
7	----------------------------------	---	---

Probably no further comment is necessary concerning the above group. Let us proceed with the statutory group.

Literacy Group	Home First (7 Cases)	Home Recidivists (25 Cases)	First Away (11 Cases)	Recidivists Away (26 Cases)
1	---	4.	---	---
2	omit	24.	omit	7.7
3	omit	24.	omit	38.5
4	omit	36.	omit	38.5
5	omit	12.	omit	7.7
6	omit	---	omit	7.7
7	omit	---	omit	---

The first offenders were altogether too few to be divided in the above comparison, but we can probably consider them in a combination.

Literacy Group	Percentage First (18 Cases)	Percentage Recidivists (51 Cases)
1	---	2.
2	44.4	15.7
3	33.3	31.4
4	22.2	37.3
5	---	10.
6	---	4.
7	---	---

The recidivists are superior in literacy. The first offenders are few, but uniformly inferior in literacy. Let us proceed with the physical injury group.

Literacy Group	Home First (118 Cases)	Home Recidivists (43 Cases)	First Away (69 Cases)	Recidivists Away (23 Cases)
1	3.4	2.4	5.8	4.3
2	19.5	26.2	23.2	8.7
3	35.6	23.8	30.4	26.1
4	31.3	45.2	29.	17.4
5	5.1	2.4	7.2	17.4
6	4.2	---	4.3	21.7
7	.8	---	---	4.3

The recidivists incarcerated outside their home state seem to be superior in literacy to the other recidivists or first offenders. Let us make the comparison in combination.

Literacy Group	Percentage First (187 Cases)	Percentage Recidivists (66 Cases)
1	4.3	3.1
2	20.7	20.
3	33.7	24.6
4	30.5	35.4
5	5.9	7.7
7	.5	1.5
6	4.3	7.7

The superiority of the recidivists in general is caused by the presence of those incarcerated outside their home state and who are recidivists.

Since there are so few recidivists in the social dereliction group, we shall omit the percentages and give only the cases. That will offer opportunity for casual inspection. The cases are as follows:

Literacy Group	Home First	Home Recidivists	First Away	Recidivists Away
1	--	--	1	--
2	4	1	7	--
3	3	1	6	1
4	5	--	13	2
5	3	--	6	--
6	1	--	2	1
7	--	--	--	--

The recidivists are so few that comment is unnecessary and superfluous. Let us proceed to the sex group.

Literacy Group	Home First (60 Cases)	Home Recidivists (19 Cases)	First Away (46 Cases)	Recidivists Away (2 Cases)
1	1.7	---	2.2	---
2	20.	42.1	21.7	---
3	40.	15.8	30.4	omit
4	26.6	36.8	41.3	omit
5	5.	5.3	2.2	---
6	5.	---	2.2	---
7	1.7	---	---	---

The combination is as follows:

Literacy Group	Percentage First (106 Cases)	Percentage Recidivists (21 Cases)
1	1.9	---
2	18.9	38.1
3	35.8	19.
4	33.	38.1
5	3.8	5.
6	3.8	---
7	.9	---

The recidivists are even less literate than are the first offenders.

Let us now compare a combination of all the first offenders of all type groups with a combination of all the recidivists of all the same groups.

Literacy Group	Home First	Home Recidivists	First Away	Recidivists Away
1 _____	3.3	3.9	2.1	1.8
2 _____	18.	21.9	19.6	14.7
3 _____	33.4	26.6	22.1	26.3
4 _____	33.	39.3	35.1	36.8
5 _____	7.3	7.7	13.4	12.6
6 _____	4.1	1.1	6.5	6.6
7 _____	.8	---	1.3	1.

If we now combine the above we have:

Literacy Group	Percentage First (978 Cases)	Percentage Recidivists (653 Cases)
1 _____	2.7	2.9
2 _____	18.8	18.7
3 _____	27.9	26.4
4 _____	34.	38.1
5 _____	10.3	10.
6 _____	5.3	3.5
7 _____	1.	.5

As can be seen, the first offenders and the recidivists are remarkably similar in literacy. In fact, a purely chance distribution of the literacy scores would not furnish two series more nearly alike.

5. The Literacy of Habitual Offenders.

The 205 habitual offenders give the following literacy distribution:

Literacy Group	Percentage of Habitual Offenders (205 Cases)
1 _____	2.9
2 _____	20.
3 _____	26.3
4 _____	34.6
5 _____	10.7
6 _____	3.9
7 _____	1.5

This distribution is even more similar to the distribution of the first offenders than is the distribution of the recidivists in general. But a comparison with the Army norms will reveal the inferiority of the habitual offenders in literacy.

We are forced to conclude that any differentiating general statement concerning the habitual criminal in terms of literacy is bound to be of little value.

6. *The Comparative Literacy of Criminals from the West, the North, and the South.*

These three groups, as previously differentiated in this work, compare in literacy as follows:

Literacy Group	Percentage of West (92 Cases)	Percentage of North (422 Cases)	Percentage of South (132 Cases)
1	.3	2.4	3.5
2	13.4	15.9	23.6
3	25.7	24.9	25.1
4	38.8	36.9	29.4
5	14.4	12.4	12.
6	7.3	5.6	4.2
7	---	1.8	2.3

It is interesting that the West should furnish so few of the low literates and at the same time so few of the high literates. It can scarcely be purely a matter of chance, since the number of case is sufficient. It is also interesting that the South should furnish so many high literates and so many low literates at the same time. But it is seen that all three of the groups are inferior to the Army norms. It might also be pointed out that the South is inferior to the other two groups in the percentage of men completing either the graded school or high school. But in the case of the college graduates or near graduates, in the case of the South, it is of whimsical interest to recall the efforts in that part of the country to suppress in the colleges the teaching of evolution. It is strange that such moral perfection should not be reflected in the data on college criminals. But perhaps it is.

It might be of value, and certainly will be of interest, to compare the literacy of the first offenders and recidivists in each of the above three groups. Following is the distribution of the western criminals:

Literacy Group	Percentage First (64 Cases)	Percentage Recidivists (28 Cases)
1	---	10.
2	19.	30.
3	13.8	30.
4	51.7	16.6
5	8.6	13.3
6	7.9	---
7	---	---

More than half of the first offenders are graduates of the graded school. The recidivists are superior in higher literates, yet are very numerous in the third group. Even though there are none in the seventh group, the first offenders and the recidivists are quite literate.

The northern criminals are distributed as follows:

Literacy Group	Percentage First (264 Cases)	Percentage Recidivists (158 Cases)
1	1.9	1.8
2	21.3	13.8
3	24.	27.
4	31.	37.7
5	13.2	10.
6	7.7	7.8
7	.7	1.8

The reverse differences in the second and the fourth groups are the only real differences, but the interpretation of their significance will not be attempted.

The southern criminals are distributed as follows:

Literacy Group	Percentage First (87 Cases)	Percentage Recidivists (45 Cases)
1	6.1	---
2	19.5	30.
3	26.8	21.3
4	31.7	34.
5	10.9	8.5
6	2.4	4.3
7	2.4	2.1

The lack of lowest grade literates among the recidivists should be noted. Otherwise there is little to choose between the first offenders and the recidivists.

Tentative Conclusions:

1. The criminal is much less literate than was the American Army. However, the migratory criminals are much more literate than home-grown ones.

2. Literacy does not vary with intelligence in all the type-groups. College trained men and even high school graduates are totally lacking in some type-groups while abundantly present in others.

3. The lowest grades of literacy are not found among recidivists.

CHAPTER 8

CHRONOLOGICAL AGE

This is really a difficult subject to discuss. It is not known just when the individual becomes a criminal, nor is it known with accuracy how many previous convictions are involved. Also the age usually obtained is the one recorded on the admission card. In this chapter it is the latter age that is used exclusively. There are many possible criticisms of such a method, but it is at least consistent.

1. *The Gross Distribution of Age Groups.*

For the convenience of discussion it will be necessary to number the age groups as follows:

Age Group	Years
1	15-20
2	21-25
3	26-30
4	31-35
5	36-40
6	41-50
7	51-X

There were not legally supposed to be any men less than eighteen years of age, but a few of sixteen were found. The reader must not suppose that the writer considers seven a sacred number. It merely happens to be a convenient number in several of the classifications in this book.

The gross distribution of the nearly four thousand cases under discussion is as follows:

Age Group	Percentage of Total (3942 Cases)
1	20.9
2	26.
3	17.7
4	13.8
5	9.4
6	8.6
7	3.6

This is not a distribution that can be made into a "normal curve." No attempt was made by the writer to make such a distribution, since it is obviously impossible. The extreme youthfulness of the criminal group is the fact that strikes one most in the above distribution. Nearly half of the entire criminal population is twenty-five years of age or less. Approximately 88% of the criminal group is composed of young men less than the age of forty years.

But there are geographical concomitants here also. Let us compare the home-grown and migratory groups.

Age Group	Percentage at Home (2376 Cases)	Percentage Away (1566 Cases)
1	23.6	16.8
2	26.2	25.5
3	17.1	18.8
4	13.1	14.1
5	9.	10.
6	7.6	10.
7	3.	4.

The differences here are probably what one might expect. Migration usually does not begin till the individual becomes an adult, and may continue as long as life lasts. Such an explanation seems easy and obvious, but is incorrect, like other easy and obvious things. In criminology there can be no assumptions more daring than the multiplication table—and even that should be looked upon with suspicion.

2. *The Age of Type Groups.*

We shall compare the home-grown group with the migratory group in each of the seven type groups, taking the fraud group first.

Age Group	Percentage of Home (181 Cases)	Percentage Away (150 cases)	Percentage of Total (331 cases)
1	19.1	7.6	13.8
2	24.5	15.2	20.2
3	15.3	17.1	16.1
4	13.7	22.8	17.9
5	10.	12.7	11.1
6	14.2	15.2	14.7
7	3.3	9.5	6.1

One should especially notice the very small percentage of the migratory group in the first age group and the large percentage in the fourth and seventh groups. In fact, this distribution of the fraudulent migratory group is quite the opposite of the general distribution of the criminal group. Even the home-grown group contains large percentages in the upper ranges of years. In fact, the fraud group is an older group—a group composed largely of mature men. And these are not men who serve long terms in prison. On the contrary, two or three years is an average term for such men to serve. Intelligent, educated, mature, but criminals!

Let us next consider the distribution of the force group of criminals.

Age Group	Percentage of Home (950 Cases)	Percentage Away (592 Cases)	Percentage of Total (1542 Cases)
1	26.7	21.6	24.9
2	29.5	31.6	30.3
3	17.2	18.4	17.6
4	15.2	12.2	14.1
5	6.8	8.1	7.3
6	3.3	5.8	4.2
7	1.3	2.2	1.7

Here we find a much younger group of criminals. More than 55% are only 25 years of age or younger, while only 34% of the fraud group was composed of men so young. It is also remarkable that in the lower range of years the migratory group is not much less numerous than the home grown group, being even more numerous in the second age group. But here, as in most of the other groups, the old men are usually incarcerated outside their home state.

Let us consider the thievery group in the same way.

Age Group	Percentage of Home (572 Cases)	Percentage Away (420 Cases)	Percentage of Total (992 Cases)
1	30.	22.4	26.8
2	30.	26.3	28.5
3	14.5	18.2	16.2
4	11.7	12.1	12.
5	7.6	10.	8.7
6	5.	7.9	6.3
7	1.9	3.	2.4

This group is still younger than the force group, in so far as the home cases are concerned. But the migratory group is not quite so young. It is significant that nearly a third of the home group should be only 20 years of age or younger. As far as maturity is concerned, this group is almost like a freshman class in college. Mere youths, yet carved with the stigma of everlasting shame!

The statutory offenses are distributed as follows:

Age Group	Percentage of Home (110 Cases)	Percentage Away (77 Cases)	Percentage of Total (187 Cases)
1	34.8	17.1	27.7
2	33.	42.8	36.6
3	14.7	17.1	15.5
4	7.3	4.3	6.1
5	4.6	8.6	6.1
6	4.6	7.1	5.5
7	1.	2.8	1.6

Here is the picture of youth in conflict with the dictates of a minority group. As a matter of course, all statutes are bound to be the expression of minority ideas. These ideas are flouted chiefly by the young. It is the habit of youth to flout the dictations of age. Watch the little child of three. But the child of three and the child of nineteen are punished differently. The one is spanked, while the other has all the fine things of human life taken away from him forever. The spanked child of three is forgiven readily by loving parents. The incarcerated child of nineteen is never forgiven, is never trusted again. Such a ruined child is not likely to commit statutory offenses again. He looks for bigger game next time, and for such as he the hunting season will never again be closed. Notice that approximately 60% of the recidivists are only 25 years of age or younger. Not yet old enough to think of getting married, and yet veterans in crime—men who should die because normal life is ended.

Let us consider the physical injury group next.

Age Group	Percentage of Home (334 Cases)	Percentage Away (187 Cases)	Percentage of Total (521 Cases)
1	10.	7.1	9.1
2	14.5	17.	15.4
3	23.7	21.7	23.1
4	16.3	17.	16.6
5	14.2	10.6	13.
6	13.6	16.5	14.6
7	7.4	9.4	8.1

Here is a picture of maturity, age with its wisdom! They are not old because sentences are long and the pardon boards are heartless. These are the men as they come to the prisons. They have lived long, but none too well. And they are not veterans in crime. Most of them have come into conflict with the law for the first time. The age between forty and fifty is the critical age for mature men, while between twenty-five and thirty is the critical age for the more youthful. Those are the two ages of struggle, the struggle to get a start in life and the struggle not to admit the truth concerning one's success. The latter age is dominated by the migratory individuals, and in this case it happens that they are chiefly veterans in crime who are fugitives from the scenes of previous derelictions.

The social dereliction group is distributed as follows:

Age Group	Percentage of Home (53 Cases)	Percentage Away (66 Cases)	Percentage of Total (119 Cases)
1	9.2	2.9	5.7

2	_____ 11.1	14.7	13.1
3	_____ 13.	22.1	18.
4	_____ 14.8	19.1	17.2
5	_____ 22.2	17.6	19.7
6	_____ 18.5	17.6	18.
7	_____ 11.1	4.9	8.2

Only between twenty-five and thirty-five is the migratory group in the majority. We see again the lack of youth with its impetuosity and the large presence of age with its time for reflection. Gentlemen may break such laws as are classified under the statutory group, but gentlemen would hesitate to break the laws of this group. But the individuals who have had the most time in which to become gentlemen are the ones chiefly found here. But these are not veterans in crime. There are only half a dozen individuals in the entire group who ever committed any crime before. The disillusionments of protracted experience are too much for the peculiar emotional characters of the individuals who comprise this group. The science of criminology is sadly in need of some objective test of emotional types. Such tests will probably not be forthcoming till the emotions figure more prominently in experimental and systematic psychology. There are signs in that direction at the present time.

The sex group is distributed as follows:

Age Group	Percentage of Home (170 cases)	Percentage Away (83 cases)	Percentage of Total (253 cases)
1	_____ 12.6	3.4	9.4
2	_____ 20.4	11.2	17.2
3	_____ 16.2	19.1	17.6
4	_____ 8.4	19.1	12.1
5	_____ 13.2	12.3	13.3
6	_____ 21.6	23.6	22.3
7	_____ 6.6	11.2	8.2

The man in the prime of life, between forty and fifty, is the one most likely to commit these crimes. As in the case of crimes of physical injury, there are two chief periods for such crimes, and the two periods are the same in the two type groups. The emotional characters of the two type groups must be largely similar. In intelligence the two groups are similar also.

3. The Age of Recidivists and First Offenders.

In this discussion the reader should be on the alert to detect the migration of the home-grown first offender from his original group to the group of the migratory recidivist. It is the more intelligent criminal who thus migrates, and he is more likely to be found in some type groups than in others. The reader should remember also that the recidivist is not necessarily an individual older in chronological age than is the first offender. The difference between the first offender and the recidivist is not a difference that can be stated in terms of time at all. The difference is probably chiefly an emotional difference, the expression of which must wait on further developments in psychology.

Taking each of the seven type groups in turn, we shall give the distributions in such manner as to make most clear the actual differences. The following is the distribution of the fraud group:

Age Group	Home First (30 cases)	Home Recidivists (34 cases)	Away First (56 cases)	Away Recidivists (24 cases)
1	18.7	23.5	5.2	---
2	18.7	29.4	12.1	4.
3	12.5	11.8	17.2	11.5
4	21.9	14.7	18.9	26.9
5	12.5	5.9	15.6	15.4
6	15.6	8.8	20.8	26.9
7	---	5.9	10.4	15.4

Here is a most interesting study. In the home group the recidivists are much more numerous than are the first offenders, more than half of recidivism taking place before the age of twenty-five is reached. It seems almost a contradiction in terms of first offenders to be largely older men while the recidivists are largely younger men. The probable explanation is that fraud has been an incurable disease. The young first offenders continue sick, the old first offenders take their disease to other states. It looks like a migration of the older first offenders, but, of course, looks are very deceptive in psychology. In the case of the migratory group, susceptibility for the disease increases with age. Is it increasing wisdom on the part of the criminal, or does he have no wisdom at all?

Following is the distribution of the total first offenders and total recidivists of the same group:

Age Group	Percentage First (86 cases)	Percentage Recidivists (58 cases)
1	10.	13.3
2	14.4	18.3
3	15.5	11.6
4	20.	20.
5	14.4	10.

6 -------------------------------------	18.8	16.6
7 -------------------------------------	6.6	10.

Here we see clearly that the difference between the first offender and the recidivists is not a difference that can be stated in terms of time.

Let us continue with the distribution of the force group.

Age Group	Home First (130 cases)	Home Recidivists (107 cases)	Away First (144 cases)	Away Recidivists (93 cases)
1 ------------	25.4	17.3	21.	7.5
2 ------------	29.7	31.7	35.7	30.
3 ------------	27.	13.5	23.1	30.
4 ------------	11.5	16.3	9.8	15.
5 ------------	5.4	12.5	5.6	7.5
6 ------------	1.5	6.7	3.5	5.3
7 ------------	---	2.	1.4	4.2

The robbers and burglars are most numerous between twenty and twenty-five, whether they be first offenders or recidivists. But the old men either die or learn better methods. Following is the total distribution of the group:

Age Group	Percentage First (274 cases)	Percentage Recidivists (200 cases)
1 -------------------------------------	23.1	12.7
2 -------------------------------------	32.6	31.
3 -------------------------------------	24.9	21.3
4 -------------------------------------	10.6	15.8
5 -------------------------------------	5.5	10.1
6 -------------------------------------	2.6	6.1
7 -------------------------------------	.7	3.

Here we see to best advantage the clustering of cases in the second age group.

Let us continue with the thievery group.

Age Group	Home First (138 cases)	Home Recidivists (138 cases)	Away First (118 cases)	Away Recidivists (113 cases)
1 ------------	27.3	22.3	21.2	18.6
2 ------------	31.4	31.7	37.3	28.3
3 ------------	14.7	15.8	13.6	23.
4 ------------	14.	12.2	11.	8.8
5 ------------	5.8	9.3	6.8	8.8
6 ------------	5.8	7.2	7.6	9.7
7 ------------	1.4	1.5	2.6	2.6

Here again we see the clustering cases in the second age group. In fact, it is the clustering of such cases in the force and thievery groups that determines such clustering in the total criminal group. More than half of all criminals must be classified in one or the other of the two groups. That merely indicates the easy and obvious method of attack that appeals to the average criminal. Following is the total distribution of this group:

Age Group	Percentage First (256 cases)	Percentage Recidivists (251 cases)
1	24.5	20.6
2	34.1	30.1
3	14.2	19.
4	12.6	10.7
5	6.1	9.1
6	6.5	8.3
7	1.9	2.

Clearly this is not an old man's game. But the disease and rigors of prison life, together with the easy charity meted out to the aged, may make such precarious behavior impossible or unnecessary.

In the case of the statutory group we shall give the number of cases instead of percentages. The reason for this is obvious.

Age Group	Home First	Home Recidivists	Away First	Away Recidivists
1	1	2	1	3
2	2	11	4	13
3	2	2	4	5
4	1	3	--	1
5	1	2	--	1
6	--	4	2	1
7	--	--	--	--

The cases are chiefly recidivists and most of them are between the ages of twenty and twenty-five. Following is the total distribution of this group:

Age Group	Percentage First (18 cases)	Percentage Recidivists (51 cases)
1	11.1	10.4
2	33.3	50.
3	33.3	14.5
4	5.5	8.3
5	5.5	6.2
6	11.1	10.4
7	---	---

The percentage of recidivists less than twenty-five years of age is greater than in the case of the first offenders. In this respect this group resembles the fraud group. But the general youthfulness of the group resembles the force and thievery groups.

Let us continue with the distribution of the physical injury group.

Age Group	Home First (118 cases)	Home Recidivists (43 cases)	Away First (69 cases)	Away Recidivists (23 cases)
1	9.4	9.3	11.6	---
2	10.1	25.6	18.8	13.
3	18.8	23.2	21.7	21.7
4	14.4	9.3	14.5	21.7
5	19.5	14.	11.6	13.
6	16.1	14.	11.6	21.7
7	11.9	4.6	10.1	9.

In the home group the first offenders predominate in the upper age levels, while the opposite is the case in the migratory group. This is also the case where the young first offender is likely to belong to the migratory group.

The total distribution of this group is as follows:

Age Group	Percentage First (187 cases)	Percentage Recidivists (66 cases)
1	10.1	6.
2	13.6	21.2
3	20.	22.7
4	14.4	13.6
5	16.5	13.6
6	14.4	16.6
7	11.2	6.

The reader should remember that there are only about a third as many recidivists as first offenders in this group. But those recidivists are widely distributed from youth to old age, just as the first offenders are.

In the case of the social dereliction group we shall give the number of cases instead of percentages. Its distribution is as follows:

Age Group	Home First	Home Recidivists	Away First	Away Recidivists
1	2	1	--	--
2	2	1	7	--
3	2	--	9	2
4	3	--	8	--
5	4	--	8	--
6	1	--	3	1
7	--	--	1	1

The total distribution is as follows:

Age Group	Cases of First	Cases of Recidivists
1	2	1
2	9	1
3	11	2
4	11	--

```
5 ------------------------------------ 12        --
6 ------------------------------------  4         1
7 ------------------------------------  1         1
```

The vast majority of the cases occur between twenty-five and forty years of age, and usually occur but once.

The sex group is distributed as follows:

Age Group	Home First (60 cases)	Home Recidivists (19 cases)	Away First (46 cases)	Away Recidivists (2 cases)
1	11.1	5.5	2.2	---
2	19.	5.5	13.	---
3	17.5	33.3	21.7	omit
4	6.3	16.6	19.6	omit
5	12.6	16.6	15.2	---
6	19.	22.2	19.6	---
7	14.3	---	8.7	---

There are no recidivists after the age of fifty, but the fires still smolder in the first offenders. But it is the game of mature men all the way through, not the expected abandoned irresponsibility of youth. Sex passion seems to develop psychologically long after the obvious biological causes have been taken away. But a large percentage of older people can probably testify to this fact. The total distribution of the group is as follows:

Age Group	Percentage First (106 cases)	Percentage Recidivists (21 cases)
1	7.3	5.
2	16.5	5.
3	19.3	35.
4	11.9	20.
5	13.8	15.
6	19.3	20.
7	11.9	---

Probably no further comment is necessary at this time concerning this group.

It might be well to give a distribution of the total recidivists and first offenders. Following is such distribution:

Age Group	Home First (497 cases)	Home Recidivists (367 cases)	Away First (480 cases)	Away Recidivists (283 cases)
1	19.5	18.	14.1	10.7
2	23.1	30.8	27.3	26.5
3	19.1	16.1	20.1	24.1
4	13.2	13.6	13.4	13.1
5	10.8	10.8	10.3	10.3
6	9.2	9.4	10.	10.3
7	4.9	1.1	4.3	4.8

This distribution differs chiefly in the lower age levels. It is really remarkable how closely the percentages vary together in passing from one age group to a higher one, except in the lower levels.

The total distribution of the total recidivists and total first offenders is as follows:

Age Group	Percentage First (977 cases)	Percentage Recidivists (650 cases)
1	16.9	14.8
2	25.1	28.9
3	19.6	19.7
4	13.3	13.4
5	10.6	10.6
6	9.6	9.8
7	4.8	2.8

These two percentage distributions look strangely alike, and demonstrate the truth of the statement that the difference between first offenders and recidivists is a difference that can scarcely be expressed in terms of crime.

4. *The Age of Criminals from the West, the North and the South.*

The percentages of 1296 cases are as follows:

Age Group	Percentage West (299 cases)	Percentage North (739 cases)	Percentage South (258 cases)
1	14.6	15.3	21.6
2	25.6	27.	25.9
3	16.	20.8	19.2
4	17.	14.4	12.1
5	11.6	8.7	9.
6	9.	9.7	8.2
7	6.	3.9	4.7

The South leads in youthful criminals. The West is least in youthful criminals and leads in mature criminals. This is interesting in the light of the comparative intelligence of these three groups.

Tentative Conclusions:

1. The criminal group is relatively youthful. But the fraud group, which is the most intelligent group, is the oldest. The force group is composed of extremely young men. Statutory crimes are committed chiefly by young men, while crimes of physical violence are committed chiefly by older men. Sex crimes are chiefly committed by mature men.

2. Recidivists are not older than are first offenders. In some type-groups the recidivists are even much younger than are the first offenders. But, on the whole, the difference between the recidivists and the first offender is a difference that can scarcely be expressed in terms of time.

CHAPTER 9

INDUSTRIAL OCCUPATIONS

In arranging material for this chapter it was difficult to decide just what to select, there were so many occupations with just a few representatives. It was finally decided that only a few of the more representative occupations would be discussed. On page 828 of the Memoirs are found distributions of a large number of occupations, the followers of which had found their way into the Army. We shall use those distributions for our norms, and shall compare with them the distributions of nineteen industrial occupations which were followed by criminals before conviction. We shall follow no logical order, since none occurs to us, but shall present the data as it occurs in our notes.

There are 15 cases of expert accountants among the criminals. Their distribution in the Army letter grades, as compared with expert accountants in the army, is as follows:

Letter Grade	Percentage Army Cases	Percentage of Criminals
E	---	---
D	---	---
C—	.5	6.6
C	5.5	---
C+	26.2	13.3
B	39.1	33.3
A	28.7	46.6

To be sure, there are only fifteen cases of the criminals in this group, but the way they are clustered in the upper ranges of Alpha leaves little doubt concerning the probable distribution of a larger number of cases. Only the more intelligent of the expert accountants get to prison. It may be that they are in position to be subjected to greater temptations. Or it may be that they have a keener yearning for the things that money will buy. Most discussions of the causes of success and failure leave out of account the influence of the presence or the absence of burning desires. Such desires may be much stronger than mere intelligence.

Following is the distribution of the general clerks:

Letter Grade	Percentage Army Cases	Percentage of Criminals
E	.3	---
D	.9	.9
C—	5.2	5.9
C	19.7	24.1
C+	33.6	33.7
B	25.	21.4
A	15.3	14.1

There are 220 general clerks among the criminals examined, so the above distribution should be fairly accurate. There seems little to choose between the two distributions. There are very few general clerks of low intelligence in prison, and the reason is that there are no such general clerks among the population. But there certainly is no indication that the clerks who commit crime and get convicted are the less intelligent ones. In fact, intelligence seems to play no part whatever in determining the criminal behavior of clerks—at least no greater part than it plays in determining that certain individuals become clerks.

Following is the comparative distribution of musicians:

Letter Grade	Percentage Army Cases	Percentage of Criminals
E	1.	---
D	4.5	1.9
C—	12.3	11.5
C	26.3	15.4
C+	28.6	23.1
B	18.5	36.5
A	8.8	11.5

There are 52 of the musicians among the criminals. It It seems that among musicians the temptations to commit crime is greater among the more intelligent ones. It would be interesting to know the kinds of crimes that musicians commit. The writer will not give that information in this place, as it is contained in the original data that is published as part of this book. Such questions are of importance. But all such questions cannot be answered in this book. The writer hopes that others will make use of his data and help in answering some of the countless questions that legitimately can be asked on the basis of the data presented. The limitations of this book, as has been pointed out elsewhere, determine that it be suggestive rather than complete.

Following is the comparative distribution of the general mechanics:

Letter Grade	Percentage Army Cases	Percentage of Criminals
E	4.3	2.5
D	11.6	4.4
C—	16.7	12.6
C	28.3	27.7
C+	24.6	25.8
B	14.5	20.8
A	---	6.3

The criminal mechanics seem quite superior in the upper

ranges, as compared to the general run of mechanics. It should also be noted that the criminal mechanics are more highly selected in the lower ranges. The modes of the two distributions are approximately equal. The group differs in this respect from the group of general clerks. No attempt will be made now to interpret the significance of these facts. Of course, the facts are significant. Criminal behavior is certainly vitally related with the every-day industrial and social behavior of men not yet criminals. Information that is sufficiently comprehensive will reveal the relations, but such information is not yet at hand. Neither the mechanistic nor the vitalistic explanations will suffice alone, but a proper combination of the two should give an adequate explanation of all behavior. There are 159 criminal mechanics.

Following is the comparative distribution of the general machinists:

Letter Grade	Percentage Army Cases	Percentage of Criminals
E	4.1	1.6
D	10.8	1.6
C—	22.7	16.8
C	29.2	37.5
C+	21.2	28.2
B	9.3	8.1
A	3.	6.

Here again we see a marked superiority of the criminal machinists, as compared to the general run of machinists. The lack of low grade criminal machinists is especially marked. There are 184 cases of criminal machinists—a number sufficient for fairly accurate comparison.

Following is the comparative distribution of the chauffeurs:

Letter Grade	Percentage Army Cases	Percentage of Criminals
E	2.3	4.8
D	8.5	12.
C—	21.	14.6
C	31.3	28.1
C+	22.5	34.6
B	10.2	9.2
A	4.1	2.1

There are 185 chauffeurs in the criminal group. The criminal chauffeurs seem rather inferior to the general run of chauffeurs. But neither group is inferior to the general population. It is important to observe what types of occupations furnish superior criminals, and what types furnish inferior ones—relatively speaking. This may become clearer at the end of this chapter.

Following is the comparative distribution of the criminal farmers:

Letter Grade	Percentage Army Cases	Percentage of Criminals
E	6.4	11.6
D	20.6	10.
C—	26.8	27.
C	26.4	29.
C+	12.6	16.3
B	5.2	5.6
A	1.9	1.3

There are 303 cases of criminal farmers. The farmer group in both distributions is not a single grade group by any means. But, with the exception of the relatively small number of cases in the D group, the criminals are inferior to the general run of farmers. But the difference is not great, since there are more criminals in the C+ group. The general farmer group is rather inferior, because there are no failures dropping out of farming. In most trades and professions the failures drop out altogether, leaving the group with a higher average ability. But the farmer who fails with his own farm merely becomes a tenant on the other man's farm, and thus continues to be a farmer. Failure of the inferior farmers does not tend to raise the average ability of the general farmer group.

Following is the comparative distribution of the criminal tailors:

Letter Grade	Percentage Army Cases	Percentage of Criminals
E	8.4	11.1
D	25.5	2.2
C—	24.7	2.2
C	20.9	15.5
C+	14.2	44.4
B	4.6	17.6
A	1.7	8.8

There are only 45 of the criminal tailors, but they are immensely superior to the general run of tailors. Language difficulty is probably the explanation of the large percentage of criminals in the E group. The unusually large percentage of criminals in the C+ should especially be noticed, and the reader will remember that such phenomenon has been observed before in certain groups of criminals.

Following is the comparative distribution of the criminal barbers:

Letter Grade	Percentage Army Cases	Percentage of Criminals
E	6.6	4.3
D	18.8	2.9
C—	26.5	26.1
C	26.3	33.3
C+	14.9	24.6
B	6.1	5.8
A	.8	2.9

The superiority of the criminal barbers is evident. There are 69 cases of the criminal barbers.

Following is the comparative distribution of the criminal carpenters:

Letter Grade	Percentage Army Cases	Percentage of Criminals
E	3.3	6.6
D	10.5	8.3
C—	24.1	11.6
C	31.9	33.3
C+	20.7	23.3
B	7.6	15.
A	1.9	1.6

The two distributions differ chiefly in the C— and the B groups. There are 60 cases of the criminal carpenters, and they contain more of the high grade men and fewer of the low grade men, speaking in percentages, than do the Army norms.

The comparative distribution of the criminal cooks is as follows:

Letter Grade	Percentage Army Cases	Percentage of Criminals
E	6.2	4.5
D	16.8	10.6
C—	22.1	27.2
C	29.	22.7
C+	17.9	24.2
B	7.3	6.
A	.7	4.5

There are 66 cases of the criminal cooks, and they show a marked superiority to the general run of cooks.

Following is the comparative distribution of criminal painters:

Letter Grade	Percentage Army Cases	Percentage of Criminals
E	4.8	9.5
D	12.2	6.
C—	22.5	20.
C	33.	31.
C+	18.2	26.7
B	7.7	6.
A	1.5	.8

There are 116 painters. Except that the criminals have a larger percentage in the C+ group, there is little to choose between the two distributions.

Following is the comparative distribution of the criminal blacksmiths:

Letter Grade	Percentage Army Cases	Percentage of Criminals
E	5.4	9.1
D	13.9	9.1
C—	20.5	21.2
C	31.3	33.3
C+	18.8	24.2
B	8.2	3.
A	1.7	---

There are 33 of the criminal blacksmiths, and they contain fewer of the highest grade men and more of the lowest grade men than do the Army norms. Rather an inferior group.

Following is the comparative distribution of the criminal laborers:

Letter Grade	Percentage Army Cases	Percentage of Criminals
E	11.4	21.3
D	24.6	13.3
C—	25.1	22.5
C	24.2	27.5
C+	10.7	12.5
B	3.5	3.8
A	.6	.3

There are 608 of the criminal laborers. They differ from the general run of laborers chiefly in the larger percentage of men in the E group. Men who are incapable of doing any kind of work well can still classify themselves as laborers.

Following is the comparative distribution of criminal miners:

Letter Grade	Percentage Army Cases	Percentage of Criminals
E	9.7	10.
D	20.3	14.4
C—	26.4	30.6
C	26.7	25.2
C+	11.7	14.4
B	4.1	5.4
A	.9	---

There are 111 of the criminal miners. Miners are about as inferior as laborers, a fact which indicates the amount of skill necessary for the occupation of miner. The criminal miners are in some respects superior to the Army norms.

The comparative distribution of the criminal teamsters is as follows:

Letter Grade	Percentage Army Cases	Percentage of Criminals
E	9.4	12.1
D	19.7	7.5
C—	24.9	25.4
C	27.9	33.5
C+	12.5	15.6
B	4.3	4.6
A	1.3	1.1

There are 173 of the criminal teamsters. The two groups are about on an equality, though there is a great discrepancy in the percentages of the D groups. In the case of the criminals, language difficulties probably explain the large percentage of E cases. None of the low grade Alpha men were reclassified in the higher ranges of Beta.

The comparative distribution of criminal engineers is as follows:

Letter Grade	Percentage Army Cases	Percentage of Criminals
E	1.8	2.5
D	12.7	2.5
C—	21.8	12.8
C	32.7	17.9
C+	27.3	25.6
B	3.6	10.3
A	---	20.5

The criminal engineers, 39 in number, are very much superior to the Army norms. The Army norms may be unusually low, since engineers were exempt from army service. That is, the railroads were allowed to keep any engineers they wished. I am inclined to think that the Army norms for engineers are too low.

Following is the comparative distribution of criminal brakemen:

Letter Grade	Percentage Army Cases	Percentage of Criminals
E	7.5	6.5
D	9.2	10.4
C—	22.5	19.5
C	32.	30.
C+	22.5	20.8
B	8.8	10.4
A	2.4	2.6

There are 77 of the criminal brakemen, and there seems little to choose between them and the Army norms.

Following is the comparative distribution of criminal electricians:

Letter Grade	Percentage Army Cases	Percentage of Criminals
E	1.6	2.3
D	3.8	---
C—	10.4	11.3
C	28.4	29.5
C+	27.7	31.8
B	18.2	15.9
A	9.8	9.1

There are 44 of the criminal electricians. What surprised me most was the fact that electricians rank so low as compared to some of the other occupations. However, there is little to choose between the criminal electricians and the Army norms.

In addition to the nineteen groups already discussed, there is another fairly numerous group, the bookkeepers. The comparative distribution of the criminal bookkeepers is as follows:

Letter Grade	Percentage Army Cases	Percentage of Criminals
E	.2	---
D	.9	---
C—	4.4	4.
C	17.9	20.
C+	29.9	20.
B	28.6	40.
A	18.1	16.

There are 25 of the criminal bookkeepers, and there seems little to choose between them and the Army norms.

I hesitate to give the 9 cases of the criminal telegraphers, but they are as follows:

Letter Grade	Percentage Army Cases	Percentage of Criminals
E	---	---
D	1.2	---
C—	10.	11.1
C	29.1	'11.1
C+	32.2	22.2
B	20.3	33.3
A	7.3	22.2

I have two very numerous groups among the criminals for which there are no norms in the Memoirs—the salesmen and the printers. It might be well to give their distribution for future comparative purposes. They are as follows:

Letter Grade	Percentage of Salesmen	Percentage of Printers
E	1.7	---
D	.8	3.
C—	6.8	6.
C	25.	19.4

C+	25.	26.8
B	27.6	32.8
A	12.9	12.

There are 116 of the salesmen and 67 of the printers. They are both very superior criminal groups, containing practically none of the lower grades of intelligence.

As a matter of curiosity, it might be stated that seven lawyers were found in prison. Five of these lawyers rate in the A group and two of them in the C+ group.

Tentative Conclusions:

1. The representatives of some industrial occupations may be found to be more intelligent if selected from prison rather than from the Army. But the reverse is true in some cases. In prison we find more intelligent accountants, musicians, mechanics, machinists, tailors, barbers, cooks, engineers, and telegraphers than could be found in the Army—speaking in terms of percentage.

2. Criminals from the unskilled trades are about as intelligent as the other members of their trade. But criminals from the skilled trades are more intelligent than are the other members of their trade.

CHAPTER 10

SOME TECHNICAL STATISTICAL RESULTS

In preparing data for this chapter I hesitated to compute variations, correlations, and errors, on the basis of type groups. The reasons for this should be obvious to the reader. The type-group classification is hypothetical and may not be used by other workers in this field. So I have decided to base the statistical treatment on the legal classification of crimes, since such treatment may be more permanent, and may be more valuable to other workers in the field.

The question of homogeneity has also arisen. In order to conform to such requirements the data will be limited to the prisons of Ohio, Illinois, and Indiana. These three states border and the data were gathered within a period of a few weeks.

The number of cases will vary largely. There are 773 cases of burglars and only 16 cases of vagrancy or begging. For the sake of completeness, all crimes of 16 or more cases will be treated.

The M. that is reported is the median. The mean is not reported, though properly used. The standard deviation is computed from the formula—

$$\text{Sigma} = \sqrt{\frac{fd^2}{fx} - c^2}$$

The standard error of Sigma will be computed from the formula—

$$\text{S. E. Sigma} = \frac{\text{Sigma}}{\sqrt{2n}}$$

The coefficient of variation will be computed from the formula—

$$V = \frac{100\,\text{Sigma}}{M}$$

The coefficient of correlation will be computed from the formula—

$$r = \frac{\dfrac{S\,x\,y}{N} - Cx\,Cy}{\text{Sigma } x \quad \text{Sigma } y}$$

The probable error of the coefficient of correlation will be computed from the formula—

$$PE = \frac{.6745 \ (1 - r^2)}{\sqrt{N}}$$

The standard error of the coefficient of correlation will be computed from the formula—

$$S.E. \ r = \frac{1 - r^2}{\sqrt{N}}$$

The regression coefficients will be computed from the formula—

$$y = r \ \frac{Sigma \ y}{Sigma \ x} \ x$$

and the formula—

$$x = r \ \frac{Sigma \ x}{Sigma \ y} \ y$$

Alpha grades will be reported in class units of ten, chronological age in class units of four, and years in school in class units of one. The reader will remember that these units are to be preserved in the statistical report. The median and the deviations will be reported first. We shall proceed with the crimes in the order of the median, from the highest to the lowest. The median and the deviations will be of the Alpha grades, the chronological age, and the years in school.

Following are the 17 cases of conspiracy:

	Alpha Grade	Age	School
M.	86	26	8
Sigma	2.5	1.9	1.94
V.	27	33	24
S. E. Sigma	.43	.33	.33

As there are only seventeen cases of this crime, the statistical data must not be taken too seriously.

The writer should state that this chapter deals also with the criminals born in foreign countries, though limited to white men. My reasons for retaining the foreign-born in the data of this chapter are the same as those already mentioned.

The 19 cases of embezzlement are as follows:

	Alpha Grade	Age	School
M.	82	30	8
Sigma	3.93	1.94	3.03
V.	49	30	38
S. E. Sigma	.64	.32	.5

The 31 cases of the confidence game are as follows:

	Alpha Grade	Age	School
M.	79	33	9
Sigma	4.15	2.46	3.65
V.	48	34	36
S. E. Sigma	.53	.31	.46

The 35 cases of assault and battery to rob are as follows:

	Alpha Grade	Age	School
M.	73	21	7
Sigma	3.6	1.36	1.73
V.	47	28	25
S. E. Sigma	.43	.16	.21

The 516 cases of robbery are as follows:

	Alpha Grade	Age	School
M.	69	24	7
Sigma	3.71	1.42	2.27
V.	52	27	34
S. E. Sigma	.11	.04	.07

The 179 cases of forgery are as follows:

	Alpha Grade	Age	School
M.	69	28	8
Sigma	3.87	1.97	2.95
V.	50	66	34
S. E. Sigma	.2	.1	.15

The 40 cases of burglary of inhabited dwellings are as follows:

	Alpha Grade	Age	School
M.	67	34	6
Sigma	4.4	2.25	2.45
V.	60	32	37
S. E. Sigma	.49	.25	.39

There are 15 cases of issuing fraudulent check.

	Alpha Grade	Age	School
M.	66	31	8
Sigma	3.76	2.15	3.5
V.	55	32	44
S. E. Sigma	.7	.4	.64

There are 721 cases of larceny.

	Alpha Grade	Age	School
M.	66	24	7
Sigma	3.6	1.86	2.42
V.	53	36	36
S. E. Sigma	.09	.05	.01

There are 37 cases of violating automobile law.

	Alpha Grade	Age	School
M.	66	21	7
Sigma	3.	.66	1.8
V.	42	15	25
S. E. Sigma	.35	.07	.21

There are 46 cases of pocket picking.

	Alpha Grade	Age	School
M.	65	34	6
Sigma	2.96	1.7	2.1
V.	48	25	36
S. E. Sigma	.3	.17	.22

There are 60 cases of vehicle taking.

	Alpha Grade	Age	School
M.	62	21	6
Sigma	3.36	1.1	2.12
V.	48	24	32
S. E. Sigma	.308	.1	.19

There are 773 cases of burglary.

	Alpha Grade	Age	School
M.	62	24	6
Sigma	3.57	1.82	2.12
V.	55	34	34
S. E. Sigma	.09	.23	.11

There are 42 cases of entering to commit felony.

	Alpha Grade	Age	School
M.	60	24	6
Sigma	3.4	1.85	1.75
V.	53	34	28
S. E. Sigma	.37	.2	.19

There are 221 cases of murder in the first degree.

	Alpha Grade	Age	School
M.	58	32	6
Sigma	3.95	2.1	2.34
V.	64	30	41
S. E. Sigma	.19	.5	.11

There are 108 cases of assault to murder, rape or rob.

	Alpha Grade	Age	School
M.	55	30	6
Sigma	3.31	2.05	2.17
V.	61	33	39
S. E. Sigma	.22	.14	.15

There are 18 cases of bigamy.

	Alpha Grade	Age	School
M.	53	30	6
Sigma	4.02	1.6	2.78
V.	71	25	45
S. E. Sigma	.67	.26	.46

There are 102 cases of rape.

	Alpha Grade	Age	School
M.	50	32	6
Sigma	3.4	2.4	2.8
V.	62	35	48
S. E. Sigma	.23	.17	.19

There are 48 cases of abandonment.

	Alpha Grade	Age	School
M.	49	37	6
Sigma	3.34	1.82	2.1
V.	63	26	36
S. E. Sigma	.34	.18	.21

There are 25 cases of sodomy.

	Alpha Grade	Age	School
M.	46	37	6
Sigma	4.07	2.4	4.01
V.	69	32	58
S. E. Sigma	.57	.34	.56

There are 47 cases of carrying concealed weapons.

	Alpha Grade	Age	School
M.	45	27	6
Sigma	3.41	1.86	2.11
V.	66	34	36
S. E. Sigma	.35	.19	.22

There are 78 cases of manslaughter.

	Alpha Grade	Age	School
M.	42	32	5
Sigma	3.9	2.2	2.41
V.	80	34	44
S. E. Sigma	.31	.17	.19

There are 25 cases of incest.

	Alpha Grade	Age	School
M.	41	47	5
Sigma	2.51	1.72	2.5
V.	60	19	46
S. E. Sigma	.35	.24	.35

There are 97 cases of murder in the second degree.

	Alpha Grade	Age	School
M.	37	34	5
Sigma	4.	1.86	2.55
V.	80	24	46
S. E. Sigma	.28	.13	.19

There are 51 cases of cutting, stabbing, or shooting to kill or wound.

	Alpha Grade	Age	School
M.	34	30	5
Sigma	3.18	1.8	2.04
V.	78	28	41
S E. Sigma	.31	.17	.2

There are 16 cases of vagrancy.

	Alpha Grade	Age	School
M.	12	48	3
Sigma	2.45	2.67	1.8
V.	96	28	47
S. E. Sigma	.44	.48	.32

The total of 3,367 cases are as follows:

	Alpha Grade	Age	School
M.	62	26	6
Sigma	3.75	1.97	2.48
V.	58	34	39
S. E. Sigma	.04	.02	.03

The above measures of deviation have been given in detail, not because the writer believes such work to be significant and valuable, but in order that this work may be of service to those who do not agree with the writer.

We shall now proceed to the treatment of correlations, regressions, and errors, taking the crimes in the same order.

Following is the crime of conspiracy:

	Alpha and Age	Alpha and School	School and Age
r	—.05	.79	—.08
PE	.16	.06	.16
S.E. r	.24	.09	.24
y	—.04	.6	—.07
x	—.06	1.02	—.08

Following is the crime of embezzlement:

	Alpha and Age	Alpha and School	School and Age
r	.39	.74	.24
PE	.13	.07	.15
S.E. r	.19	.105	.22
y	.19	.57	.15
x	.78	.95	.37

Following is the confidence game crime:

	Alpha and Age	Alpha and School	School and Age
r	.09	.72	.44
PE	.12	.058	.09
S.E. r	.18	.086	.14
y	.05	.63	.29
x	.15	.82	.65

Following is the crime of assault and battery to rob:

	Alpha and Age	Alpha and School	School and Age
r	—.031	.65	—.26
PE	.11	.066	.11
S.E. r	.16	.097	.16
y	—.011	.31	—.2
x	—.08	1.35	—.33

Following is the crime of robbery:

	Alpha and Age	Alpha and School	School and Age
r	—.044	.56	—.22
PE	.03	.02	.027
S.E. r	.044	.032	.04
y	—.016	.34	—.14
x	—.07	.66	—.37

Following is the crime of forgery:

	Alpha and Age	Alpha and School	School and Age
r	.034	.69	.16
PE	.05	.026	.05
S.E. r	.074	.04	.07
y	.017	.52	.11
x	.066	.9	.24

Following is the crime of burglary of inhabited dwelling:

	Alpha and Age	Alpha and School	School and Age
r	—24	.63	—.19
PE	.1	.064	.1
S.E. r	.15	.095	.15
y	—.12	.35	—.17
x	—.47	1.13	—.2

Following is the crime of issuing fraudulent check:

	Alpha and Age	Alpha and School	School and Age
r	.17	.56	.09
PE	.17	.12	.11
S.E. r	.25	.18	.16
y	.09	.52	.05
x	.3	.6	.14

Following is the crime of larceny:

	Alpha and Age	Alpha and School	School and Age
r	—.11	.69	—.26
PE	.025	.013	.023
S.E. r	.037	.019	.034
y	—.057	.46	—.2
x	—.22	1.02	—.34

Following is the crime of violating automobile law:

	Alpha and Age	Alpha and School	School and Age
r	.12	.69	—.04
PE	.11	.058	.1
S.E. r	.16	.086	.16
y	.02	.41	—.014
x	.54	1.14	—.11

Following is the crime of pocket picking:

	Alpha and Age	Alpha and School	School and Age
r	—.069	.4	—.35
PE	.1	.083	.087
S.E. r	.14	.123	.12
y	—.04	.28	—.28
x	—.12	.56	—.43

Following is the crime of vehicle taking:

	Alpha and Age	Alpha and School	School and Age
r	.016	.69	.3
PE	.087	.046	.08
S.E. r	.13	.068	.12
y	.005	.43	.15
x	.049	1.09	.58

Following is the crime of burglary:

	Alpha and Age	Alpha and School	School and Age
r	—.042	.59	.37
PE	.024	.016	.02
S.E. r	.036	.023	.03
y	—.01	.35	.21
x	—.16	.99	.64

Following is the crime of entering to commit felony:

	Alpha and Age	Alpha and School	School and Age
r	—.03	.66	—.21
PE	.1	.058	.1
S.E. r	.15	.087	.15
y	—.016	.33	—.22
x	—.05	1.28	—.19

Following is the crime of first degree murder:

	Alpha and Age	Alpha and School	School and Age
r	—.33	.62	—.2
PE	.04	.028	.044
S.E. r	.062	.04	.065
y	—.17	.36	—.18
x	—.63	1.04	—.22

Following is the crime of assault to murder, rob, or rape:

	Alpha and Age	Alpha and School	School and Age
r	—.16	.6	—.2
PE	.063	.041	.062
S.E. r	.093	.061	.092
y	—.1	.4	—.19
x	—.26	.91	—.21

Following is the crime of bigamy:

	Alpha and Age	Alpha and School	School and Age
r	.23	.75	.41
PE	.15	.06	.13
S.E. r	.22	.1	.2
y	.09	.52	.23
x	.57	1.08	.71

Following is the crime of rape:

	Alpha and Age	Alpha and School	School and Age
r	—.23	.63	—.13
PE	.065	.04	.065
S.E. r	.093	.06	.097
y	—.16	.52	—.11
x	—.32	.76	—.15

Following is the crime of abandonment:

	Alpha and Age	Alpha and School	School and Age
r	—.13	.69	—.22
PE	.096	.051	.093
S.E. r	.14	.075	.13
y	—.07	.43	—.19
x	—.24	1.09	—.25

Following is the crime of sodomy:

	Alpha and Age	Alpha and School	School and Age
r	0	.96	0
PE	.13	.001	.13
S.E. r	.2	.0015	.2
y	0	.94	0
x	0	.97	0

Following is the crime of carrying concealed weapons:

	Alpha and Age	Alpha and School	School and Age
r	.13	.93	.38
PE	.097	.013	.08
S.E. r	.14	.02	.12
y	.07	.57	.33
x	.24	1.5	.43

Following is the crime of manslaughter:

	Alpha and Age	Alpha and School	School and Age
r	—.14	.73	—.032
PE	.074	.035	.076
S.E. r	.111	.053	.113
y	—.078	.45	—.029
x	—.24	1.18	—.035

Following is the crime of incest:

	Alpha and Age	Alpha and School	School and Age
r	—.17	.61	—.13
PE	.13	.08	.13
S.E. r	.19	.12	.19
y	—.11	.61	—.09
x	—.24	.61	—.19

Following is the crime of second degree murder:

	Alpha and Age	Alpha and School	School and Age
r	—.26	.68	—.16
PE	.063	.037	.047
S.E. r	.094	.054	.07
y	—.12	.43	—.11
x	—.56	1.06	—.22

Following is the crime of cutting, stabbing, or shooting:

	Alpha and Age	Alpha and School	School and Age
r	—.14	.8	—.19
PE	.09	.035	.08
S.E. r	.14	.05	.12
y	—.08	.51	.16
x	—.25	.85	.21

Following is the crime of vagrancy:

	Alpha and Age	Alpha and School	School and Age
r	—.45	.48	—.29
PE	.13	.13	.15
S.E. r	.2	.19	.23
y	.49	.35	—.19
x	.41	.65	—.43

Following is the total of all the crimes:

	Alpha and Age	Alpha and School	School and Age
r	—.13	.65	—.1
PE	.01	.006	.01
S.E. r	.02	.01	.02
y	—.06	.43	.08
x	—.25	.98	.12

CHAPTER 11

RELIGION

Most criminals belong to some church, and frankly admit the fact. The big majority attend church services every Sunday morning in the prison chapel. Of the men in the Maryland Penitentiary, 43.5% belong to some Protestant church, 34.4% belong to some Catholic church, 7.8% are Hebrews, while 14.3% are frankly agnostic.

1. *Intelligence of the Religious Groups.*

Let us first conpare the four groups of Catholics, Protestants, agnostics, and Hebrews. Using the Army letter grades, the four groups compare as follows:

Letter Grade	Catholic (87 cases)	Protestant (108 cases)	Hebrew (20 cases)	Agnostic (38 cases)
E	10.3	7.3	---	2.7
D	8.	10.	---	5.3
C—	13.8	19.1	10.	18.4
C	32.2	23.6	30.	21.
C+	24.1	15.4	30.	21.
B	8.	13.6	10.	21.
A	3.4	9.1	20.	10.5

The Hebrews and the agnostics certainly seem to demonstrate a much greater ability to make high scores in the Alpha test than do the Catholics and the general Protestant group. However, the Protestants demonstrate much greater ability in this respect than do the Catholics.

It might be well to give the number of cases of all the religous denominations represented in the Maryland Penitentiary. The cases are as follows:

Catholics	87	Agnostics	38
Episcopalians	10	Lutherans	14
Christians	6	Presbyterians	8
Methodists	41	Christian Science	6
Hebrews	20	Congregational	1
Baptists	21	I. B. S. A.	1

Ignoring those of less than eight cases, the following groups are arranged in the order of combined A and B percentages:

	A	B	C+	C	C—	D	E
Presbyterian	25.	25.	25.	25.	---	---	---
Episcopal	30.	10.	10.	20.	30.	---	---
Agnostic	10.5	21.	21.	21.	18.4	5.3	2.7
Hebrew	20.	10.	30.	30.	10.	---	---
Methodist	4.9	14.6	22.	9.7	22.	14.6	12.2
Baptist	4.8	9.5	14.3	52.4	14.3	---	4.8
Lutheran	---	14.3	---	21.4	42.8	7.1	14.3
Catholic	3.4	8.	24.1	32.2	13.8	8.	10.3

The writer has no desire to furnish powder for religious propagandists to shoot one another with. The figures certainly reveal interesting religious concomitants, but give to no group anything to be proud of.

The geographical concomitants are present, even in the religious groups. Let us compare the Catholics born in the State of Maryland with the Catholics born outside the state. There are 30 Catholics born outside the state and 57 Catholics who were born in the state.

Letter Grade	Percentage of Home Catholics	Percentage Born Away
E	10.5	10.
D	5.2	13.3
C—	14.	13.3
C	36.8	23.3
C+	26.3	20.
B	7.	10.
A	---	10.

Of the Methodists, there are 26 born in Maryland and 15 born outside the state. They compare as follows:

Letter Grade	Percentage of Home Methodists	Percentage Born Away
E	11.5	13.3
D	19.2	6.6
C—	26.9	13.3
C	11.5	6.6
C+	23.1	20.
B	7.7	26.6
A	---	13.3

There is an interesting exception in the case of the agnostics. They compare as follows:

Letter Grade	Percentage of Home Agnostics	Percentage Born Away
E	---	4.1
D	---	8.3
C—	---	29.1
C	35.7	12.5
C+	28.6	16.6
B	28.6	16.6
A	7.1	12.5

To be sure, there are only 24 of the migratory agnostics and 14 of the home-grown ones, but the figures can be added to in the future.

2. *The Literacy of the Various Religious Groups.*

As could be expected, the literacy of the religious groups correlates highly with the Alpha scores. Following is the literacy distribution of the Maryland criminals, the religious groups being in the same order as in the Alpha distribution.

	1	2	3	4	5	6	7
Presbyterian _____	---	---	12.5	25.	27.5	---	25.
Episcopal _____	---	---	40.	30.	10.	---	20.
Agnostic _____	7.9	18.4	23.7	34.2	7.9	5.	2.6
Hebrew _____	---	20.	---	35.	30.	10.	5.
Methodist _____	4.9	26.8	31.7	14.6	10.	10.	2.4
Baptist _____	---	4.7	19.	38.1	19.	19.	---
Lutheran _____	7.1	7.1	28.5	35.7	7.1	14.3	---
Catholic _____	4.6	23.	32.2	26.4	8.	5.7	--

The above comparison has some interesting features. The agnostics are not nearly so well educated as one might have thought, on the basis of the Alpha scores. The Baptists are much better educated than the agnostics, though not nearly so intelligent. The Presbyterians and the Episcopalians agree most closely with the Alpha scores. The literacy of the various groups is about what one would expect from one's observation and experience in general social life.

3. Religion and Types of Crime.

Let us consider the percentage of each religion that commits each type of crime.

	Fraud	Force	Thievery	Physical Injury	Derelic.	Sex
Presbyterian ___	50.	37.5	12.5	---	---	---
Episcopal _____	30.	40.	20.	10.	---	---
Agnostic _____	2.6	60.5	13.2	23.7	---	---
Hebrew _____	25.	30.	35.	10.	---	---
Methodist _____	12.2	22.	34.1	22.	---	10.
Baptist _____	18.2	45.4	18.2	2.4	9.1	2.4
Lutheran _____	---	42.8	21.1	28.6	---	7.1
Catholic _____	5.7	42.5	23.	13.8	4.6	9.2

The Methodists and Catholics comprise approximately 50% of the prison population, but commit more than 85% of all sex crimes. The Presbyterians, Episcopalians, and Hebrews are strong on fraud. The agnostics, Methodists and Lutherans are inclined to be strong on crimes of physical injury. The Baptists and agnostics are superior in obtaining property by force. The vast majority of agnostics follow the law of force —being either robbers or murderers. The Methodists and Hebrews are superior as plain thieves. To what extent the mode of the distribution of each religious group reflects a typical characteristic from the history of that religious group is a question that we are forced to leave to the students of ecclesiastical history.

4. The Religion of Recidivists.

The case distribution of the recidivists in the Maryland Penitentiary is as follows:

Religious Group	Number of Cases	Religious Group	Number of Cases
Presbyterian	--	Methodist	9
Episcopal	3	Baptist	6
Agnostic	10	Lutheran	4
Hebrew	5	Catholic	20

It is seen that the Presbyterians do not tend to become recidivists, while the agnostics and the Catholics furnish the large number of recidivists. However, for real comparison, we should compare the percentage of the total prison population in each religious group with the percentage of the total number of recidivists in each religious group.

Religious Group	Percentage of Total Prisoners	Percentage of Recidivists
Presbyterian	3.2	---
Episcopal	4.	5.2
Agnostic	14.3	17.5
Hebrew	7.8	8.8
Methodist	16.2	15.8
Baptist	8.3	10.5
Lutheran	5.5	7.
Catholic	34.4	35.1

There seems to be little of significance in the above distribution. There are no Presbyterians among the recidivists, but there are very few Presbyterians in the prison population. The agnostics are the only ones that show a decided increase among the recidivists, but the increase is not large enough to be significant. It does not appear that any religion or ecclesiastical group has any advantage over the others in ability to halt a career of crime.

5. *The Relation of Criminal Intelligence to Religious Inbreeding and Outbreeding.*

Does it make any difference in criminal intelligence whether both parents belong to the same church or to different churches? To be sure, the number of cases is small, but a comparison may prove valuable for further work in this direction. The writer has no weapon to grind or theory to prove in any of these comparisons. A large number of concomitants not mentioned in this book are of great importance, but this study is unable to consider all possible influences.

In terms of Alpha, let us compare the intelligence of the criminals both of whose parents belonged to the same religious group, and the intelligence of the criminals both of whose parents did not belong to the same religious group. We are not interested in the religious group that the criminal himself belongs to, or whether he belongs to any religious group. Did his parents belong to identical churches, or did they belong to different churches? In terms of religious belief, is the criminal himself an inbred product or is he a combination of religious belief, and which is the more intelligent? We find 189 criminals who are the children of parents with identical religious belief, and 44 who are the children of parents with opposing religious belief. They compare as follows:

Letter Grade	Percentage from Same Religious Sources	Percentage from Different Sources
E	7.9	6.8
D	9.5	4.5
C—	20.1	6.8
C	26.4	27.2
C+	19.6	18.2
B	11.1	20.5
A	5.3	15.9

Tentative Conclusions:

1. The criminal is religious, the vast majority belonging to some established religious demonination. The religious demoninations vary widely in intelligence, the Hebrews and the agnostics seeming to be more intelligent than are the Catholics and the Protestants.

2. But the agnostics rank very low in literacy. The Presbyterians and the Episcopalians are much more literate than are the Hebrews.

3. The Presbyterians incline to fraud, while the agnostic inclines to force. Nearly all cases of sex crimes are committed by Catholics and Methodists.

4. The recidivists are recruited chiefly from the ranks of the Catholics and the agnostics, while there are none at all among the Presbyterians.

5. Outbreeding of religious belief seems to produce a more intelligent criminal than does inbreeding.

CHAPTER 12

SEASONAL DISTRIBUTION

Much has been written in the literature of crime concerning the distribution through the various seasons of the year of crime frequencies. The study of this problem should proceed in connection with the study and analysis of the local social customs. Without reference to the year, the men in the Maryland Penitentiary committed their crimes in the following months of the year:

Name of Month	Number of Cases	Name of Month	Number of Cases
January	23	July	17
February	17	August	16
March	23	September	23
April	21	October	18
May	17	November	28
June	22	December	30

There is a decided variation. The months of February, May, July, August, and October are months of diminished criminal behavior. The peaks seem to be reached in the months of March, June, September, and December. These months begin the seasons and are months of temperature and other seasonal changes.

The distribution of cases, as to month and Alpha letter grade, is as follows:

	A	B	C+	C	C—	D	E
January	2	3	5	7	4	1	1
February	2	3	7	3	0	0	2
March	0	4	8	8	0	3	0
April	4	3	4	5	3	1	1
May	1	2	4	3	4	1	2
June	3	0	2	7	6	3	1
July	2	3	2	6	2	2	0
August	3	1	2	7	2	1	0
September	1	3	4	5	3	3	4
October	1	1	4	5	2	3	2
November	1	6	6	7	4	2	2
December	1	4	4	9	9	0	3

The writer is unable to see any significant clustering of intelligence levels according to season. It may be that a much larger number of cases, all taken from the same year, might show something of significance. It seems unnecessary to state the above cases in terms of percentages, and such procedure would probably bore the reader.

However, in spite of the above quite negative results, it is possible that types of crime may be more likely to be committed in some seasons rather than others. A great deal has been written on this subject, and much that has been written has proved worthless. Let us make a case distribution of types of crime according to month.

	Fraud	Force	Thievery	Physical Injury	Derel.	Sex
January	--	16	6	1	--	--
February	5	7	4	1	--	--
March	1	13	5	3	1	--
April	1	5	5	5	1	4
May	1	11	4	1	--	--
June	3	4	4	6	3	2
July	1	8	5	1	--	2
August	4	4	3	5	--	--
September	2	7	6	6	--	2
October	2	4	7	3	--	2
November	2	14	6	6	--	--
December	5	12	3	5	3	2

The physical injury and thievery groups do not seem to cluster at all. April seems the big month for sex crimes. June and December claim nearly all the cases of social dereliction. There seems little significant grouping of the fraud cases. The force group clusters about the winter months and the month of May. But the interpretation of the above groupings should wait for the accumulation of a large number of cases and the study of local social customs. The former has been reported many times before, and is included here for completeness and for the sake of future additions. On the whole, there seems little significant seasonal distribution of criminal intelligence.

CHAPTER 13

‚LENGTH OF INCARCERATION

Some of my enthusiastic friends have ventured the opinion that criminals as a group would be still higher in general intelligence if it had not been for the degenerating effects of long prison life. That raises a distinct problem. Does the ability to make a high score in a mental test undergo degeneration in proportion to the length of incarceration? I found that criminals themselves were convinced that such is the case. I found large numbers of intelligent prisoners who were resigned to becoming feeble-minded or insane as a result of long prison terms. Men's imaginations feed greedily on the few crumbs of information that reach them in those great massive mausoleums for the living.

For convenience in making the distributions let us agree upon the following numbers for the time intervals:

Time Group	Years of Imprisonment
1	Six months or less
2	Seven months to one year
3	Thirteen months to two years
4	Twenty-five months to three years
5	Thirty-seven months to five years
6	More than five years

In the Maryland Penitentiary there are the following numbers of cases in the various time groups:

Time Group	Number of Cases
1	69
2	59
3	50
4	24
5	35
6	18

If now we will make a percentage distribution of the time groups, in terms of the Army letter grades for Alpha, we can observe the influence of incarceration on ability to make scores in Alpha. Such distribution is as follows:

Letter Grade	1	2	3	4	5	6
E	5.8	6.8	8.	4.2	5.7	16.6
D	7.2	6.8	6.	4.2	11.4	11.1
C—	18.8	18.6	18.	12.5	11.4	16.6
C	27.5	30.5	22.	20.8	34.2	22.2
C+	21.8	17.	22.	20.8	20.	22.2
B	11.6	15.3	22.	12.5	5.7	---
A	7.2	5.1	2.	25.	11.4	11.1

If any deterioration of intelligence is indicated by the comparative scores, the writer fails to see it. The men who have been in prison between two and three years are by far the most intelligent men in the prison population.

For easier comparison let us compare the men who have been in prison two years or less with the men who have been in prison more than two years.

Letter Grade	Percentage Two Years or less	Percentage More Than Two Years
E	6.7	7.8
D	6.7	9.1
C—	18.5	13.
C	27.	27.2
C+	20.2	20.7
B	15.7	6.5
A	5.	1ɔ.ɔ

If there is any distinction in the two distributions it is all to the advantage of the long term man. There is no indication at all that intelligence is injured by length of incarceration.

CHAPTER 14

HEIGHT AND WEIGHT

1. *The Height of the Criminal.*

We found no criminal less than 60 inches tall, and very few were more than 72 inches. For convenience, let us adopt seven height groups, as follows:

Height Group	Height in Inches
1	60-61
2	62-63
3	64-65
4	66-67
5	68-69
6	70-71
7	72-X

The percentage of each crime group to be found in each height group would then be as follows:

	1	2	3	4	5	6	7
(27) Fraud	3.7	11.1	7.4	26.	30.	18.5	3.7
(105) Force	--	3.8	20.9	28.5	27.6	13.3	4.7
(58) Thievery	3.4	8.6	19.	31.	27.6	10.3	---
(43) Physical In.	--	4.6	18.6	20.9	41.8	9.3	4.6
(7) Dereliction	--	12.5	12.5	25.	25.	25.	---
(14) Sex	--	---	21.4	28.6	28.6	14.3	---

The fraud group comprises the largest range of physical height, while the sex group comprises the lowest range.

Some of the crime groups show a marked distinction between the home-grown and the migratory elements of their constituents. The force group, for example, shows the migratory individuals much taller as a rule than are the home-grown individuals. Following is the comparison.

Height Group	Percentage of Home Grown (48 cases)	Percentage of Migratory (57 cases)
1	---	---
2	4.1	3.5
3	29.1	14.
4	31.2	26.3
5	29.1	28.1
6	4.1	21.
7	2.1	7.

There are 48 of the home-grown individuals in the above group and 57 of the migratory individuals.

Following we find the opposite results in the physical injury group:

Height Group	Percentage of Home Grown (28 cases)	Percentage of Migratory (15 cases)
1	---	---
2	---	13.3
3	14.3	26.6
4	17.8	26.6
5	50.	26.6
6	10.7	6.6
7	7.1	---

The following case distribution of the sex group shows similarity with the physical injury group:

Height Group	Cases of Home Grown	Cases of Migratory
1	--	--
2	--	1
3	3	--
4	2	2
5	3	1
6	2	--
7	--	--

However, the thievery group shows practically a dead heat. Its distribution is as follows:

Height Group	Percentage of Home Grown (35 cases)	Percentage of Migratory (23 cases)
1	2.8	4.3
2	8.6	8.7
3	17.1	21.7
4	34.3	26.1
5	25.7	30.4
6	11.4	8.7
7	---	---

The above distribution has 35 cases of home-grown individuals and 23 cases of migratory individuals.

The fraud group probably had best be reported in a case distribution. Percentages are misleading when dealing with so few cases. The fraud group case distribution is as follows:

Height Group	Percentage of Home Grown	Percentage of Migratory
1	--	1
2	2	1
3	--	2
4	4	3
5	2	6
6	3	2
7	--	1

It is seen that the wide range of the fraud group is caused by the migratory element.

Exact results in this field must wait on the examination of larger numbers of cases.

2. *The Weight of the Criminal.*

Let us now decide upon seven weight groups, as follows:

Weight Group	Pounds
1	X-120
2	121-130
3	131-140
4	141-150
5	151-160
6	161-170
7	171-X

These seven groups have no particular significance, and are not designed to give any particular type of distribution. They are merely for convenience.

The percentage distribution of the six crime groups being considered is as follows:

	1	2	3	4	5	6	7
(27) Fraud	11.1	11.1	11.1	29.6	14.8	7.4	14.8
(105) Force	3.8	13.3	26.6	32.3	6.6	12.4	8.5
(58) Thievery	5.2	15.5	29.3	20.7	18.9	6.8	3.4
(43) Physical In.	2.3	11.6	20.9	13.9	13.9	13.9	13.9
(7) Dereliction	---	1.	1.	1.	2.	1.	1.
(14) Sex	---	7.1	35.7	21.4	7.1	14.3	14.3

It is seen that the fraud group has the greatest range of real proportions. The murder brigade in the physical injury group are the consistently big and heavy men of the criminal population. The modern murderer may be a more recent version of the ancient hero and warrior, or he may possess a physical organism too powerful for his mental equipment. But even in the latter case he might approximate the ancient hero. The Old Testament abounds in such characters, and so do the writings of Homer.

There seem to be two distinct groups in sex crimes. One is composed of the big fellows, while there is a second very large group of men below the average in weight. The latter group is by far the larger and more significant.

Chapter 15

SOME MARITAL CONCOMITANTS

For the data of this chapter we are limited to the cases from the Maryland Penitentiary. The widowers and the divorced cases are so few we shall have to eliminate them from the discussion. So, in this chapter, we shall be confined to the discussion of single men and married men. There are 143 single men and 93 married men. That is, the single men and the married men occur approximately in the proportion of 60 to 40. If the marital state has no relation to types of crime, single men and married men should occur in approximately that proportion in any type group. We shall compare single men and married men as to intelligence, types of crime, recidivism, and literacy.

1. *The Comparative Intelligence of Single and Married Men.*

For the suggestive purposes of this chapter, the number of cases being so small, we shall use the Army letter grades in reporting Alpha. The numbers are percentages.

	Percentage of Single (143 cases)	Percentage of Married (93 cases)
E	6.3	8.6
D	7.	7.5
C—	18.1	9.7
C	29.3	24.7
C+	20.3	21.5
B	14.	14.
A	4.9	14.

The married men certainly seem superior in intelligence to the single men. They are far superior in the highest grade. The comparison in the lower grades is quite interesting, the married men being in the majority in the lowest grades, but very scarce in C— group.

It might be interesting to compare the home-grown type with the migratory type. The comparison is as follows:

	Single at Home (74 cases)	Single Away (69 cases)	Married at Home (51 cases)	Married Away (42 cases)
E	6.7	5.8	11.7	4.7
D	9.4	4.5	7.8	7.1
C—	18.9	17.3	9.8	9.5
C	36.5	21.7	25.5	23.8
C+	17.5	23.2	27.4	14.3
B	9.4	18.8	13.7	14.3
A	1.3	8.7	3.9	26.2

The most casual glance at the above comparisons shows the very significant differences that exist in the four groups. The migratory group of single men is more intelligent than the home-grown group of married men, but with much less intelligence than the migratory group of married men. There are 74 cases of the home-grown single men and 69 cases of the migratory single men. There are 51 cases of the home-grown married men and 42 cases of the migratory married men. The differences in the respective numbers of cases would not account for the very significant differences in the percentages. The writer does not assume that marriage brings about a growth of intelligence. In this chapter, as in the remainder of the book, the discussion is concerning concomitants.

2. *The Marital State and Types of Crime.*

In this section we shall consider the relative proportions of single men and married men committing each of the various types of crime. However, there is no discussion of statutory offenses, since the laws of Maryland do not seem to supply such cases to the penitentiary. Social dereliction will be omitted also, since definition practically confines this group to married men. In this section the comparisons are made in relative percentages—the sum of each pair being 100. Remember that single men are to married men as 60 to 40, as far as numbers are concerned. Just remember that if the law of probability is the only selective influence, approximately 60% of the cases in any type group will be single men, and approximately 40% will be married men. Just associate 60 with single men and 40 with married men. Then observe figures that actually occur. First, we have the total:

	Single Men (143 cases)	Married Men (93 cases)
Fraud	35	65
Force	69	31
Thievery	69	31
Physical Inj.	56	44
Sex	60	40

It is seen that only in sex crimes is the relative proportion of single men and married men as 60 to 40. The married men are almost overwhelmingly in the majority in the fraud group —the percentages being practically reversed. The less intelligent the group, the greater the likelihood that the law of probability will determine the relative proportions of single and married men. The more intelligent the group, the less the likelihood that the law of probability will determine the proportions. It is interesting that fraud and the married state should be so highly correlated.

Let us make the comparison also in terms of home-grown and migratory groups.

	Single at Home (74 cases)	Single Away (69 cases)	Married at Home (51 cases)	Married Away (42 cases)
Fraud	27	40	73	60
Force	64	73	36	27
Thievery	68	72	32	28
Physical Inj.	54	58	46	42
Sex	63	1 case	37	1 case

There are ten cases of widowers, but eight of these are concerned with physical injury and sex, that is, the less intelligent groups. It is seen that the home-grown married men are the ones who are especially inclined to fraud. That is, the group that presumably should be the most orthodox and conservative is the one most inclined to fraud. That is probably what we should expect, since radicalism and revolution are more closely associated with physical violence. Speaking symbolically, the fraud group is recruited chiefly from the old blue-blooded stock. The lower groups are recruited from any old source. The hierarchy of criminal groups is so similar to the hierarchy of other social groups!

3. *The Marital State and Recidivism.*

Of course we are forced to confine ourselves to recidivists that happen to be in the one prison in Maryland. There are only fifty-four of them, if we do not count the widowers and divorced prisoners. The proportion of married men and single men among the fifty-four recidivists is as follows:

	Single Men	Married Men
Recidivists	62	38

It is seen that the law of probability seems to function here. It is significant, however, that marriage does not deter the criminal from becoming a recidivist. Either that, or marriage is no bar to the recidivist.

The home-grown and the migratory groups compare as follows:

	Recidivists
Single at Home	60
Single Away	64
Married at Home	40
Married Away	36

Of the sixteen habitual criminals, ten are single and six are married. It certainly seems that the marital state has no relation to recidivisim. The comparative percentages are as nearly purely probable as one could expect from the small number of cases. If marriage will not prevent a criminal from becoming a recidivist, it is doubtful if any other human institution, brought to bear up the same conditions would meet with any greater success.

4. *Literacy and the Marital State.*

Here, also, we shall use comparative percentages in each literacy group for the reporting of single and married cases. The reader will recall that there are seven literacy groups. The total is distributed as follows:

Literacy Group	Percentage of Single (143 cases)	Percentage of Married (93 cases)
1	50	50
2	69	31
3	60	40
4	73	27
5	50	50
6	37	63
7	14	86

The home-grown and migratory groups compare as follows:

Literacy Group	Single at Home (74 cases)	Single Away (69 cases)	Married at Home (51 cases)	Married Away (42 cases)
1	50	50	50	50
2	71	67	29	33
3	57	67	43	33
4	70	77	30	23
5	56	48	44	52
6	--	50	100	50
7	--	20	100	80

Tentative Conclusions:

1. There are more single men than married men, but the married men seem more intelligent. The migratory married men seem especially intelligent.

2. Married men tend chiefly to commit crimes of fraud.

3. The marital state seems to have no relation to recidivism.

4. Not only do the married men seem more intelligent, but they are vastly more literate than are the single men.

PART III

White Foreign-Born Men Criminals

CHAPTER 16

SOME GEOGRAPHICAL CONCOMITANTS

The total number of foreign born criminals with which this and following articles are to be concerned is 761. This is not a large number of cases for statistical treatment, but is as large as could be obtained at the present time by ordinary influences of admission to state prisons.

Let us first compare the distribution of the Alpha scores of foreign born criminals with the distribution of Alpha scores of foreign born recruits in the draft as reported on page 695 Volume 15 of the Memoirs of the National Academy of Sciences. The reader will remember that we are dealing with 761 cases of criminals and 4,737 cases of recruits in the draft army, both groups being foreign born.

Following is the comparative distribution of the two groups:

Alpha Score	Criminal Cases	Percentage of Criminal Cases	Percentage of White Draft
0- 9	116	15.2	8.3
10- 14	59	7.7	6.0
15- 19	44	5.8	4.7
20- 24	45	5.9	6.4
25- 34	91	11.9	12.1
35- 44	73	9.6	11.9
45- 59	95	12.5	15.4
60- 74	93	12.2	11.4
75- 89	53	7.0	8.8
90-104	39	5.1	6.1
105-119	28	3.7	4.0
120-134	14	1.8	2.3
135-149	6	.8	1.3
150-212	5	.7	1.2

Transferring the above distribution in letter grades we have the following:

Leter Grades	Percentage of foreign born draft	Percentage of foreign born criminals
E	14.3	22.9
D	11.1	11.7
C—	24.0	21.5
C	26.8	24.7
C+	14.9	12.1
B	6.3	5.5
A	2.5	1.5

It will be observed that the foreign born draft seems superior to the foreign born criminals. In the case of the draft we have 23.7 per cent. superior to C while only 19 per cent. of the foreign born criminals are superior to C. Also 49.4 per cent. of the foreign born draft are inferior to C while 56.1 per cent. of the foreign born criminals are inferior to C. It will be remembered that the result of this comparison is quite different from the comparison of native born white criminals with the native born members of the draft. Does it follow from this fact that the old concept of feeble-mindedness in a realm of criminal behavior is a truer concept in the case of foreign born criminals than in the case of our own native born criminals? 'Can the above results be used as an argument against the admission of the foreign born into America? The writer has no desire to play the part of the propagandist in this report but does wish to prevent the drawing of false conclusions. For the sake of proper insight into the problems involved let us remember the wide variation in the geographical distribution of intelligence in the American draft army and compare the distribution of the intelligence of foreign born criminals with the distribution of intelligence of the Arkansas draft and the North Carolina draft as reported on pages 689 and 690 of the*Memoirs of the National Academy of Sciences,* Vol. 15.

Letter Grades	Percentage of foreign born criminals (761 cases)	Percentage of Arkansas draft (710 cases)	Percentage of North Carolina draft (702 cases)
E	22.9	15.9	14.3
D	11.7	17.2	17.1
C—	21.5	26.2	28.2
C	24.7	24.6	22.5
C+	12.1	12.7	12.5
B	5.5	2.8	3.8
A	1.5	.5	1.9

It will be seen that the foreign born criminals compare very favorably in the distribution of their Alpha scores with the native born white members of the North Carolina and Arkansas draft. With the 19.1 percentage of foreign born criminals superior to C let us compare the 16 per cent. of the Arkansas draft superior to C and the 18.2 per cent. of the North Carolina draft superior to C. With the 56.1 per cent. of foreign born criminals inferior to C let us compare the 59.3 per cent. of the Arkansas draft inferior to C and the 59.6 per cent of the North Carolina draft inferior to C. That is, in spite of the seemingly obvious inferiority of foreign born criminals we find that their ability to make scores in the Army Alpha Test is equal if not superior to the ability of the native born white recruit from North Carolina and Arkansas to make scores in the same test. And yet there is the obvious handicap of language which the foreign born criminal undoubtedly is struggling against. Such inferiority as is read into the Alpha performances of the foreign born criminals must also be read into the Alpha performances of the white native born recruits from Arkansas and North Carolina.

But now the question arises whether the geographical distribution of intelligence which seems so marked in the case of the many records as reported in Volume 15 of the *Memoirs of the National Academy of Sciences* and is existing so obviously, as pointed out by the author in his article in the *Journal of Criminal Law and Criminology,* does not function just as significantly in the case of the foreign born whether criminals or members of the army draft. It is extremely unfortunate that the voluminous report of mental testing in the army does not indicate to us the variation in the intelligence of foreign born members of the draft tested in different camps. That is, there is a perfectly obvious possibility that a given nationality tested at Camp Sherman might vary considerably from the same nationality tested at Camp Devens. The army report does not give us that information so we shall have to be satisfied with whatever probability might be established in considering the variation in the intelligence of the foreign born criminals tested in different states. Following is such a comparison of the distribution of Alpha scores made by the foreign born criminals tested in the five states of Ohio, Illinois, Indiana, New Jersey and Maryland.

	P. C. of Ohio foreign born criminals (291 cases)	P. C. of Ill. foreign born criminals (191 cases)	P. C. of Ind. foreign born criminals (43 cases)	P. C. of N. J. foreign born criminals (206 cases)	P. C. of Md. foreign born criminals (30 cases)
0- 9	16.1	6.3	9.3	24.2	10.0
10- 14	9.3	4.0	2.3	9.7	10.0
15- 19	5.8	4.0	9.3	6.8	3.3
20- 24	9.6	3.7	9.3	2.4	3.3
25- 34	13.0	12.6	4.7	11.1	13.3
35- 44	9.6	10.0	7.0	10.7	3.3
45- 59	13.4	14.7	2.3	11.1	13.3
60- 74	10.0	16.3	34.9	6.8	13.3

75- 89-------------- 3.8	12.6	4.7	5.8	13.3
90-104-------------- 4.8	5.3	9.3	4.8	3.3
105-119------------- 2.4	6.8		2.9	6.6
120-134------------- 1.4	1.5	2.3	2.4	3.3
135-149------------- .7	1.5	2.3		
150-212-------------	.5	2.3	.9	3.3

Transferring this distribution into letter grades the variations become even more obvious.

Letter Grades	P. C. of Ohio foreign born criminals	P. C. of Ill. foreign born criminals	P. C. of Ind. foreign born criminals	P. C. of N. J. foreign born criminals	P. C. of Md. foreign born criminals
E --------------	25.4	10.4	11.6	33.9	20.0
D --------------	15.4	7.7	18.6	9.2	6.6
C— -------------	22.6	22.6	11.7	21.8	16.6
C --------------	23.4	31.0	37.2	17.9	26.6
C+ -------------	8.6	17.9	14.0	10.6	16.6
B --------------	3.8	8.3	2.3	5.3	9.9
A --------------	.7	2.0	4.6	.9	3.3

In the above distribution we find that the percentage of E grades varies all the way from 10.3 per cent. to 33.9 per cent. and that the A grades vary all the way from .7 per cent. to 4.6 per cent. Even in the case of the C grades we find a variation from 17.9 per cent. to 37.2 per cent. We find that of the Ohio criminals only 13.1 per cent. are superior to C while 28.2 per cent. of the Illinois foreign born criminals give grades superior to C. Also we find that 63.4 per cent of the Ohio foreign born criminals are inferior to a grade of C while only 40.6 per cent. of the Illinois foreign born criminals are inferior to C. This variation in the intelligence of foreign born criminals examined in different states is almost as marked as is the variation in intelligence of native born criminals examined in different states. That is, it is just as invalid to speak of the foreign born criminal as representing a type as it would be to speak of the native born criminal as representing a type or even to speak of the native born criminal as representing a type or even to speak of the criminal class as a type.

The problem of geographical distribution of the intelligence of foreign born criminals and foreign born members of the army draft might become somewhat more simplified if we compare the criminals of various nationalities with the army draft quota from the same nationalities. That is, it might be illuminating instead of speaking of the foreign born in general terms to speak definitely of the German born criminals and German born members of the American army, the Italian born criminals and Italian members of the army, etc. Following this plan let us first compare the intelligence distributed in terms of letter grades of the foreign born criminals born in England, Scotland, Canada and Ireland with the foreign born draft born in these same countries. Following is a comparison:

Letter Grades	P. C. of foreign born draft born in England Scotland Canada Ireland (695 cases)	P. C. of criminals born in England Scotland Canada Ireland (125 cases)
E	10.8	8.0
D	9.7	6.4
C—	20.0	12.0
C	28.8	32.8
C+	18.2	24.0
B	8.6	11.2
A	4.0	5.6

It will be seen that a definite comparison bears the characteristics pointed out in previous publications concerning the intelligence of white native born criminals. That is, criminals born in England, Scotland, Canada and Ireland seem definitely superior to the members of the draft born in these same countries. While 40.8 per cent. of the criminals made a grade superior to C, only 30.8 per cent. of the foreign born draft in the same countries made a grade superior to C. While 26.4 per cent. of the criminals born in the different countries made a grade inferior to C, 40.5 per cent. of the foreign born draft from these same countries made a grade inferior to C. Does the similarity of this comparison with the comparison of native born criminals and members of the draft indicate that among the English speaking and native born peoples tested by the Army Alpha the problem of intelligence is of more relative importance while among the non-English speaking foreign born peoples the problem of feeble-mindedness is of greater relative importance in the investigation of criminal behavior? But before we come to any conclusions in this matter let us consider some of the other nationalities.

Following is a comparison of the German born criminals with the German members of the draft:

Letter Grades	P. C. of foreign born draft born in Germany (217 cases)	P. C. of criminals born in Germany (84 cases)
E	6.0	4.7
D	11.5	10.7
C—	26.7	14.2
C	27.6	32.1
C+	17.1	28.6
B	6.4	8.4
A	4.6	1.2

We find in the case of the Germans that 38.2 per cent. of the criminals are superior to C while only 28.1 per cent. of the German born draft is superior to C. 29.6 per cent of the German born criminals are inferior ot C while 44.2 per cent. of the German born draft is inferior to C. So in the case of the Germans also we are justified in assuming that the criminals not only are not inferior mentally to the draft group but are even perceptibly superior in their ability to make scores in the Army Alpha test.

Proceeding to a comparison of the Italian born criminals with the Italian members of the draft we have the following:

Letter Grades	P. C. of foreign born draft born in Italy (724 cases)	P. C. of criminals born in Italy (143 cases)
E	30.4	41.2
D	15.1	14.0
C—	26.6	27.3
C	19.2	11.2
C+	6.2	4.2
B	1.8	2.1
A	.7	

In the case of the Italians only 6.3 per cent. of the criminals made a grade superior to C while 8.7 per cent. of the Italian born members of the draft made a grade superior to C. We also find that 82.5 per cent. of the Italian born criminals made a score inferior to C while 82.1 per cent. of the Italian born members of the draft made a grade inferior to C. So in the case of the Italians there seems to be a distinct mental inferiority even though both distributions reveal a mode which lies in C.

Now let us make the same comparison of the Austrian criminals and members of the army draft. Following is such a comparison:

Letter Grades	P. C. of foreign born draft born in Austria (126 cases)	P. C. of criminals born in Austria (100 cases)
E	8.0	30.0
D	8.7	13.0
C—	37.3	19.0
C	28.6	25.0
C+	11.9	10.0
B	2.4	3.0
A	1.6	1.0

It is observed that 14 per cent. of the Austrian born criminals made a score superior to C while 15.9 per cent of the Austrian born draft made a score superior to C. It is also observed that 62 per cent. of the Austrian born criminals made a score inferior to C while 54 per cent. of the Austrian born members of the draft made a score inferior to C. So it is seen that in the case of the Austrians the criminals are not markedly inferior to the Austrian born members of the draft but that that the Austrian born criminals give a decided bi-modal distribution of Alpha scores. That is, 30 per cent. of the Austrian born criminals made a score of E while only 8 per cent. of the Austrian born members of the draft made a score of E. It will also be observed that while 19 per cent. of the Austrian born criminals made a score of C—, 37.3 per cent. of the Austrian born members of the draft made a score of C—. The resulting very decided differences of the forms of the two distribution curves make it very difficult to determine whether Austrian born criminals are inferior, superior or generally equal to the Austrian born members of the draft.

Let us proceed to the Russian born criminals and members of the draft. Following is a comparison of the two groups:

Letter Grades	P. C. of foreign born draft born in Russia (709 cases)	P. C. of criminals born in Russia (80 cases)
E	17.2	26.2
D	12.0	9.9
C—	25.7	16.2
C	24.0	36.2
C+	13.2	6.2
B	7.2	3.7
A	1.7	1.2

It will be seen that 11.1 per cent. of the Russian born criminals made a score superior to C while 22.1 per cent. of the Russian born members of the draft made a score superior to C. It will also be observed that 52.3 per cent. of the Russian born criminals made a score inferior to C while 54.9 per cent. of the Russian born members of the draft made a score inferior to C. Here we have the interesting spectacle of one distribution showing a larger percentage of both superior and inferior individuals than the other distribution shows. That is, the Russian born members of the draft show both a larger percentage of superior individuals and a larger percentage of inferior individuals than the Russian born criminals show. It will be seen that this distribution is brought about by the unusually large number of Russian criminals who made a score of C. It should also be observed that both the different distributions are bi-modal, the distribution of criminals being especially so. Here also we find it difficult to decide whether the criminals are more intelligent, less intelligent or of equal intelligence with the members of the draft. But along with this difference as in the case of the Austrians there is a decided bi-modality of the distribution curves.

Letter Grades	P. C. of foreign born draft born in Italy Greece Austria-Hungary Russia Poland (1,809 cases)	P. C. of criminals born in Italy Greece Austria-Hungary Russia Poland (430 cases)
E	22.5	32.6
D	13.8	13.0
C—	27.6	23.7
C	22.1	21.2
C+	9.2	6.0
B	3.9	3.0
A	1.1	.4

A definite lumping of cases shows us 9.4 per cent of foreign born criminals from Southern and Eastern Europe making a score superior to C and 14.2 per cent. of the foreign born members of the draft coming from the same countries making a score superior to C. It also shows 69.3 per cent. of such criminals making a score inferior to C and 63.9 per cent. of such members of the foreign born draft making a score inferior to C. That is, we find among such criminals a relatively larger percentage of very low grade individuals mentally and a relatively higher percentage of high grade individuals than is revealed in the distribution of the foreign born draft. That is, in so far as there is any difference in average Alpha scores such foreign born criminals are certainly not superior to such foreign born members of the draft but in other words are distinctly inferior.

Now if we will make the same comparison of criminals born in so-called Central, Northern and Western Europe with the foreign members of the draft from the same countries we will get somewhat different results. Following is the comparison:

	P. C. of foreign born draft born in Germany England Scotland Denmark Sweden Norway Holland Ireland (2,055 cases)	P. C. of criminals born in Germany England Scotland Denmark Sweden Norway Holland Ireland (188 cases)
Letter Grades		
E	9.5	6.9
D	8.8	7.4
C—	22.6	14.3
C	30.0	32.9
C+	18.4	27.0
B	7.3	8.0
A	3.1	3.2

In a definite comparison we find 38.2 per cent. of such criminals making scores superior to C and 28.8 per cent. of such foreign born members of the draft making scores superior to C. We also find 28.6 per cent. of such criminals making scores inferior to C and 41.1 per cent. of such foreign born members of the draft making scores inferior to C. So in this comparison the relative superiority of the criminals is more marked.

Probably we are justified in assuming for the time being at least that the question previously raised may be answered in the affirmative. That is, the so-called superior races and nationalities give us still more superior criminals while so-called inferior races and nationalities give us still more inferior criminals. Certainly this complicates to a tremendous degree the entire problem of criminal intelligence.

It might be interesting at this point to consider a comparison of the Canadian born criminals with the Canadian born members of the draft. Following is such a comparison:

Letter Grades	Canada P. C. of foreign born draft born in (702 cases)	Canada P. C. of crimi- nals born in (46 cases)
E	6.1	8.7
D	9.7	8.7
C—	18.8	10.8
C	31.2	34.8
C+	20.0	17.4
B	9.8	15.2
A	4.5	4.4

In the above comparison we find 37 per cent. of the Canadian born criminals making a score superior to C while 34.3 per cent. of the Canadian born members of the draft made a score superior to C. Also that 28.2 per cent. of the Canadian born criminals made a score inferior to C while 34.6 per cent. of the Canadian born members of the draft made a score inferior to C. So a comparison of the Canadian born criminals with the Canadian born members of the draft indicates at least a slight superiority on the part of the criminals. Of course Canada is settled chiefly by emigrants from Western Europe.

CHAPTER 17

TYPES OF CRIME

1. The writer, in discussing the intelligence and types of crime committed by white native born criminals, *Journal of Criminal Law and Criminology,* August, 1924, made the following suggestion concerning the classification of types of crime: "The writer suggests that the seventy-two crimes, for purposes of comparison, be classified into seven groups as follows: (1) Obtaining property through deception and fraud, known legally as forgery, embezzlement, false pretenses, conspiracy, confidence games, receiving stolen property, blackmail, counterfeiting, and uttering fraudulent checks. (2) Obtaining property through force, known legally as robbery, burglary, assault to rob, breaking and entering, entering to commit felony, burglary and larceny, safe blowing, attempted burglary, kidnapping, child stealing, house-breaking, attempt to rob, and burglary of inhabited dwelling. (3) Obtaining property through common thievery, known legally as larceny, pocket picking, vehicle taking, horse stealing and automobile stealing. (4) Statutory offenses, known legally as unlawful use of motor vehicle, illegal sale of drugs, illegal sale or possession of intoxicating beverages, carrying concealed weapons, unlawful use of explosives, operating motor vehicle without owner's consent, violating automobile law, having burglar tools, concealing weapons to aid escape, escaping prison, and removing railroad property. (5) Crimes of physical injury, known legally as murder, maiming, manslaughter, assault to murder, accessory to murder, cutting, shooting or stabbing to kill or wound, arson, and malicious destruction of property. (6) Crimes of social dereliction, known legally as abandonment, desertion, vagrancy, begging, non-support, neglect of minor child, child abandonment, bigamy, lewdness, seduction, perjury, publishing of obscene writing, abduction, and receiving earnings of prostitute. (7) Sex crimes, known legally as rape, sodomy, indecent liberty with child, incest, assault to rape, crime against nature, assault to commit crime against nature, crime against child, adultery, and carnal abuse." For the sake of uniformity and ease of comparison we will follow that same grouping in this discussion dealing with foreign born white criminals.

If the relative percentages of native born whites and foreign born whites committing each of the seven types of crime are compared, we get the following interesting differences.

	Number of native born whites	Number of foreign born	Percentage of native born whites	Percentage of foreign born
Deception	331	48	8.1	6.3
Force	1542	269	39.1	35.4
Thievery	992	132	25.1	17.4
Statutory	187	39	4.7	5.1
Physical Injury	521	199	13.2	26.2
Dereliction	119	19	3.	2.5
Sex	253	54	6.4	7.1

It will be observed that the significant differences between native born and foreign born whites, as far as types of crime are concerned, are to be found in the relative percentage committing crimes of thievery and crimes of physical injury. It is found that foreign born whites are much less likely to commit crimes of thievery than are native born whites. It is also seen that foreign born whites are very much more likely to commit crimes of physical injury than are native born whites. The variations in the case of the other crime groups are slight in comparison. However, the reader should be cautioned here, as he has been cautioned elsewhere in these various reports, against accepting a general conclusion concerning an entire group as applying with equal force to all the individuals in that group. For example, it may be found later that foreign born criminals from Borneo and from Alaska do not vary in the same direction from native born whites, so that any general statement concerning the foreign born can not possibly apply with equal force to both of them.

2. Before taking up the problems of the variation of nationalities in the various crime groups, let us first consider the distribution of Alpha grades made by the combined foreign born criminals in the various crime groups. It must be assumed, of course, that the reader is acquainted with the previous articles in this series appearing in this journal and in the *Journal of Criminal Law and Criminology,* and that the reader is also acquainted with the general nature of the Army Alpha Test.

Proceeding further, let us first consider the distribution of the Alpha percentages of foreign born criminals committing crimes of deception, this crime being the first of the seven groups of types of crime.

Alpha	Number of Cases	Percentage	Alpha	Number of Cases	Percentage
0- 9	2	4.2	60- 74	8	16.6
10-14	1	2.1	75- 89	2	4.2
15-19	1	2.1	90-104	5	10.4
20-24	1	2.1	105-119	8	16.6
25-34	6	12.5	120-134	2	4.2
35-44	4	8.3	135-149		
45-59	6	12.5	150-212	2	4.2

Translating into the traditional letter grades:

Letter Grades	Percentage of foreign born criminals
E	6.3
D	4.2
C—	20.8
C	4.2
C+	20.8
B	29.1
A	14.6

It will be noticed, in the case of this group, that 25 per cent achieve a ranking of A or B. It will be recalled from Chapter 16, Page 162, that only 7 per cent of the entire foreign born criminal group achieve such ranking. It will be observed also that only 10.5 per cent of the members of the deception group achieve ranking as low as D or E. It will be recalled that the article referred to above revealed that 34.6 per cent of the entire foreign born criminal group achieve that low ranking. That is, foreign born criminals who commit crimes of deception are very superior as compared to the entire foreign born criminal group, and in this way are similar to the white native born criminals who commit similar crimes. In fact, it might be interesting to compare the letter grades of the foreign born criminals committing crimes of deception with the letter grades of the native born criminals committing similar crimes. Taking from page 59, the letter grades and the percentages of white native born criminals committing crimes of deception, and arranging them parallel with the letter grades and percentages of the above foreign born criminals committing similar crimes, we get the following interesting comparison:

Letter Grades	Percentage of white native born Criminals	Percentage of white foreign born Criminals
E	2.4	6.3
D	8.2	4.2

C—	--------------------- 11.4	20.8
C	--------------------- 25.1	29.1
C+	--------------------- 24.8	14.6
B	--------------------- 15.8	20.8
A	--------------------- 12.3	4.2

The marked superiority of the foreign born criminals committing crimes of deception becomes even more startling in the following comparison of the group with the white native born members of the Arkansas draft as reported on Page 689, Vol. 15, of the *Memoirs of the National Academy of Sciences.*

Letter Grades	Percentage of Arkansas draft	Percentage of white foreign born Criminals
E	--------------------- 15.9	6.3
D	--------------------- 17.2	4.2
C—	--------------------- 26.2	20.8
C	--------------------- 24.6	29.1
C+	--------------------- 12.7	14.6
B	--------------------- 2.8	20.8
A	--------------------- .5	4.2

Certainly the prevailing fear that the low intelligence of the immigrant tides has resulted and will continue to result in an increase of criminal behavior is far from being substantiated by the above figures.

Let us make a similar distribution of the Alpha scores and percentages of foreign born criminals committing crimes of force, which is the second group in the classification of seven types.

Alpha Scores	Number of Cases	Percentage	Alpha Scores	Number of Cases	Percentage
0- 9	18	6.6	60- 74	44	16.3
10-14	16	6.	75- 89	30	11.1
15-19	12	4.4	90-104	19	7.
20-24	14	5.1	105-119	12	4.4
25-34	31	11.5	120-134	6	2.2
35-44	21	7.7	135-149	2	.7
45-59	43	16.	150-212	1	.4

Translating into the traditional letter grades:

Letter Grades	Percentage of foreign born criminals
E	--------------------------12.6
D	-------------------------- 9.5
C—	--------------------------19.2
C	--------------------------32.3
C+	--------------------------18.1
B	-------------------------- 6.6
A	-------------------------- 1.1

As can be observed, this group also is much superior to the

general distribution of foreign born criminals, both in increased percentage of cases superior to C, and in decreased percentage of cases inferior to C. A slight amount of cross reference on the part of the reader will show that this group also is far superior to the native born white draft from Arkansas, from North Carolina, and from other entire states.

Proceeding to a similar distribution of the percentages of foreign born criminals committing crimes of thievery, which is the third group in the classification of seven types:

Alpha Score	Number of Cases	Percentage	Alpha Score	Number of Cases	Percentage
0- 9	17	12.9	60- 74	20	15.1
10-14	7	5.3	75- 89	10	7.6
15-19	9	6.8	90-104	8	6.
20-24	5	3.8	105-119	5	3.8
25-34	15	11.3	120-134	2	1.5
35-44	17	12.9	135-149	1	.8
45-59	15	11.3	150-212	1	.8

Translating into the traditional letter grades:

Letter Grades	Percentage of foreign born criminals
E	18.2
D	10.6
C—	24.2
C	26.4
C+	13.6
B	5.3
A	1.6

Here, of course, we have an increased percentage of inferior individuals as compared to crimes of deception or of force. But we must remember, however, that foreign born criminals are not so likely to commit crimes of thievery as are native born whites. But in spite of the increased percentage of inferior individuals, this group is still somewhat superior to the white native born draft from either Arkansas or North Carolina.

Considering next the distribution of Alpha grades and percentages of foreign born criminals committing statutory crimes, which is the fourth group in the classification of seven types:

Alpha Score	Number of Cases	Percentage of foreign born Criminals	Alpha Score	Number of Cases	Percentage of foreign born Criminals
0- 9	6	15.4	60- 74	5	12.8
10-14	3	7.7	75- 89	1	2.6
15-19	3	7.7	90-104	1	2.6
20-24	1	2.6	105-119	1	2.6
25-34	4	10.2	120-134	2	5.1

35-44----------5	12.8	135-149---------1		2.6
45-59----------6	15.4	150-212---------		

Translating into the traditional letter grades:

Letter Grades	Percentage of foreign born criminals
E	------------------------- 23.1
D	------------------------- 10.3
C—	------------------------- 23.
C	------------------------- 28.2
C+	------------------------- 5.2
B	------------------------- 7.7
A	------------------------- 2.6

In this group we find a very large increase of inferior individuals. However, the group differs from the distribution of the entire foreign born criminal group chiefly in the small percentage of C+ individuals. Yet the group compares favorably to the white native born draft from Arkansas or from North Carolina.

Let us consider next the most interesting group of all the foreign born criminals, the group committing crimes of physical injury, which is group 5 in the classification of the seven types:

Alpha Score	Number of Cases	Percentage of foreign born Criminals	Alpha Score	Number of Cases	Percentage of foreign born Criminals
0- 9----------56		28.	60- 74----------9		4.5
10-14----------26		13.	75- 89----------8		4.
15-19----------15		7.5	90-104----------4		2.
20-24----------21		10.5	105-119----------1		.5
25-34----------25		12.5	120-124----------1		.5
35-44----------15		7.5	135-149----------2		1.
45-59----------15		7.5	150-212----------1		.5

Translating into the traditional letter grades:

Letter Grades	Percentage of foreign born criminals
E	------------------------- 41.
D	------------------------- 18.
C—	------------------------- 20.
C	------------------------- 12.
C+	------------------------- 6.
B	------------------------- 1.
A	------------------------- 1.5

Foreign born criminals are twice as likely to be found in this group as are native born white criminals. At the same time it is observed that 41 per cent of this group made a grade of E in the Alpha test and that only 2.5 percent made a grade of A or B. This group is very inferior indeed when compared to the distribution of the entire foreign born criminal group, or when compared to the other six groups in the classification of seven types, or when compared to samples of the white native born draft. It is the one group, more than any other, that tends to support the prevailing hysteria concerning the mentality of foreign born elements in America. However, the reader must remember that this group consists of only approximately two hundred cases, which is only slightly more than one-fourth of the foreign born criminal group discussed in this paper. The reader should also be on his guard against assuming that all foreign born nationalities are equally prone to commit this type of crime. It is necessary that further analysis be made of the national and racial elements comprising this group. However, it is interesting to remember that the relatively low intelligence of this group coincides with the relatively low intelligence of white native born criminals committing similar crimes. (Page 61).

A similar distribution of the Alpha scores and percentages of foreign born criminals committing crimes of social dereliction, which is group 6 in the classification of seven types:

Alpha Score	Number of Cases	Percentage of foreign born Criminals	Alpha Score	Number of Cases	Percentage of foreign born Criminals
0- 9	2	10.	60- 74	2	10.
10-14	3	15.8	75- 89	2	10.
15-19	1	5.	90-104		--
20-24	1	5.	105-119		--
25-34	5	26.3	120-134		--
35-44			135-149		--
45-59	3	15.8	150-212		--

Translating into the traditional letter grades:

Letter Grades	Percentage of foreign born criminals
E	25.8
D	10.
C—	26.3
C	25.8
C+	10.
B	
A	

There are only nineteen cases in this group, and it is therefore precarious to discuss the distribution of percentages. However, it is well to observe that there is no case achieving a rank of A or B.

Proceeding to the distribution of Alpha scores and percentages of foreign born criminals committing sex crimes, which is group 7 in the classification of seven types:

Alpha Score	Number of Cases	Percentage of foreign born Criminals	Alpha Score	Number of Cases	Percentage of foreign born Criminals
0- 9	15	27.7	60- 74	5	9.2
10-14	2	3.7	75- 89		--
15-19	3	5.6	90-104	2	3.7
20-24	2	3.7	105-119	1	2.
25-34	5	9.2	120-134	1	2.
35-44	11	20.4	135-149		--
45-59	7	13.	150-212		--

Translating into the traditional letter grades:

Letter Grades	Percentage of foreign born criminals
E	31.4
D	9.3
C—	29.6
C	22.2
C+	3.7
B	4.
A	--

Here also we find that no individual achieves a ranking of A.

For the purpose of convenient comparison and cross reference, let us assemble the various distributions of Alpha scores and percentages in the case of all seven of the type groups, and arrange with them the distribution of the entire foreign born draft and of the entire foreign born criminal group:

Alpha Score	Deception	Force	Thievery	Statutory	Physical Injury	Dereliction	Sex	Percentage of foreign born draft	Percentage of foreign Criminals
0- 9	4.2	6.6	12.9	15.4	28.	10.	27.7	8.3	15.2
10- 14	2.1	6.	5.3	7.7	13.	15.8	3.7	6.0	7.7
15- 19	2.1	4.4	6.8	7.7	7.5	5.	5.6	4.7	5.8
20- 24	2.1	5.1	3.8	2.6	10.5	5.	3.7	6.4	5.9
25- 34	12.5	11.5	11.3	10.2	12.5	26.3	9.2	12.1	11.9
35- 44	8.3	7.7	12.9	12.8	7.5	___	20.4	11.9	9.6
45- 59	12.5	16.	11.3	15.4	7.5	15.8	13.	15.4	12.5
60- 74	16.6	16.3	15.1	12.8	4.5	10.	9.2	11.4	12.2
75- 89	4.2	11.1	7.6	2.6	4.	10.	___	8.8	7.
90-104	10.4	7.	6.	2.6	2.	___	3.7	6.1	5.1
105-119	16.6	4.4	3.8	2.6	.5	___	2.	4.0	3.7
120-134	4.2	2.2	1.5	5.1	.5	___	2.	2.3	1.8
135-149		.7	.8	2.6	1.	___	___	1.3	.8
150-212	4.2	.4	.8	___	.5	___	___	1.2	.7

Translating into the traditional letter grades:

Letter Grades	Deception	Force	Thievery	Statutory	Physical Injury	Dereliction	Sex	Percentage of foreign born draft	Percentage of foreign born Criminals
E	6.3	12.6	18.2	23.1	41.	25.8	31.4	14.3	22.9
D	4.2	9.5	10.6	10.3	18.	10.	9.3	11.1	11.7
C−	20.8	19.2	24.2	23.	20.	26.3	29.6	24.	21.5
C	29.1	32.3	26.4	28.2	12.	25.8	22.2	26.8	24.7
C+	14.6	18.1	13.6	5.2	6.	10.	3.7	14.9	12.1
B	20.8	6.6	5.3	7.7	1.	---	4.	6.3	5.5
A	4.2	1.1	1.6	2.6	1.5	---	---	2.5	1.5

The large array of type groups is relatively very similar to a similar array in the case of white native born criminals, (Page 62). However, there is one important difference,—superior foreigners practically do not commit crimes of physical injury, social dereliction, or sex, while these three crimes are committed by relatively large numbers of superior native born whites. This may indicate that the educative effects of some alien social institutions are somewhat more obvious in a direct comparison than are our own. The problem of criminal behavior can certainly not become clarified by the application of so simple a concept as that of low intelligence.

We will now consider the percentages of the various nationalities that commit each type of crime. We will consider only the more numerous nationalities, since they are obviously of greater importance, and will include in one group the natives of England, Scotland, Canada and Ireland. This method should enable us to determine which nationalities are responsible for the large percentage of inferior individuals committing crimes of physical injury, for example, and also will give us an insight into the various national elements that support the more intelligent types of crime.

Let us first consider the percentage of Germans committing each of the seven types of crime:

Crime	Number of Cases	Percentage
Deception	8	9.5
Force	29	34.5
Thievery	22	26.2
Statutory	4	4.7
Physical Injury	14	16.6

Dereliction	3	3.6
Sex	4	4.7

It is impossible to discuss arrays of this sort except for the purpose of comparison with other arrays of a similar nature, so we will proceed with a distribution of the percentages of Italians committing each of the seven types of crime.

Crime	Number of Cases	Percentage
Deception	3	2.1
Force	36	25.
Thievery	14	10.
Statutory	10	7.
Physical Injury	68	47.2
Dereliction	2	1.4
Sex	77	7.6

Following is the distribution of the percentages of Austrians committing each of the seven types of crime:

Crime	Number of Cases	Percentage
Deception	4	4.
Force	49	49.
Thievery	77	11.
Statutory	6	6.
Physical Injury	24	24.
Dereliction	--	---
Sex	7	7.

Following is the distribution of the percentages of Russians committing each of the seven types of crime:

Crime	Number of Cases	Percentage
Deception	4	5.
Force	41	51.2
Thievery	12	15.
Statutory	5	6.2
Physical Injury	13	16.2
Dereliction	3	3.8
Sex	2	2.5

Following is the distribution of the percentages of English, Scotch, Canadians and Irish committing each of the seven types of crime:

Crime	Number of Cases	Percentage
Deception	13	10.
Force	47	36.4
Thievery	23	17.1
Statutory	6	4.6
Physical Injury	23	17.1
Dereliction	5	3.9
Sex	12	9.3

It will now be convenient to assemble the various distributions of percentages of each nationality committing each of the seven types of crime, and compare these distributions with the percentage of the entire foreign born criminal group committing each type of crime.

Crime	Percentage of foreign born criminals	Percentage of German criminals	Percentage of Italian criminals	Percentage of Austrian criminals	Percentage of Russian criminals	Percentage of English, Scotch, Canadian and Irish criminals	Percentage of white native born criminals
Deception	6.3	9.5	2.1	4.	5.	10.	8.1
Force	35.4	34.5	25.	49.	51.2	36.4	39.1
Thievery	17.4	26.2	10.	11.	15.	17.1	25.1
Statutory	5.1	4.7	7.	6.	6.2	4.6	4.7
Physical Injury	26.2	16.6	47.2	24.	16.2	17.1	13.2
Dereliction	2.5	3.6	1.4	---	3.8	3.9	3.
Sex	7.1	4.7	7.6	7.	2.5	9.3	6.4

We shall probably be inclined to accept the percentages of white native born criminals committing each type of crime as our basic norms. Comparing the percentage of foreign born criminals committing each type of crime with the basic norms, we get a point of departure for the consideration of the various national groups. We find, for example, that the group consisting of English, Scotch, Canadians and Irish is more prone to crimes of deception than is any other national group, and that the German criminals are a close second. We also find that the Italian criminals are least inclined of all the national groups to crimes of deception. This supports very markedly previous conclusions concerning the presence in deceptive criminal behavior of high levels of intelligence.

An examination of the above assembly also indicates that the Russian and the Austrian criminals are more inclined to commit crimes of force than are any of the other nationalities. This can not be assumed to be entirely because of relatively low intelligence on the part of this nationality, since the Italian criminals are least likely of all national groups to commit crimes of force.

In the case of the thievery group we find that Italians, Austrians and Russians are much more scarce than are the other nationalities. Approximately one-half of the Austrian and Russian criminals have been convicted for obtaining property by force. A very small percentage indeed, as compared to native born criminals and German criminals, have been convicted of obtaining property by theft. It was pointed out at the beginning of this article that foreign born criminals are much less likely to commit crimes of thievery than are native born white criminals, and the credit for this belongs to the Italians, Austrians and Russians.

In the case of statutory crimes there are no outstanding significant variations in the various national groups.

We find very interesting variations in the case of crimes of physical injury. Native born white criminals are less likely to commit crimes of this type than are any other nationalities. In fact the likelihood of any nationality being largely represented in this group is in direct proportion to the extent to which it deviates below the intelligence norms of the white native born criminal group. We find that nearly one-half of all the Italian criminals with which we are dealing have been convicted of this type of crime. Remembering the large number of inferior individuals committing this type of crime and considering the exceedingly large percentage of Italians committing the same type of crime, it is valid to assume just that much validity in the prevailing social hysteria concerning the relation of crime waves and immigration. But one should not forget the fact that Italians are almost not represented in crimes of social dereliction, indicating a greater respect on their part for social institutions than their general criminal behavior would tend to indicate.

In the case of sex crimes it is interesting to observe that those most likely to commit such crimes are immigrants from England, Scotland, Canada and Ireland, and those least likely to commit such crimes are the immigrants from Russia.

Perhaps we can make these national differences even more striking by comparing the percentages of each nationality committing crimes against property and crimes against the person.

	Property		Person	
	No. of cases	Percent	No. of cases	Percent
Foreign born criminals	508	66.7	253	33.3
German	66	78.6	18	21.4
Italian	65	45.2	79	54.8
Austrian	70	70.	31	31.
Russian	65	81.2	15	18.8
English, Scotch, Canadian and Irish	94	73.	35	27.
Native born criminals	3171	80.	774	20.

It can be seen at a glance that the probability of committing crimes against property is approximately equal for native born criminals, Russians and Germans; that the likelihood is much less in the case of the English group and the Austrian group; and is least of all in the case of the Italian group. On the other hand, the probability of committing crimes against the person is least in the case of native born criminals, Russians and Germans; greater in the case of the English group and the Austrian group; and greatest of all in the case of the Italian group. This clarifies to a certain extent the distinctions which to the general reader might have been somewhat obscure in the array of types of crime.

4. For the sake of more exact comparison, and also for the purpose of showing the variations in the nationalities themselves, it is necessary to consider the distribution of Alpha scores made by each nationality in each type of crime. But since this involves a large number of tables and might lead to unprofitable tediousness, we shall consider the Alpha scores and percentages of each national group committing only two types of crime, crimes against property and crimes against the person. Crimes against the person consist of the crimes of physical injury and sex crimes, while all of the other types of crimes are considered crimes against property.

Following is the distribution of Alpha scores and percentages of German criminals committing crimes against property and against the person:

Alpha Score	Property		Person	
	No. of Cases	Percentage	No. of Cases	Percentage
0- 9	—	—	—	—
10- 14	3	4.5	7	5.5
15- 19	7	1.5	4	22.
20- 24	3	4.5	7	5.5
25- 34	3	4.5	3	16.5
35- 44	5	7.6	7	5.5
45- 59	77	16.6	2	11.
60- 74	10	15.2	4	22.
75- 89	13	20.	7	5.5
90-104	10	15.2	—	—
105-119	4	6.	7	5.5
120-134	2	3.	—	—
135-149	7	1.5	—	—
150-212	—	—	—	—

Translating into the traditional letter grades:

Letter Grades	Percentages	
	Property	Person
E	4.5	5.5
D	6.	27.5
C—	12.1	22.
C	31.8	33.
C+	35.2	5.5
B	9.	5.5
A	1.5	—

Following is the distribution of Alpha scores and percentages of Italian criminals committing crimes against property and against the person:

Alpha Score	Property		Person	
	No. of Cases	Percentage	No. of Cases	Percentage
0- 9	77	17.4	32	39.5
10- 14	8	12.7	8	9.9
15- 19	6	9.5	3	3.7
20- 24	4	6.3	6	7.4
25- 34	14	22.2	9	11.1
35- 44	6	9.5	77	13.6
45- 59	4	6.3	4	4.9
60- 74	5	7.9	3	3.7
75- 89	2	3.2	2	2.4
90-104	7	1.6	7	1.2
105-119	2	3.2	—	—
120-134	—	—	7	1.2
135-149	—	—	—	—
150-212	—	—	—	—

Translating into the traditional letter grades:

Letter Grades	Percentages	
	Property	Person
E	30.1	49.4
D	15.8	11.1
C—	31.7	24.7
C	14.2	8.6
C+	4.8	3.6
B	3.2	1.2
A	—	—

Following is the distribution of Alpha scores and percentages of Austrian criminals committing crimes against property and against the person:

Alpha Score	Property		Person	
	No. of Cases	Percentage	No. of Cases	Percentage
0- 9	7	10.	10	32.3
10- 14	3	4.3	8	25.8
15- 19	3	4.3	2	6.4
20- 24	6	8.6	3	9.6

25- 34	13	18.6	7	3.2
35- 44	5	7.1	7	3.2
45- 59	14	20.	2	6.4
60- 74	8	11.4	7	3.2
75- 89	5	7.1	2	6.4
90-104	3	4.3	—	—
105-119	3	4.3	—	—
120-134	—	—	—	—
135-149	—	—	7	3.2
150-212	—	—	—	—

Translating into the traditional letter grades:

Letter Grades	Percentages	
	Property	Person
E	14.3	58.1
D	12.9	16.
C—	25.7	6.4
C	31.4	9.6
C+	11.4	6.4
B	4.3	—
A	—	3.2

Following is the distribution of Alpha scores and percentages of Russian criminals committing crimes against property and against the person:

Alpha Score	Property		Person	
	No. of Cases	Percentage	No. of Cases	Percentage
0- 9	8	12.	4	28.6
10- 14	5	7.6	4	28.6
15- 19	3	4.5	—	—
20- 24	4	6.	7	7.1
25- 34	3	4.5	4	28.6
35- 44	5	7.6	7	7.1
45- 59	13	20.	—	—
60- 74	16	24.2	—	—
75- 89	3	4.5	—	—
90-104	2	3.	—	—
105-119	7	1.5	—	—
120-134	2	3.	—	—
135-149	7	1.5	—	—
150-212	—	—	—	—

Translating into the traditional letter grades:

Letter Grades	Percentages	
	Property	Person
E	19.6	57.2
D	10.5	7.1
C—	12.1	35.7
C	44.2	—
C+	7.5	—
B	4.5	—
A	1.5	—

Following is the distribution of Alpha scores and percentages of English, Scotch, Canadian and Irish criminals committing crimes against property and against the person.

Alpha Score	Property		Person	
	No. of Cases	Percentage	No. of Cases	Percentage
0- 9	2	2.2	5	13.5
10- 14	3	3.2	7	2.7
15- 19	2	2.2	7	2.7
20- 24	4	4.4	2	5.4
25- 34	8	8.7	2	5.4
35- 44	3	3.2	2	5.4
45- 59	13	14.1	7	19.
60- 74	18	19.5	5	13.5
75- 89	77	12.	3	8.1
90-104	77	12.	5	13.5
105-119	6	6.5	7	2.7
120-134	6	6.5	7	2.7
135-149	2	2.2	7	2.7
150-212	3	3.2	7	2.7

Translating into the traditional letter grades:

Letter Grades	Percentages	
	Property	Person
E	5.4	16.2
D	6.6	8.1
C—	11.9	10.8
C	33.6	32.5
C+	24.	21.6
B	13.	5.4
A	5.4	5.4

These arrays of Alpha scores and percentages made by the various national groups committing crimes against property and against the person may be assembled for easier comparison. Let us report the percentages in grades greater than C and grades less than C in each case.

		Percentages	
		Less than C	Greater than C
German	Property	22.6	45.7
	Person	55.	11.
Italian	Property	77.6	8.
	Person	85.2	4.8
Austrian	Property	50.9	15.7
	Person	80.5	9.6
Russian	Property	42.2	13.5
	Person	100.	—
English, Scotch, Canadians and Irish	Property	23.9	42.4
	Person	35.1	32.4

In the case of each national group the individuals committing crimes against property tend to rank higher in mental test scores than the individuals committing crimes against the person. This agrees with the findings of the author in the case of the native born white criminals. The difference between the criminals committing crimes against property and those committing crimes against the person are greater in some national groups than in others. For example, the differences are very marked in the case of the Germans and also in the case of the Russians. The differences are very obvious, but not quite so marked, in the case of the Austrians. The Italian group, however, and the group of English, Scotch, Canadian and Irish criminals do not show such marked differences. Whether the above differences are influenced by political and other social institutions is difficult to say, but it certainly appears as if democratic forms of government are associated with nationalities in which mental distinctions are not so great between types of crime; and that the more monarchical forms of government are associated with nationalities that show great mental differences between types of crime.

CHAPTER 18

RECIDIVISM

We will now compare the scores made in the Army Alpha Test by foreign born first offenders, second offenders, and habitual offenders. This will make it possible to consider the relative intelligence of the three groups, and will contribute information as to whether or not the recidivists are more or less intelligent than are first offenders.

For the first gross comparison we will consider the Alpha use of data from the prisons of Indiana, Maryland and New Jersey. We only have two hundred and seventy-nine cases to deal with. This is not a large number, but is quite large enough for a beginning in the discussion of this problem.

For the first gross comparison we will consider the Alpha score distribution of the first offenders and of the recidivists. The recidivists consist of both the second offenders and those who have been convicted of crime three or more times.

Alpha Score	First Offenders (187 cases)	Recidivists (92 cases)
0-9	24.1	13.0
10-14	9.6	6.5
15-19	8.6	3.2
20-24	3.7	3.2
25-34	10.0	12.0
35-44	7.4	13.0
45-59	10.0	9.7
60-74	12.3	10.9
75-89	5.3	8.7
90-104	2.7	10.9
105-119	3.2	2.2
120-134	2.1	3.2
135-149	---	1.1
150-212	7.0	2.2

Translating into the traditional letter grades:

Letter Grades	First Offenders	Recidivists
E	33.7	19.5
D	12.3	6.4
C—	17.4	25.0
C	22.3	20.6
C+	8.0	19.6
B	5.3	5.4
A	1.0	3.3

Obviously, in terms of Alpha grades, the recidivists are markedly superior to the first offenders. Of the first offenders only 14.3 per cent. are superior to C, while among the recidivists 28.3 per cent. are superior to C. Among the first offenders the two lowest letter grades represent 46 per cent. of the entire group, while the same two letter grades only represent 25.9 per cent. of the recidivists. This distinction between foreign born first offenders and recidivists is in agreement with a similar distinction in the case of native born white criminals as reported in Chapter 6. It is impossible to hold that recidivism and feeble-mindedness have any general relation. Certainly it seems more in line with the facts to hold the opposite point of view.

But since recidivists are individuals who have been convicted of crime more than once, it is possible that there may be some type of correlation existing between mental test scores and number of previous convictions. In order to consider this possibility let us divide the recidivists into two groups, second offenders and habitual offenders, the habitual offenders being those who have been convicted three or more times. Now let us arrange in parallel columns the Alpha distributions of the three groups, first offenders, second offenders, and habitual offenders.

Alpha Scores	First Offenders (187 cases)	Second Offenders (52 cases)	Habitual Offenders (40 cases)
0-9	24.1	17.3	7.5
10-14	9.6	7.7	5.0
15-19	8.6	3.8	2.5
20-24	3.7	---	7.5
25-34	10.	11.5	12.5
35-44	7.4	17.3	7.5
45-59	10.0	7.7	12.5
60-74	12.3	7.7	15.0
75-89	5.3	9.6	7.5
90-104	2.7	4.0	15.0
105-119	3.2	3.8	---
120-134	2.1	3.8	2.5
135-149	---	1.9	---
150-212	7.0	---	5.0

Translating into the traditional letter grades:

Letter Grades	First Offenders	Second Offenders	Habitual Offenders
E	33.7	25.0	12.5
D	12.3	3.8	10.0
C—	17.4	28.8	20.0
C	22.3	15.4	27.6
C+	8.0	17.3	22.5

B	----------- 5.3	7.6	2.5
A	----------- 1.0	1.9	5.0

The above increase in intelligence, as we pass from first offenders to recidivists, seems to be continued in the ordered array of first offenders, second offenders, and habitual offenders. The first offenders furnish 14.3 per cent. superior to C, the second offenders furnish 26.8 per cent. superior to C, while the habitual offenders furnish 30 per cent. superior to C. In the two lowest letter grades we find 46 per cent. of the first offenders, 28.8 per cent. of the second offenders, and only 22.5 per cent. of the habitual offenders. That is, it appears that in the case of foreign born criminals the more frequently they have been convicted of crime the more intelligent they are likely to be. But this seemingly obvious conclusion is not one that we can agree to assume in a consideration of this problem, for it leaves out of consideration certain racial and national facts that may vitiate the validity of the assumption. That is, it is possible that the habitual offenders may come from certain racial or national groups that, because of language or other similar factors, are capable of making scores in tests such as the Alpha.

In consideration of this possibility let us consider the percentages of the first, second, and habitual offenders already considered that happen to have been born in each of the following countries:

Country	First Offenders (125 cases)	Second Offenders (40 cases)	Habitual Offenders (30 cases)
England, Scoland, Canada and Ireland (52 cases)	18.7	16.3	32.4
Germany (43 cases)	14.	28.6	13.5
Italy (59 cases)	25.1	24.5	10.8
Austria (18 cases)	6.4	8.2	8.1
Russia (20 cases)	8.8	4.1	8.1

The above table indicates that approximately one-third of all the foreign born habitual offenders were born in English speaking countries, and consequently would be more likely to make a high score in the Alpha Test than would the representatives from the non-English speaking countries. But that does not vitiate the important fact that criminals born in English speaking countries are three times as likely to become habitual offenders as criminals born in Italy, for example. In the above table we find that Italy furnishes a greater number of first offenders than does the group represented by England,

Scotland, Canada and Ireland, but furnishes less than one-third
as many habitual offenders as does the English speaking group.
It certainly is highly significant that the English speaking
group should be the only group that furnishes a significantly
larger percentage of habitual offenders than should normally be
expected according to the law of chance. The facts become
more significant when we consider the percentages of first,
second, and habitual offenders born in Central, Western and
Northern Europe, and the percentages of first, second, and
habitual offenders born in Southern and Eastern Europe.

Area	First Offenders (171 cases)	Second Offenders (49 cases)	Habitual Offenders (37 cases)
Central, Western, and Northern (113 cases)	39.8	51.	54.1
Southern and Eastern (144 cases)	60.2	49.	45.9

It will be observed that Central, Western and Northern
Europe, the so-called superior area of Europe, furnishes a
much smaller percentage of first offenders than is furnished by
Southern and Eastern Europe, the so-called inferior area. But
the reverse is the case with second offenders and with habitual
offenders.

Tentative Conclusions:

1. A comparison in terms of Alpha grades of foreign born
first offenders and recidivists indicates a superiority on the
part of the recidivists. This superiority increases with degree
of recidivism, but can be explained very largely in terms of
national and racial differences, the so-called superior races
and nationalities presenting a greater tendency toward recidivism than do the so-called inferior races and nationalities.

CHAPTER 19

LITERACY

This report deals with 762 cases of foreign born white criminals. The sixteen years of normal school life extending through college will be reported in seven literacy groups as previously used in these reports, and which are as follows:

Group	Grade or Years
1	0-2
2	3-4
3	5-6
4	7-8
5	9-11
6	12-14
7	15-16

1. *Gross Comparison of White Foreign Born Criminals with the White Foreign Born Draft.*

On page 758, Volume V, of the *Memoirs of the National Academy of Sciences,* 1912, will be found the data concerning the literacy of the white foreign born draft, the sample consisting of 9,498 cases. When we compare the literacy distribution of the 762 cases of white foreign born criminals, we get the following results:

Literacy Group	Percentage of white foreign born draft (9,498 cases)	Percentage of white foreign born criminals (762 cases)
1	22.5	16.9
2	20.6	24.5
3	21.4	25.3
4	26.2	22.8
5	6.6	6.3
6	2.8	3.0
7	.8	1.0

It is obvious that the white foreign born criminals are quite similar in literacy distribution with the white foreign born draft. There certainly seem to be no significant literacy distinctions between the two groups. However, one observes with great surprise the low literacy of both groups, in this respect the foreign born draft and foreign born criminals being somewhat similar to the literacy distribution of the negro draft and negro criminals, which will be reported in Chapter 24. That the reader may see at a glance the significantly low literacy of the foreign born criminals and foreign born draft, we will exhibit the following table which shows in parallel columns the literacy distribution of the native born white draft, native born white criminals, foreign born draft, and foreign born white criminals.

Literacy Group	Percentage of native born draft (51,620 cases)	Percentage of native born criminals (3,932 cases)	Percentage of foreign born draft (9,498 cases)	Percentage of foreign born criminals (762 cases)
1	1.0	2.9	22.5	16.9
2	7.2	16.6	20.6	24.5
3	20.0	27.8	21.4	25.3
4	44.7	36.4	26.2	22.8
5	16.0	11.6	6.6	6.3
6	8.4	3.8	2.6	.8

It is obviously true that white foreign born criminals are much less literate than are white native born criminals, but this cannot be argued as a causal factor in the making of such criminals, since the low literacy is no more marked in the case of white foreign born criminals than in the case of the white foreign born members of the draft.

2. *The Literacy of White Foreign Born Criminal Recidivists.*

In this case we are limited to 821 cases taken from the prisons of Indiana, Maryland, and New Jersey. We can best consider the literacy distributions of recidivists by presenting the following table which shows in parallel columns the literacy distribution of first offenders, second offenders, and habitual offenders.

Literacy Group	Percentage of First Offenders (188 cases)	Percentage of Second Offenders (53 cases)	Percentage of Habitual Offenders (40 cases)
1	26.6	5.6	5.0
2	23.9	22.6	25.0
3	20.8	30.2	20.0
4	18.0	30.2	40.0
5	6.2	3.8	7.5
6	2.6	1.9	2.5
7	1.6	3.8	---

The outstanding characteristic of the above table is the relatively low literacy of first offenders and the relatively high literacy of second offenders and habitual offenders. It would seem that in so far as literacy is a causative factor in the criminal behavior of white foreign born men that there is a positive correlation between amount of literacy and amount of recidivism.

3. *The Literacy Comparison of Criminals from Southern and Eastern Europe with Criminals from Northern and Western Europe.*

For this comparison we exhibit 437 cases from Italy, Greece, Austria, Hungary, Russia and Poland, and 179 cases from Germany, England, Scotland, Denmark, Sweden, Norway, Holland and Ireland. These two groups are previously referred to as Southern and Eastern Europe and Northern and Western Europe, and such countries as do not lend themselves to this classification have been left out of account altogether.

Literacy Group	Italy, Greece, Austria, Hungary, Russia, Poland, (437 cases)	Germany, England, Scotland, Denmark, Sweden, Norway, Holland, Ireland (179 cases)
1	23.8	3.9
2	28.1	15.5
3	26.8	25.0
4	16.4	38.3
5	3.0	10.0
6	1.4	5.5
7	.4	1.1

Certainly the two geographical divisions vary very much in the amount of literacy their migrating criminals possess. The criminals from Northern and Western Europe are found slightly superior in literacy to the native born white criminals, while the criminals from Southern and Eastern Europe compare in literacy very favorably with negro criminals. For differences in types of crime committed by criminals from these two divisions of Europe the reader is referred to Chapter 17.

4. *The Literacy of the Various Type Groups Among the White Foreign Born Criminals.*

The seven type groups used throughout this report will be followed in this case. The following table shows the literacy distribution in terms of percentage and gives the number of cases in each of the seven type groups.

Literacy Group	Fraud (53 cases)	Force (270 cases)	Thievery (133 cases)	Statutory (34 cases)	Physical Injury (199 cases)	Social Dereliction (12 cases)	Sex (61 cases)
1	2.0	10.4	13.6	30.0	26.5	2 cases	27.8
2	11.3	18.5	27.4	20.6	34.5	6 cases	20.
3	19.0	28.8	27.0	23.5	21.5	1 case	31.1
4	34.0	31.5	22.0	17.6	13.0	3 cases	11.4
5	13.2	7.0	8.3	8.8	2.0	-------	6.5
6	17.0	2.6	.7	---	2.0	-------	3.3
7	4.0	1.1	1.5	---	---	-------	---

It will be observed that the Fraud group is by far the most literate of all the crime groups among the white foreign born criminals, and that this group is closely followed by the Force group, and then the Thievery group. The other groups are of relatively low literacy. This comparison of the crime groups in terms of literacy distribution shows the same characteristics observed in the case of white native born criminals.

Tentative Conclusions:

1. Low literacy cannot be argued as a causal factor in the making of criminals among the foreign born whites, since low literacy is just as marked among the white foreign born members of the army draft as among the white foreign born criminals.

2. So far is low literacy from being a positive factor in the making of criminals among the white foreign born men, that there even seems to be a positive correlation between amount of literacy and amount of recidivism.

3. The criminals from Northern and Western Europe are far superior in literacy to the criminals from Southern and Eastern Europe.

4. Just as in the case of white native born criminals, the most literate crime group among the foreign born white criminals is the Fraud group, followed closely by the Force group, and then the Thievery group, the other groups being of relatively low literacy.

5. In so far as the causative effect of literacy can be expressed in terms of the above data, it seems valid to state that literacy correlates positively with the number of criminal convictions, and with the degree of deception and fraud involved.

CHAPTER 20

CHRONOLOGICAL AGE

We are dealing here with 761 cases of white foreign-born criminals from the prisons of Ohio, Indiana, Illinois, Maryland, and New Jersey. The age-group classification to be followed in this report is as follows:

Age Group	Years of Age
1	15-20
2	21-25
3	26-30
4	31-35
5	36-40
6	41-50
7	51-x

A direct comparison of the foreign-born criminals with the native-born white criminals and with the negro criminals in the same prisons reveals no obviously significant differences in the arrays of age percentages. The decreased percentage of foreign-born cases in the first age-group might be explained by the age of migration, especially since this deficiency is offset by an increased percentage in the second age-group.

Age Group	Percentage of Foreign-born Group (761 cases)	Percentage of Negro Criminals (1254 cases)	Percentage of Native-born White Criminals (3932 cases)
1	15.0	12.9	20.9
2	20.1	27.1	26.0
3	19.4	18.4	17.7
4	15.6	17.1	13.8
5	13.4	11.4	9.4
6	12.1	10.6	8.6
7	4.3	2.5	3.6

An analysis of crime-groups in terms of age-groups reveals some very striking differences:

Percentage of Each Crime-group to be Found
In Each Age-group

Age Group	Fraud. (48)	Force. (271)	Thievery. (133)	Statutory. (43)	Physical Injury. (192)	Social Dereliction. (18)	Sex. (56)
1	4.1	23.6	18.0	21.0	5.7	5.5	5.4
2	18.8	24.7	21.0	18.6	18.2	---	10.7
3	8.3	20.3	20.3	16.3	21.9	39.0	10.7
4	16.7	11.0	16.5	23.2	20.3	11.1	14.3
5	18.8	11.0	15.8	11.6	14.1	22.2	10.7

| 6 | 27.1 | 7.0 | 4.5 | 9.3 | 14.6 | 5.5 | 37.5 |
| 7 | 6.3 | 2.2 | 3.7 | --- | 5.2 | 16.6 | 10.7 |

The physical-injury and the fraud groups, just as in the case of the white native-born criminals, show a decreased percentage of the very youthful cases as compared with the force and thievery groups, and an increased percentage of the older cases. It seems significant that more than a third of the sex cases should be located in the sixth age-group.

Some of these differences are obscured and some are accentuated if we compare the property with the person group:

Age Group	Percentage of Property Group (160 cases)	Percentage of Person Group (96 cases)
1	8.7	6.2
2	27.5	15.6
3	21.2	10.4
4	17.5	21.8
5	15.6	14.5
6	6.2	21.8
7	3.1	9.3

The problem of recidivism is not cleared up to any extent by a comparison of the respective ages of first offenders and recidivists, this being also true of the native-born white criminals. There seems to be a significant difference in percentages of first offenders and recidivists in the third age-group, but seemingly not elsewhere.

Age Group	First Offenders. (173 cases)	Recidivists. (83 cases)
1	9.8	3.6
2	22.5	24.2
3	12.1	27.7
4	20.2	17.0
5	16.2	13.2
6	12.1	12.1
7	6.9	2.4

The difference in the percentages of first offenders and recidivists in the third age-group is in no way obscured by a reclassification into property and person groups:

Age Group	Crimes Against Property		Crimes Against the Person	
	First Offenders. (93 cases)	Recidivists. (67 cases)	First Offenders. (80 cases)	Recidivists. (16 cases)
1	11.8	4.5	7.5	---
2	31.2	22.4	12.5	31.2
3	15.0	29.8	8.7	18.7
4	18.3	16.4	22.5	18.7

5	15.0	16.4	17.5	---
6	5.4	7.4	20.0	31.2
7	3.2	3.0	11.2	---

The interesting question of the geographical distribution of mental traits makes its appearance here also.

Age Group	Southern and Eastern Europe Italy, Greece, Austria, Hungary, Russia, Poland. (433 cases)	Northern and Western Europe Germany, England, Scotland, Denmark, Sweden, Norway, Holland, Ireland. (190 cases)
1	19.1	8.0
2	23.8	12.6
3	19.0	21.0
4	15.9	15.3
5	12.5	15.3
6	8.5	20.5
7	1.1	7.4

The northern and western European groups show a marked increase in the percentage of older groups as compared to the southern and eastern European groups.

Tentative Conclusions:

1.   There seem to be no significant differences in the general distribution of chronological ages of foreign-born as compared with native-born white criminals.

2.   The physical-injury and the fraud groups, just as in the case of the white native-born criminals, show a decreased percentage of the very youthful cases as compared with the force and thievery groups, and an increased percentage of the older cases.

3.   These recidivists are not significantly older than are first offenders. There seems to be a significantly reduced percentage of first offenders in the third age-group, this reduction not being obscured by a classification into property and person groups.

4.   The northern and western European groups show a marked increase in the percentage of older groups and a decrease in the percentage of younger groups as compared to the southern and eastern European groups.

PART IV

Negro Men Criminals

CHAPTER 21

SOME GEOGRAPHICAL CONCOMITANTS

This series of reports will deal with negro criminal intelligence as it was measured in the state penitentiaries and reformatories of Ohio, Illinois, Maryland and New Jersey. The report will deal with 1351 cases.

1. *Gross Comparisons.*

To get the problem clearly before us it might be well to consider in parallel columns the Alpha score distributions of the negro draft, the white draft, and the foreign born draft, as reported in Volume 15 of the *Memoirs of the National Academy of Sciences,* Tables 205, 211, and 254.

	Cases in order of		White	Percentages in order of		White
Alpha Score	Negro Draft	White Draft	Foreign Draft	Negro Draft	White Draft	Foreign Draft
0- 9	2051	1774	394	32.4	4.0	8.3
10- 14	730	1535	282	11.5	3.5	6.0
15- 19	620	1855	221	9.8	4.2	4.7
20- 24	479	2040	302	7.5	4.6	6.4
25- 34	767	4640	575	12.1	10.5	12.1
35- 44	529	4810	565	8.3	10.9	11.9
45- 59	495	6754	731	7.8	15.3	15.4
60- 74	285	5913	541	4.5	13.4	11.4
75- 89	194	4684	420	3.1	10.6	8.8
90-104	94	3609	289	1.4	8.2	6.1
105-119	43	2618	189	.7	5.9	4.0
120-134	24	1703	107	.4	3.8	2.3
135-149	9	1118	64	.1	2.5	1.3
150-212	7	1170	57	.1	2.6	1.2

Transferring into the traditional letter grades:

Percentages in the order of

Letter Grades	Negro Draft	White Draft	White Foreign Draft
E	43.9	7.5	14.3
D	17.3	8.8	11.1
C—	20.4	21.4	24.0
C	12.3	28.7	26.8
C+	4.5	18.8	14.9
B	1.1	9.7	6.3
A	.2	5.1	2.5

The above tables emphasize very drastically the great difference in the distributions of the three parallel columns. The problem of the relatively low intelligence of the negro is made very evident, and from the revelation conclusions of varying degrees of validity may follow.

Certain significant facts have already been discovered involving the probable superiority in terms of mental test scores of criminals as compared to samples of the general population. These facts have already been discussed in the case of white native born criminals and in the case of white foreign born criminals. Similar facts may or may not be observed in a comparison of negro criminals with samples of the negro population.

Alpha Score	Negro Criminal Cases	Percentage of Negro Criminal Cases	Percentage of Negro Draft
0- 9	227	16.8	32.4
10- 14	164	12.1	11.5
15- 19	104	7.6	9.8
20- 24	127	9.4	7.5
25- 34	184	13.6	12.1
35- 44	146	10.9	8.3
45- 59	144	10.6	7.8
60- 74	109	8.0	4.5
75- 89	59	4.4	3.1
90-104	39	2.8	1.4
105-119	24	1.8	.7
120-134	14	1.0	.4
135-149	7	.5	.1
150-212	3	.2	.1

Translating into the traditional letter grades:

Letter Grade	Negro Criminal Cases	Percentage of Negro Criminal Cases	Percentage of Negro Draft
E	391	28.9	43.9
D	231	17.0	17.3
C—	330	24.5	20.4
C	253	18.6	12.3
C+	98	7.2	4.5
B	38	2.8	1.1
A	10	.7	.2

The above tables indicate that among negro criminals there is a much smaller percentage of the most inferior cases and a larger percentage of the relatively more superior cases. This is in direct agreement with facts already found concerning white criminals, both native and foreign born.

Let us remember, however, that gross comparisons very easily lead to false conclusions. It is probably not valid to compare the entire negro criminal group, with which we are dealing, with negro draft tables as given in Volume 15 of the *Memoirs of the National Academy of Sciences*. It is not necessary at this time to go into the question of the extent to which the negro army draft was representative of the general negro

Population. That question has been discussed in Chapter 3. It is only necessary to point out here the great geographical differences in the distribution of negro intelligence, as measured in groups coming from different states. For example, let us compare a sample of the negro draft coming from Mississippi with a sample of negro draft coming from Tennessee, the samples being those reported in Vol. 15, *Memoirs of the National Academy of Sciences.*

Alpha Score	Negro Draft Mississippi Cases	Tennessee Negro Draft Cases	Mississippi Negro Draft Percentage	Tennessee Negro Draft Percentage
0- 9	381	61	49.3	12.1
10- 14	113	39	14.6	7.7
15- 19	57	50	7.3	9.9
20- 24	43	53	5.5	10.5
25- 34	74	98	9.6	19.4
35- 44	43	55	5.5	10.9
45- 59	33	69	4.3	13.7
60- 74	14	31	1.8	6.1
75- 89	10	29	1.3	5.7
90-104	5	12	.6	2.4
105-119	0	3	0	.6
120-134	0	1	0	.2
135-149	0	1	0	.2
150-212	0	2	0	.4

Translating into the traditional letter grades:

Letter Grade	Mississippi Negro Draft Percentage	Tennessee Negro Draft Percentage
E	63.9	19.8
D	12.8	20.4
C—	15.1	30.3
C	6.1	19.8
C+	1.9	8.1
B	0	.8
A	0	.6

To be sure, the Tennessee negro draft is not by any means overwhelmingly superior, but is very much more superior than the Mississippi negro draft. The differences between the two groups are so great that neither one can be accepted as a true sample of general negro intelligence. However, there is no reason for supposing that the sample from Tennessee is not representative of the general negro population in that state. Neither is there any reason for supposing that the sample from Mississippi is not representative of the general negro population in that state. The problem of negro intelligence should always be stated as negro intelligence *where.*

The same point is brought out in the comparison of the Alabama negro draft sample and the Ohio negro draft sample, both taken from the above sources.

Alpha Score	Alabama Negro Draft Cases	Ohio Negro Draft Cases	Alabama Negro Draft Percentage	Ohio Negro Draft Percentage
0- 9	62	9	22.8	5.5
10- 14	33	9	12.2	5.5
15- 19	41	13	15.1	7.9
20- 24	19	13	7.0	7.9
25- 34	42	15	15.5	9.2
35- 44	24	22	8.8	13.5
45- 59	24	20	8.8	12.2
60- 74	16	22	5.9	13.5
75- 89	5	16	1.8	9.8
90-104	4	8	1.4	4.9
105-119	1	5	.4	3.0
120-134	0	5	.0	3.0
135-149	0	4	0	2.4
150-212	0	2	0	1.2

Translating into the traditional letter grades:

Letter Grade	Alabama Negro Draft Percentage	Ohio Negro Draft Percentage
E	35.0	11.0
D	22.1	15.8
C—	24.3	22.7
C	14.7	25.7
C+	3.2	14.7
B	.4	6.0
A	0	3.6

The differences are much greater in the comparison of Alabama and Ohio than they are in the case of Mississippi and Tennessee. The reader should remember, however, that the draft reports from Camp Sherman were not included in the distribution tables in Volume 15 of the *Memoirs of the National Academy of Sciences,* and as a result the Ohio cases appearing in these tables are cases of Ohio men reported from other camps.

In order to show that these same geographical differences are found in the negro criminal data also, let us compare the negro criminal cases from Tennessee with the negro criminals born in Ohio.

Alpha Score	Tennessee Negro Criminal Cases	Ohio Negro Criminal Cases	Tennessee Negro Criminal Percentage	Ohio Negro Criminal Percentage
0- 9	14	10	16.1	6.0
10- 14	10	15	11.5	9.0

15- 19_____ 5	6	5.7	3.6
20- 24_____ 16	13	18.4	7.9
25- 34_____ 15	19	17.2	11.5
35- 44_____ 12	18	13.8	10.9
45- 59_____ 7	28	8.0	16.9
60- 74_____ 3	23	3.4	14.
75- 89_____ 3	11	3.4	6.6
90-104_____ 2	8	2.3	4.9
105-119_____ 0	7	0	4.2
120-134_____ 0	3	0	1.8
135-149_____ 0	2	0	1.2
150-212_____ 0	1	0	.6

Translating into the traditional letter grades:

Letter Grade	Tennessee Negro Criminal Percentage	Ohio Negro Criminal Percentage
E	_____ 27.6	15.0
D	_____ 24.1	11.5
C—	_____ 31.0	22.4
C	_____ 11.4	30.9
C+	_____ 5.7	11.5
B	_____ 0	6.0
A	_____ 0	1.8

It is evident that the Ohio negro criminals are much more capable of making scores in the Alpha test than are the Tennessee negro criminals. It is obvious that geographical concomitants should be taken into consideration in any discussion concerning negro intelligence or concerning negro criminal intelligence.

There are other matters to be taken into consideration also. The geographical concomitants and intelligence of the white native born population make it difficult for a direct comparison to be made of white and negro intelligence. Almost any conclusion can be invalidated by the proper selection of geographical groups. For example, let us compare the white draft from Arkansas with the negro draft from Ohio, the figures being taken from Volume 15, *Memoirs of the National Academy of Sciences.*

Alpha Score	White Draft Cases in Arkansas	Negro Draft Cases in Ohio	White Draft Arkansas Percentage	Negro Draft Ohio Percentage
0- 9_____	59	9	8.3	5.5
10- 14_____	54	9	7.6	5.5
15- 19_____	58	13	8.2	7.9
20- 24_____	64	13	9.0	7.9
25- 34_____	115	15	16.2	9.2
35- 44_____	71	22	10.0	13.5
45- 59_____	103	20	14.5	12.2
60- 74_____	72	22	10.1	13.5

75- 89_____ 57	16	8.0	9.8
90-104_____ 33	8	4.6	4.9
105-119_____ 15	5	2.1	3.0
120-134_____ 5	5	.7	3.0
135-149_____ 3	4	.4	2.4
150-212_____ 1	2	.1	1.2

Translating into the traditional letter grades:

Letter Grade	White Draft Arkansas Percentage	Negro Draft Ohio Percentage
E	15.9	11.0
D	17.2	15.8
C—	26.2	22.7
C	24.6	25.7
C+	12.6	14.7
B	2.8	6.0
A	.5	3.6

The Ohio negro draft is quite plainly superior, in terms of Alpha grades, to the white draft from Arkansas. Such facts should be taken into consideration in any investigation that deals with racial factors and questions of superiority.

Since it is possible to question, though mildly, the sample of the Ohio draft, it might be well to make a similar comparison substituting the white draft from North Carolina and the negro draft from New York.

Alpha Score	White Draft Cases in North Carolina	Negro Draft Cases in New York	North Carolina White Draft Percentage	New York Negro Draft Percentage
0- 9_____	55	20	7.8	10.1
10- 14_____	44	17	6.2	8.6
15- 19_____	54	10	7.7	5.0
20- 24_____	66	20	9.4	10.1
25- 34_____	100	30	14.2	15.2
35- 44_____	97	22	13.8	11.2
45- 59_____	89	23	12.7	11.7
60- 74_____	69	21	9.8	10.6
75- 89_____	50	19	7.1	9.6
90-104_____	38	8	5.4	4.0
105-119_____	21	2	3.0	1.0
120-134_____	6	3	.8	1.5
135-149_____	9	2	1.2	1.0
150-212_____	4	0	.6	0

Translating into the traditional letter grades:

Letter Grade	North Carolina White Draft Percentage	New York Negro Draft Percentage
E	14.0	18.7
D	17.1	15.1
C—	28.0	26.4
C	22.5	22.3

C+	12.5	13.6
B	3.8	2.5
A	1.8	1.0

If the designation of the above two groups were unknown, it would be impossible to tell by inspection which was the white group and which the negro group. It is well that such facts cause us to be guarded in the terms which we use when we speak of general negro intelligence as compared to general white intelligence.

2. Comparison of the Negro Criminal Population of a given state with the Negro Draft from the same state.

It is obvious that in comparing a criminal group with a population group we must select groups from the same geographical area in so far as it is possible. If we fail to select our groups, it is quite possible by selective designation to prove almost anything by direct comparison of groups. Since we do not have any data concerning the negro criminal population of the state of Indiana, we will compare the criminal population of New Jersey, Illinois, Maryland and Ohio with the negro draft groups from the same states.

Following is a comparison of the New Jersey negro criminals with the New Jersey negro draft. The reader should remember that all draft figures are taken from Volume XV, *Memoirs of the National Academy of Sciences.*

Alpha Score	New Jersey Negro Criminal Cases	New Jersey Negro Draft Cases	Negro Criminal Percentage	Negro Draft Percentage
0- 9	61	21	24.2	20.0
10- 14	22	7	8.7	6.6
15- 19	21	9	8.3	8.5
20- 24	34	9	13.4	8.5
25- 34	18	6	7.1	5.7
35- 44	24	19	9.5	18.0
45- 59	26	12	10.3	11.4
60- 74	23	5	9.1	4.7
75- 89	8	10	3.1	9.5
90-104	2	6	.8	5.7
105-119	7	0	2.7	0
120-134	4	0	1.5	0
135-149	2	1	.8	.9
150-212	0	0	0	0

Translating into the traditional letter grades:

Letter Grade	Negro Criminal Percentage	Negro Draft Percentage
E	32.9	26.6
D	21.7	17.0

C—	----------------------	16.6	23.7
C	----------------------	19.4	16.1
C+	----------------------	3.9	15.2
B	----------------------	4.2	0
A	----------------------	.8	.9

The above direct comparison indicates that the negro draft from the state of New Jersey possessed a larger percentage of relatively superior individuals than exist in the criminal group from the same state, and also a less percentage of relatively inferior individuals than exist in the criminal group from the same state. This is just the reverse of what we found to be true in comparing the entire group of negro criminal cases with which we are dealing with the entire negro draft from the country at large.

Following are the distributions from the State of Illinois:

Alpha Score	Illinois Negro Criminal Cases	Illinois Draft Cases	Negro Criminal Percentage	Negro Draft Percentage
0- 9	22	11	8.8	7.9
10- 14	17	10	6.8	7.2
15- 19	17	12	6.8	8.7
20- 24	14	8	5.6	5.8
25- 34	40	20	16.1	14.5
35- 44	36	13	14.8	9.4
45- 59	32	18	12.9	13.0
60- 74	28	23	11.2	16.6
75- 89	15	15	6.0	10.9
90-104	17	3	6.8	2.0
105-119	6	1	2.4	.7
120-134	1	3	.4	2.0
135-149	2	0	.8	0
150-212	1	1	.4	.7

Translating into the traditional letter grades:

Letter Grade	Negro Criminal Percentage	Draft Negro Percentage
E	15.6	15.1
D	12.5	14.5
C—	30.9	23.9
C	24.1	29.6
C+	12.8	12.9
B	2.8	2.7
A	1.2	.7

In the case of Illinois the two groups have a fairly similar distribution, no superiority can be perceived in either group as compared to the other group.

Following is a similar distribution from the state of Ohio:

Alpha Score	Ohio Negro Criminal Cases	Ohio Draft Cases	Ohio Criminal Percentage	Ohio Draft Percentage
0- 9	87	9	14.4	5.5
10- 14	87	9	14.4	5.5
15- 19	39	13	6.5	7.9
20- 24	65	13	10.8	7.9
25- 34	90	15	14.9	9.2
35- 44	61	22	10.1	13.5
45- 59	72	20	11.9	12.2
60- 74	47	22	7.8	13.5
75- 89	25	16	4.1	9.8
90-104	13	8	2.2	4.9
105-119	8	5	1.3	3.0
120-134	4	5	.6	3.0
135-149	3	4	.5	2.4
150-212	0	2	.0	1.2

Translating into the traditional letter grades:

Letter Grades	Negro Criminal Percentage	Negro Draft Percentage
E	28.8	11.0
D	17.3	15.8
C—	25.0	22.7
C	19.7	25.7
C+	6.3	14.7
B	1.9	6.0
A	.5	3.6

In the case of Ohio, the negro draft group is very much superior to the criminal group in the same state. This also is the reverse of what we have found in comparing the entire negro criminal group with the entire negro draft from the country at large. The reader is cautioned, however, to remember that mental test figures from Camp Sherman, Ohio, are not included in the report of Ohio negro draft cases in Volume 15 of the *Memoirs of the National Academy of Sciences*.

Following is a comparison of negro criminals and negro draft in the state of Maryland:

Alpha Score	Maryland Negro Criminal Cases	Maryland Negro Draft Cases	Negro Criminal Percentage	Negro Draft Percentage
0- 9	57	32	22.8	21.6
10- 14	38	18	15.2	12.1
15- 19	27	17	10.8	11.4
20- 24	14	13	5.6	8.8
25- 34	36	19	14.4	12.8
35- 44	25	15	10.0	10.1
45- 59	14	13	5.6	8.8

60- 74_____ 11	10	4.4	6.7
75 -89_____ 11	5	4.4	3.3
90-104_____ 7	4	2.8	2.7
105-119_____ 3	1	1.2	.7
120-134_____ 5	1	2.0	.7
135-149_____ 0	0	0	0
150-212_____ 2	0	.8	0

Translating into the traditional letter grades:

Grades Letter	Negro Criminal Percentage	Negro Draft Percentage
E _____	38.0	33.7
D _____	16.4	20.2
C— _____	24.4	22.9
C _____	10.0	15.5
C+ _____	7.2	6.0
B _____	3.2	1.4
A _____	.8	0

It is difficult to see in the case of the Maryland groups any distinct advantage of one group as compared to the other. The criminal group has a somewhat larger percentage of the most inferior individuals. It would be impossible to decide, by comparison of groups from Maryland only, whether negro criminals are more or less intelligent than the general population of negroes.

Combining the negro draft cases from the above four states, and also combining the negro criminal cases from the same four states, and comparing the two groups in parallel columns, we get the following:

Alpha Score	Negro Criminal Cases in Maryland, New Jersey, Illinois and Ohio	Negro Draft Cases in New Jersey, Maryland, Illinois and Ohio	Negro Criminal Percentage	Negro Draft Percentage
0- 9_____227	73	16.8	13.2
10- 14_____164	44	12.1	7.9
15- 19_____104	51	7.6	9.2
20- 24_____127	43	9.4	7.7
25- 34_____184	60	13.6	10.8
35- 44_____146	69	10.9	12.4
45- 59_____144	63	10.7	11.3
60- 74_____109	60	8.0	10.8
75- 89_____ 59	46	4.3	8.3
90-104_____ 39	21	2.9	3.7
105-119_____ 24	7	1.8	1.2
120-134_____ 14	9	1.0	1.6
135-149_____ 7	5	.5	.9
150-212_____ 3	3	.2	.5

Translating into the traditional letter grades:

Letter Grades	Negro Criminal Percentage in New Jersey, Maryland, Illinois and Ohio	Negro Draft Percentage in New Jersey, Maryland, Illinois and Ohio
E	28.9	21.1
D	17.0	16.9
C—	24.5	23.2
C	18.7	22.1
C+	7.2	12.0
B	2.8	2.8
A	.7	1.4

Neither group has a decided advantage, the negro draft having such advantage as exists. It shows 16.2 percent superior to C, while the criminal group shows only 10.7 percent superior to C. The draft group also has a smaller percentage of the more inferior individuals. This result coincides with the tentative conclusion reached in the case of foreign born white criminals (Chapter 16, Page 169): "That is, the so-called superior races and nationalities give us still more superior criminals, while so-called inferior races and nationalities give us still more inferior criminals."

3. *Possible Factors of Distance, Climate, Industrial Opportunity, etc.*

It should be interesting to compare negro criminals from the Southern states with the negro draft from the same states. The states designated as Southern are Virginia, Louisiana, South Carolina, North Carolina, Tennessee, Alabama, Mississippi, Florida and Georgia.

Alpha Score	Negro Criminals in Southern States	Negro Draft Cases in Southern States	Negro Criminal Percentage	Negro Draft Percentage
0- 9	101	1385	21.0	38.4
10- 14	73	465	15.2	12.9
15- 19	42	345	8.7	9.5
20- 24	61	263	12.7	7.3
25- 34	67	419	13.7	11.6
35- 44	42	258	8.7	7.1
45- 59	38	223	7.9	6.2
60- 74	35	111	7.3	3.1
75- 89	11	76	2.3	2.1
90-104	3	36	.6	.9
105-119	4	15	.8	.4
120-134	2	3	.4	.08
135-149	1	1	.2	.03
150-212	0	3	0	.08

Translating into the traditional letter grades:

Letter Grades	Negro Criminal Percentage in Southern States	Negro Draft Percentage in Southern States
E	36.2	51.3
D	21.4	16.8
C—	22.4	18.7
C	15.2	9.3
C+	2.9	3.0
B	1.2	.48
A	.2	.11

In the case of the Southern states, it is clear that the negro criminal group has a decided advantage, in terms of Alpha scores, over the negro draft group.

Let us now make a similar comparison of the negro criminals and the negro draft group in the borderline states bounding the Southern group on the North and West in an unbroken line, consisting of Maryland, West Virginia, Kentucky, Arkansas and Texas:

Alpha Score	Negro Criminal Cases in Borderline States	Negro Draft Cases in Borderline States	Negro Criminal Percentage	Negro Draft Percentage
0- 9	54	530	19.3	36.5
10- 14	39	176	13.9	12.1
15- 19	27	157	9.6	10.8
20- 24	23	109	8.2	7.5
25- 34	43	170	15.3	11.7
35- 44	28	114	10.0	7.8
45- 59	32	103	11.4	7.1
60- 74	15	43	5.4	2.9
75- 89	9	25	3.2	1.7
90-104	6	16	2.1	1.1
105-119	1	7	.3	.5
120-134	3	3	1.1	.2
135-149	2	0	.7	0
150-212	0	0	0	0

Translating into the traditional letter grades:

Letter Grades	Negro Criminal Percentage in Borderline States	Negro Draft Percentage in Borderline States
E	33.2	48.6
D	17.8	18.3
C—	25.3	19.5
C	16.8	10.0
C+	5.3	2.8
B	1.4	.7
A	.7	0

In the borderline states also we find the negro criminal group superior in terms of alpha scores to the negro draft group from the same states.

Let us now make a similar comparison of the negro criminal group with the negro draft group from all the other states of the country, these states lying North and West of the Southern and borderline states.

Alpha Score	Negro Criminal Cases in Northern and Western States	Negro Draft Cases in Northern and Western States	Negro Criminal Percentage	Negro Draft Percentage
0- 9	51	136	10.4	10.7
10- 14	43	89	8.7	7.0
15- 19	23	118	4.6	9.3
20- 24	37	107	7.5	8.4
25- 34	59	178	11.9	14.0
35- 44	65	157	13.2	12.3
45- 59	65	169	13.2	13.3
60- 74	58	131	11.8	10.3
75- 89	33	93	6.7	7.3
90-104	27	42	5.5	3.3
105-119	17	21	3.4	1.6
120-134	8	18	1.6	1.4
135-149	4	8	.8	.6
150-212	2	4	.4	.3

Translating into the traditional letter grades:

Letter Grades	Negro Criminal Percentage in Northern and Western States	Negro Draft Percentage in Northern and Western States
E	19.1	17.7
D	12.1	17.7
C—	25.1	26.3
C	25.0	23.6
C+	12.2	10.6
B	5.0	3.0
A	1.2	.9

In the case of the Northern and Western states we do not find that the negro criminal group has so decided an advantage over the draft group.

For a closer comparison and cross reference let us assemble the percentages of the negro criminal cases and the negro draft from the above three sections of the country.

	Percentages of Negro Criminals in order of			Percentages of Negro Draft in Order of		
Alpha Score	South	Border-line	Northern and Western	South	Border-line	North and West
0- 9	21.0	19.3	10.4	38.4	36.5	10.7
10- 14	15.2	13.9	8.7	12.9	12.1	7.0
15- 19	8.7	9.6	4.6	9.5	10.8	9.3
20- 24	12.7	8.2	7.5	7.3	7.5	8.4
25- 34	13.7	15.3	11.9	11.6	11.7	14.0
35- 44	8.7	10.0	13.2	7.1	7.8	12.3
45- 49	7.9	11.4	13.2	6.2	7.1	13.3
60- 74	7.3	5.4	11.8	3.1	2.9	10.3
75- 89	2.3	3.2	6.7	2.1	1.7	7.3
90-104	.6	2.1	5.5	.9	1.1	3.3
105-119	.8	.3	3.4	.4	.5	1.6
120-134	.4	1.1	1.6	.08	.2	1.4
135-149	.2	.7	.8	.03	0	.6
150-212	0	0	.4	.08	0	.3

Translating into the traditional letter grades:

Letter Grades	Percentage of Negro Criminals			Percentage of Negro Draft		
	South	Borderline	West	South	Borderline	West
E	36.2	33.2	17.7	51.3	48.6	17.7
D	21.4	17.8	17.7	16.8	18.3	17.7
C—	22.4	25.3	26.3	18.7	19.5	26.3
C	15.2	16.8	23.6	9.3	10.0	23.6
C+	2.9	5.3	10.6	3.0	2.8	10.6
B	1.2	1.4	3.	.48	.7	3.0
A	.2	.7	.9	.11	0	.9

It is obvious that the negro criminals from the Southern group of states are inferior to those from the other two groups, and that the individuals from the borderline states comprise a distribution very much inferior to the Northern and Western group. That is, the negro criminals are relatively more intelligent the further away from the Southern group of states the sampling is taken. Along with the progressive increase in the ability of the negro criminal to make a score in the Alpha test, we find a concomitant decrease in the superiority of the negro criminal to the draft group from the same geographical area. This should not be interpreted by the reader as invalidating the previous tentative conclusion that so-called inferior national groups contribute still more inferior criminals. The reader must remember that negro criminals from the Southern states were imprisoned and tested in states far removed from their home state. It is quite possible that, if the negro criminals actually imprisoned in prisons actually located in the same Southern states were tested and their scores compared with the scores of the negro draft from the same states, the draft might prove to be superior.

To emphasize further the possible factor of distance let us compare in the case of each of the four states of Maryland, Illinois, Ohio and New Jersey, the negro criminals imprisoned within their home state and the negro criminals imprisoned outside their home state. Taking Ohio first:

Alpha Score	Negro Cases at Home	Negro Cases Away from Home	Percentage of Former	Percentage of Latter
0- 9	9	78	6.2	17.1
10- 14	13	74	8.9	16.3
15- 19	4	35	2.7	7.7
20- 24	11	54	7.5	11.9
25- 34	18	72	12.3	15.8
35- 44	15	46	10.3	10.1
45- 59	27	45	18.5	9.9
60- 74	22	25	15.1	5.5
75- 89	10	15	6.8	3.3
90-104	8	5	5.5	1.1
105-119	5	3	3.4	.7
120-134	2	2	1.4	.4
135-149	2	1	1.4	.2
150-212	0	0	0	0

Translating into the traditional letter grades:

Letter Grades	Percentage confined in Home State (Ohio)	Percentage confined in Ohio but born elsewhere
E	15.1	33.4
D	10.2	19.6
C—	22.6	25.9
C	33.6	15.4
C+	12.3	4.4
B	4.8	1.1
A	1.4	.2

In the case of Ohio we find that the negro criminals born in that state and imprisoned there are superior, in ability to make a score in the Alpha test, to the negro criminals born elsewhere but imprisoned in Ohio. This is exactly the reverse of what was found in the case of native born white criminals.

Following is a similar comparison of the New Jersey groups:

Alpha Score	Negro Cases at Home	Negro Cases Away from Home	Percentage of Former	Percentage of Latter
0- 9	10	52	16.9	26.9
10- 14	5	16	8.5	8.3
15- 19	5	16	8.5	8.3
20- 24	7	27	11.8	13.9
25- 34	8	10	13.5	5.2
35- 44	7	17	11.8	8.8
45- 59	4	22	6.8	11.4
60- 74	6	17	10.2	8.8
75- 89	3	5	5.1	2.6
90-104	0	2	0	1.0
105-119	2	5	3.4	2.6
120-134	2	2	3.4	1.0
135-149	0	2	0	1.0
150-212	0	0	0	0

Translating into the traditional letter grades:

Letter Grades	Percentage Confined in Home State	Percentage confined outside Home
E	25.4	35.2
D	20.3	22.2
C—	25.3	14.0
C	17.0	20.2
C+	5.1	3.6
B	6.8	3.6
A	0	1.0

In the case of New Jersey also we find the same results as in the case of Ohio.

Following is a similar comparison of the Illinois groups:

Alpha Score	Negro Cases at Home	Negro Cases Away from Home	Percentage of Former	Percentage of Latter
0- 9	4	18	7.0	9.4
10- 14	4	13	7.0	6.8
15- 19	4	13	7.0	6.8
20- 24	0	13	0	6.8
25- 34	7	33	12.3	17.3
35- 44	9	27	15.8	14.1
45- 59	8	24	14.0	12.5
60- 74	4	25	7.0	13.1
75- 89	8	7	14.0	3.6
90-104	5	12	8.8	6.3
105-119	2	4	3.5	2.1
120-134	0	1	0	.5
135-149	1	1	1.8	.5
150-212	1	0	1.8	0

Translating into the traditional letter grades:

Letter Grades	Percentage confined in Home State	Percentage confined outside Home State
E	14.0	16.2
D	7.0	13.6
C—	28.1	31.4
C	21.0	25.6
C+	22.8	9.9
B	3.5	2.6
A	3.6	.5

Here, also, we find the same results as in the case of Ohio and New Jersey.

Following is a similar distribution for the state of Maryland:

Alpha Score	Negro Cases at Home	Negro Cases Away from Home	Percentage of Former	Percentage of Latter
0- 9	28	29	21.9	23.8
10- 14	16	22	12.5	18.0
15- 19	17	10	13.3	8.2
20- 24	9	5	7.0	4.1
25- 34	19	17	14.8	13.9
35- 44	14	11	10.9	9.0
45- 59	8	6	6.3	4.9
60- 74	6	5	4.7	4.1
75- 89	5	6	3.9	4.9
90-104	3	4	2.3	3.3
105-119	1	2	.8	1.6
120-134	2	3	1.6	2.4
135-149	0	0	0	0
150-212	0	2	0	1.6

Translating into the traditional letter grades:

Letter Grades	Percentage confined in Home State	Percentage confined outside Home State
E	34.4	41.8
D	20.3	12.3
C—	25.7	22.9
C	11.0	9.0
C+	6.2	8.2
B	2.4	4.0
A	0	1.6

In the case of Maryland the negro criminal group born elsewhere shows a larger percentage of A, B and C+ scores, but also a larger percentage of E scores. In terms of superiority, there seems to be little to choose between the two groups.

Following is a composite of the cases from the four states confined within their home state, and the cases from the prisons of the four states confined outside their own state.

Alpha Score	Negro Cases Confined at Home	Negro Cases Away from Home	Percentage of former	Percentage of Latter
0- 9	51	177	13.1	18.2
10- 14	38	125	9.7	13.0
15- 19	30	74	7.7	7.7
20- 24	27	99	6.9	10.3
25- 34	52	132	13.3	13.7
35- 44	45	101	11.5	10.4
45- 59	47	97	12.0	10.1
60- 74	38	72	9.7	7.5
75- 89	26	33	6.6	3.5
90-104	16	23	4.1	2.4
105-119	10	14	2.6	1.4
120-134	6	8	1.5	.8
135-149	3	4	.8	.4
150-212	1	2	.2	.2

Translating into the traditional letter grades:

Letter Grades	Negro Percentage Confined at Home	Negro Percentage confined out- home State
E	22.8	31.2
D	14.6	18.0
C—	24.8	24.1
C	21.7	17.6
C+	10.7	5.9
B	4.1	2.2
A	1.0	.6

In the above composite the negro criminal group confined in the home state shows a fairly marked superiority, as a group, over the negro criminal group confined outside the home state.

Tentative Conclusions:

1. Some negro draft groups are superior to some white draft groups, in so far as superiority can be measured in terms of Alpha scores.

2. The group of negro criminals treated in this article gives a distribution of Alpha scores showing some superiority to the entire negro draft group. But this general conclusion must be qualified by further analysis.

3. The entire negro criminal population of a given state is inferior to the negro draft from the same state, this conclusion following from an examination of data from the four states of Illinois, Ohio, Maryland and New Jersey.

4. There is a progressive increase of negro criminal and draft intelligence from the Southern states through the borderline states to the Northern and Western states. This is partly responsible for the fact that negro criminals confined

in the home state, in the case of Illinois, Maryland and New Jersey, are superior to negro criminals confined in the same state though born elsewhere.

5. The tendency of the negro criminal group confined in the home state to make superior Alpha scores to the negro groups confined in the same state though born elsewhere, should be especially noted, since the same disagreement with white criminal tendencies will be found in further publications.

CHAPTER 22

TYPES OF CRIME

We shall consider in this article the types of crime committed by negroes, and the relative intelligence of the individuals committing such types of crime. We shall follow the classification of types as agreed upon in the Journal of *Criminal Law and Criminology,* Volume XV, No. 2, pp. 280-281, August, 1924, "The writer suggests that the seventy-two crimes, for purposes of comparison, be classified into seven groups as follows: (1) Obtaining property through deception and fraud, known legally as forgery, embezzlement, false pretenses, conspiracy, confidence games, receiving stolen property, blackmail, counterfeiting, and uttering of fradulent checks. (2) Obtaining property through force, known legally as robbery, burglary, assault to rob, breaking and entering, entering to commit felony, burglary and larceny, safe blowing, attempted burglary, kidnapping, child stealing, housebreaking, attempt to rob, and burglary of inhabited dwelling. (3) Obtaining property through common thievery, known legally as larceny, pocket-picking, vehicle taking, horse stealing and automobile stealing. (4) Statutory offenses, known legally as unlawful use of motor vehicle, illegal sale of drugs, illegal sale or possession of intoxicating beverages, carrying concealed weapons, unlawful use of explosives, operating motor vehicle without owner's consent, violating automobile law, having burglar tools, concealing weapons to aid escape, escaping prison, and removing railroad property. (5) Crimes of physical injury, known legally as murder, maiming, manslaughter, assault to murder, accessory to murder, cutting, shooting or stabbing to kill or wound, arson, and malicious destruction of property. (6) Crimes of social dereliction, known legally as abandonment, desertion, vagrancy, begging, non-support, neglect of minor child, child abandonment, bigamy, lewdness, seduction, perjury, publishing of obscene writing, abducting, and receiving earnings of prostitute. (7) Sex crimes, known legally as rape, sodomy, indecent liberty with child, incest, assault to rape, crime against nature, assault to commit crime against nature, crime against child, adultery, and carnal abuse."

For gross comparison let us consider the comparative Alpha distribution, in terms of percentages, of the individuals committing each type of crime.

Alpha Score	Fraud (36 cases)	Force (540 cases)	Thievery (252 cases)	Statutory (56 cases)	Physical Injury (389 cases)	Dereliction (15 cases)	Sex (63 cases)
0-9	13.9	13.9	15.1	23.2	20.3	26.6	20.6
10-14	5.5	11.6	11.5	10.7	13.6	20.0	12.7
15-19	---	5.7	10.3	5.4	9.0	13.3	11.1
20-24	11.1	9.2	8.7	7.1	10.8	6.7	6.3
25-34	19.5	15.0	12.3	7.1	12.1	6.7	20.6
35-44	16.7	11.5	9.9	21.4	8.7	13.3	9.5
45-59	5.5	12.2	9.9	7.1	10.5	6.7	7.9
60-74	11.1	8.7	10.3	12.5	5.6	---	4.7
75-89	5.5	4.6	4.7	3.6	4.1	---	3.2
90-104	2.8	3.9	2.3	---	2.5	---	1.6
105-119	2.8	2.2	2.8	1.8	.7	---	---
120-134	2.8	1.1	1.2	---	.5	6.7	1.6
135-149	2.8	.2	.4	---	1.0	---	---
150-212	---	---	.4	---	.5	---	---

If we state the letter grades of the seven groups of types, we have the following:

Letter Grade	Fraud	Force	Thievery	Statutory	Physical Injury	Dereliction	Sex
E	19.4	25.5	26.6	33.9	33.9	46.6	33.3
D	11.1	14.9	19.0	12.5	19.8	20.0	17.4
C—	36.2	26.5	22.2	28.5	20.8	20.0	30.1
C	16.6	20.9	20.2	19.6	16.1	6.7	12.6
C+	8.3	8.5	7.0	3.6	6.6	---	4.8
B	5.6	3.3	4.0	1.8	1.2	6.7	1.6
A	2.8	.2	.8	---	1.5	---	---

It is obvious that the seven groups of negro criminals are related in practically the same way that we found to be the case with white criminals. Crimes against property are consistently committed by groups in general superior to the groups committing crimes against the person, while the more abstract crimes against property are consistently committed by still more superior individuals. These are not new facts, having been observed long ago by various writers in the field of criminology, but have now been stated in exact figures for white native born American criminals, for foreign born criminals in America, and for American negro criminals.

It is possible to make a more startling comparison of the above groups by comparing, in the case of each crime group, the percentage making Alpha grades superior to C, and those making grades inferior to C.

Percentage Inferior to C		Type Group	Percentage Superior to C
66.7	_____	Fraud _____	16.7
66.9	_____	Force _____	12.0
67.8	_____	Thievery _____	11.8
74.9	_____	Statutory _____	5.4
74.5	_____	Physical Injury _____	9.3
86.6	_____ _____	Dereliction _____	6.7
80.8	_____	Sex _____	6.4

It is obvious that the differences between the various type groups occur chiefly in the range of more superior individuals. Each group seems to possess a very large percentage of inferior individuals, but the groups are quite different in the percentage which they possess of the superior individuals.

Let us now consider in a series of tables, one for each type, the comparative Alpha distribution, in terms of percentages, of the negroes confined in their home state, and the negroes confined outside their home state. Because of the impossibility of locating the home state of forty-seven individuals, the total number of cases considered in this section will be 1,304.

Crimes of Fraud

Alpha Score	Percentage of cases at home (12 cases)	Percentage of cases away from home (23 cases)
0-9	8.3	17.4
10-14	---	4.3
15-19	---	---
20-24	16.6	8.7
25-34	33.3	13.0
35-44	25.0	13.0
45-59	---	8.7
60-74	---	17.4
75-89	8.3	4.3
90-104	---	4.3
105-119	---	4.3
120-134	8.3	---
135-149	---	4.3
150-212	---	---

In letter grades, the percentage distribution of the above group is as follows:

Letter Grade	Percentage at Home	Percentage Away from Home
E	8.3	21.7
D	16.6	8.7
C—	58.3	26.0
C	---	26.1
C+	8.3	8.6
B	8.3	4.3
A	---	4.3

Crimes of Force

Alpha Score	Percentage of cases at home (151 cases)	Percentage of cases away from home (364 cases)
0-9	9.3	15.4
10-14	10.6	11.8
15-19	3.9	5.5
20-24	5.9	10.1
25-34	11.2	16.5
35-44	10.6	12.1
45-59	15.9	11.2
60-74	15.2	6.6
75-89	5.3	4.6
90-104	5.3	3.5
105-119	4.6	1.4
120-134	1.3	1.1
135-149	.7	---
150-212	...	---

In letter grades, the percentage distribution of the above group is as follows:

Letter Grade	Percentage at Home	Percentage Away from Home
E	19.9	27.2
D	9.8	15.6
C—	21.8	28.6
C	31.1	17.8
C+	10.6	8.1
B	5.9	2.5
A	.7	---

Crimes of Thievery

Alpha Score	Percentage of cases at home (80 cases)	Percentage of cases away from home (175 cases)
0-9	11.2	14.8
10-14	8.7	13.1
15-19	13.7	6.8
20-24	7.5	9.1
25-34	16.2	12.0
35-44	12.5	9.1
45-59	11.2	9.5
60-74	6.2	13.1
75-89	6.2	4.0
90-104	5.0	1.5
105-119	1.3	3.4
120-134	---	1.5
135-149	---	.8
150-212	---	.8

In letter grades, the percentage distribution of the above group is as follows:

Letter Grade	Percentage at Home	Percentage Away from Home
E	19.9	27.9
D	21.2	15.9

C—	_____ 28.7	21.1
C	___ _____ 17.4	22.6
C+	____. _____ 11.2	5.5
B	_____ 1.3	4.9
A	_____ ---	1.6

Statutory Crimes

Alpha Score	Percentage of cases at home (15 cases)	Percentage of cases away from home (39 cases)
0-9	13.3	28.2
10-14	---	12.8
15-19	---	7.7
20-24	---	10.2
25-34	6.6	7.7
35-44	33.3	17.9
45-59	6.6	5.1
60-74	26.6	7.7
75-89	6.6	2.5
90-104	---	---
105-119	6.6	---
120-134	---	---
135-149	---	---
150-212	---	---

In letter grades, the percentage distribution of the above group is as follows:

Letter Grade	Percentage at Home	Percentage Away from Home
E	_____ 13.3	41.0
D	_____ ---	17.9
C—	_____ 39.9	25.6
C	_____ 33.2	12.8
C+	_____ 6.6	2.5
B	_____ 6.6	---
A	_____ ---	---

Crimes of Physical Injury

Alpha Score	Percentage of cases at home (112 cases)	Percentage of cases away from home (258 cases)
0-9	17.2	22.5
10-14	12.5	14.7
15-19	8.0	9.6
20-24	8.0	12.0
25-34	11.6	10.8
35-44	8.9	7.7
45-59	10.7	10.4
60-74	4.5	5.8
75-89	8.0	2.7
90-104	3.6	1.9
105-119	.9	.8
120-134	1.8	---
135-149	2.7	.4
150-212	.9	.4

In letter grades, the percentage distribution of the above group is as follows:

Letter Grade	Percentage at Home	Percentage Away from Home
E	29.7	37.2
D	16.0	21.6
C—	20.5	18.5
C	15.2	16.2
C+	11.6	4.6
B	2.7	.8
A	3.6	.8

Crimes of Social Dereliction

Alpha	Percentage of cases at home	Percentage of cases away from home
0-9	40.0	30.0
10-14	20.0	10.0
15-19	20.0	10.0
20-24	20.0	---
25-34	---	10.0
35-44	---	20.0
45-59	---	10.0
60-74	---	---
75-89	---	---
90-104	---	---
105-119	---	---
120-134	---	10.0
135-149	---	---
150-212	---	---

In letter grades, the percentage distribution of the above group is as follows:

Letter Grade	Percentage at Home	Percentage Away from Home
E	60.0	40.0
D	40.0	10.0
C—	---	30.0
C	---	10.0
C+	---	---
B	---	10.0
A	---	---

Sex Crimes

Alpha	Percentage of cases at home (18 cases)	Percentage of cases away from home (42 cases)
0-9	16.6	21.4
10-14	11.1	14.3
15-19	16.6	7.1
20-24	---	9.5
25-34	22.2	21.4
35-44	5.5	9.5
45-59	5.5	9.5
60-74	11.1	2.4
75-89	5.5	2.4

90-104	--	2.4
105-119		---
120-134	5.5	---
135-149	- -	---
150-212	--	---

In letter grades, the percentage distribution of the above group is as follows:

Letter Grade	Percentage at Home	Percentage Away from Home
E	27.7	35.7
D	16.6	16.6
C—	27.7	30.9
C	16.6	11.9
C+	5.5	4.8
B	5.5	---
A		---

For the sake of such illumination as it might give, let us finally consider the percentage of negro criminals coming from each section of the country who become classified in each type of crime.

Types of Crime	Percentage of negroes from each section of the country committing the given type of crime, the percentage being in the order			
	Southern	Border-line	Northern & Western	Home
Fraud	2.1	1.3	3.5	3.1
Force	34.5	41.8	45.8	38.7
Thievery	15.6	16.3	21.6	20.0
Statutory	5.4	5.2	2.6	3.6
Physical Injury	36.1	30.0	21.3	28.7
Dereliction	1.4	.7	.9	1.3
Sex	4.7	4.5	4.2	4.6

To be sure, the variations of the percentages of each geographical group committing each type of crime is not extremely great. Such differences as exist are found chiefly in crimes of force and in crimes of physical injury. These two types of crime seem to vary inversely with each other when the Southern group and the Northern and Western group are compared. That is, it seems that the negro is more likely to commit crimes of force in the North and West than he is in the South, and less likely to commit crimes of physical injury in the North and West than he is in the South. This is in agreement with the findings concerning foreign born criminals The Southern negroes in types of crimes committed compare to the Northern and Western negroes somewhat as the Southern Europeans compare to the Northern and Western Europeans.

Tentative Conclusions:

1. Negroes who commit crimes against property are in general superior to the negroes who commit crimes against the person. To this extent, negro criminals bear a close resemblance to white criminals.

2. Where the number of cases is adequate, there is a decided tendency in the case of each crime group for the negro criminals imprisoned in their home state to show superiority to negro criminals imprisoned outside their home state. To this extent, the negro criminals are in decided contrast with the white criminals. There seems to be an inverse variation between crimes of force and crimes of physical injury when we compare Northern and Western negroes with the Southern negroes. To this extent, there is agreement with the contrast between Southern European criminals and Northern and Western European criminals.

CHAPTER 23

RECIDIVISM

The number of cases dealt with in this article is exactly five hundred, and is confined to the state penitentaries of New Jersey and Maryland. For various reasons data concerning negro criminal recidivists could not be obtained in the Middle Western prisons.

1. *Gross Comparison of Recidivists with First Offenders.*
Table No. 1 is a gross comparison of the first offenders with the recidivists, the recidivists showing a degree of superiority just as marked as in the case of the white criminals previously reported.

TABLE NO. 1

State Penitentiaries of New Jersey and Maryland

Alpha Score	Percentage of First Offenders (319 cases)	Percentage of Recidivists (181 cases)
0-9	25.8	15.7
10-14	13.7	9
15-19	12.2	4.4
20-24	8.7	10.7
25-34	10.3	11.7
35-44	7.8	13.4
45-59	7.2	10.9
60-74	5.3	7.7
75-89	2.2	7.8
90-104	2.2	1.2
105-119	1.2	3.4
120-134	1.2	3.1
135-149	.3	.4
150-212	.3	.7

Letter Grades	Percentage of First Offenders	Percentage of Recidivists
E.	40.5	24.7
D.	20.9	15.1
C—	18.1	25.1
C.	12.5	18.6
C+	4.4	9
B.	2.4	6.5
A.	.6	1.1

Table No. 2 shows a more detailed analysis of recidivists into second offenders and habitual offenders, the habitual offenders being those convicted three or more times. Just as in the case of white criminals previously reported, as above referred to, the negro habitual offenders show a clear superiority to the second offenders, while the second offenders show a clear superiority to the first offenders.

TABLE NO. 2

Alpha Score	First Offenders (319)	Second Offenders (123)	Habitual Offenders (58)
0-9	26.8	21.9	15.5
10-14	13.7	8.9	6.9
15-19	12.2	4.8	3.4
20-24	8.7	9.6	10.3
25-34	10.3	12.2	6.9
35-44	7.8	12.2	13.8
45.59	7.2	9.6	13.8
60.74	5.3	8.1	10.3
75-89	2.2	7.3	5.1
90-104	2.2	---	3.4
105-119	1.2	1.6	6.9
120-134	1.2	2.4	3.4
135-149	.3	---	---
150-212	.3	.8	---

Letter Grades	First Offenders	Second Offenders	Habitual Offenders
E.	40.5	30.9	22.4
D.	20.9	14.6	13.7
C—	18.1	24.3	20.7
C.	12.5	17.8	24.1
D+	4.4	7.3	8.6
B.	2.4	4.0	10.3
A.	.6	.8	---

	Inferior to C.	C.	Superior to C.
First	79.5	12.5	7.4
Second	69.8	17.8	12.1
Habitual	56.8	24.1	18.9

2. *Gross Geographical Concomitants of Recidivism.*

According to Table 3, the recidivists confined outside their home state show a slight superiority to the recidivists confined in their home state. This is in agreement with findings already published regarding white criminals, as above referred to.

TABLE NO. 3

Alpha Score	Percentage of Home Recidivists (76)	Percentage of Transient Recidivists (104)
0-9	17.1	18.2
10-14	9.2	7 7
15-19	3.9	3.8
20-24	13.1	9.6
25-34	14.4	5.7
35-44	13.1	10.5
45-59	9.2	15.3
60-74	5.2	11.5
75-89	6.5	7.7
90-104	1.3	.9
105-119	1.3	5.7
120-134	5.2	.9
135-149	——	.9
150-212	——	.9

Letter grades	Percentage at Home	Percentage away from Home
E	26.3	25.9
D	17.0	13.4
C-	27.5	16.2
C	14.4	26.8
C+	7.8	8.6
B	6.5	6.6
A	—	1.8

TABLE NO. 4

	First Offenders at Home (107)	First Offenders Away (205)
0-9	23.3	28.7
10-14	12.1	12.6
15-19	15.9	9.7
20-24	9.3	10.2
25-34	14.0	10.2
35-44	9.3	7.8
45-59	4.6	7.8
60-74	6.5	3.9
75-89	2.8	1.9
90-104	.9	2.4
105-119	.9	1.4
120-134		1.9
135-149		.4
150-212		.4

Letter Grade	Percentage at Home	Percentage Away from Home
E.	35.4	41.3
D.	25.2	19.9
C—	23.3	18.0
C.	11.1	11.7
C+	3.7	4.3
B.	.9	3.3
A.	---	.8

Table No. 4 shows a slight superiority on the part of first offenders confined outside of their home state as compared to first offenders confined in their home state. This, also, is in agreement with findings already published concerning white criminals.

TABLE NO. 5

First Offenders vs. Recidivists in the Fraud Group

Alpha	First Offenders (10)	Recidivists (4)
0-9	2	—
10-14	1	—
15-19	—	—
20-24	—	1
25-34	2	—
35-44	3	—
45-59	—	1
60-74	1	—

75-89	— ·	1
90-104	—	—
105-119	1	—
120-134	—	1
135-149	—	—
150-212	—	—

TABLE NO. 6

First Offenders vs. Recidivists in the Force Group

	Percentages	
Alpha	First (77)	Recidivists (56)
0-9	28.5	26.8
10-14	14.2	8.9
15-19	10.3	---
20-24	6.5	14.3
25-34	13.0	12.3
35.44	6.5	14.3
45-59	3.9	5.3
60 74	6.5	3.5
75-89	1.3	8.9
90-104	6.5	---
105-119	1.3	3.5
120-134	1.3	1.8
135-149	---	---
150-212	---	---

Letter Grade	Percentages	
	First	Recidivists
E	42.7	35.7
D	16.8	14.3
C—	19.5	26.6
C	10.4	8.8
C+	7.8	8.9
B	2.6	5.3
A	-- ·	---

TABLE NO. 7

First Offenders vs. Recidivists in the Common Thievery Group

	Percentage	
Alpha	First (61)	Recidivists (68)
0-9	25.8	11.7
10-14	11.2	7.3
15-19	17.7	7.3
20-24	8.0	10.3
25-34	9.6	10.3
35-44	8.0	8.8
45-59	9.6	14.7
60-74	3.2	13.2
75-89	1.6	5.8
90-104	---	1.4
105-119	--	5.8
120-134	3.2	1.4
135-149	---	1.4
150-212	---	---

Letter Grade	Percentages	
	First	Recidivists
E	37.0	19.0
D	25.7	17.6
C—	17.6	19.1
C	12.8	27.9
C+	1.6	7.2
B	3.2	7.2
A	---	1.4

TABLE NO. 8
First Offenders vs. Recidivists in the Statutory Group

	Percentages	
Alpha	First (12)	Recidivists (14)
0-9	2	2
10-14	1	2
15-19	1	--
20-24	1	1
25-34		
35-44	4	5
45-59	--	1
60-74	1	3
75-89	--	--
90-104	--	--
105-119	1	--
120-134	1	--
135-149	--	--
150-212	--	--

TABLE NO. 9
First Offenders vs. Recidivists in the Physical Injury Group

	Percentages	
Alpha	First (128)	Recidivists (34)
0-9	26.5	14.7
10-14	17.2	14.7
15-19	11.7	8.8
20-24	10.9	11.7
25-34	8.6	14.7
35-44	5.6	5.9
45-59	8.6	5.9
60-74	5.4	8.8
75-89	3.1	5.9
90-104	1.5	2.9
105-119	.7	---
120-134	---	2.9
135-149	.7	---
150-212	---	2.9

Letter Grade	Percentages	
	First	Recidivists
E	43.7	29.4
D	22.6	20.5
C—	14.2	20.6
C	14.0	14.7
C+	4.6	8.8
B	.7	2.9
A	.7	2.9

3. *Recidivism and Types of Crime.*
In this section we exhibit Tables 5-10 inclusive. In Tables
5, 8 and 10 the number of cases is so small that we exhibit
numbers rather than percentages. Causal inspection, however, in the case of these three tables, indicates superiority on
the part of the recidivists in so far as differences are indicated.
Tables 6, 7 and 9 show a marked superiority of the recidivist
group as compared to the first offenders.

TABLE NO. 10
First Offenders vs. Recidivists in the Sex Group

Alpha	First (23)	Recidivists (9)
0-9	7	2
10-14	1	--
15-19	3	1
20-24	2	1
25-34	5	2
35-44	2	1
45-59	3	1
60-74	--	--
75-89	--	--
90-104	--	--
105-119	--	--
120-134	--	1
135-149	--	--
150-212	--	--

TABLE NO. 11
First Offenders vs. Recidivists in the Northern and Western
Group

	Percentages	
Alpha	First (85)	Recidivists (79)
0-9	17.6	17.7
10-14	8.2	5.0
15-19	12.9	5.0
20-24	8.2	11.3
25-34	9.4	7.6
35-44	8.2	13.9
45-59	12.9	12.6
60-74	5.9	8.8
75-89	2.3	8.8
90-104	4.7	---
105-119	3.5	5.0
120-134	3.5	2.5
135-140	1.1	---
150-212	1.1	1.2

Letter Grade	Percentages	
	First	Recidivists
E	25.8	22.7
D	21.1	16.3
C—	17.6	21.5
C	18.8	21.4

C+	7.0	8.8
B	7.0	7.5
A	2.2	1.2

TABLE NO. 12

First Offenders vs. Recidivists in the Border States of Maryland, West Virginia, Kentucky, Arkansas and Texas

Percentages

Alpha	First (107)	Recidivists (51)
0-9	26.1	19.6
10-14	14.0	9.8
15-19	14.9	5.8
20-24	9.3	7.8
25-34	11.2	17.6
35-44	8.4	13.7
45-59	5.6	7.8
60-74	5.6	5.8
75-89	2.6	3.9
90-104	1.8	1.9
105-119	---	1.9
120-134	---	3.9
135-149	---	---
150-212	---	---

Letter Grade	Percentages	
	First	Recidivists
E	40.1	29.4
D	24.2	13.6
C—	19.6	31.3
C	11.2	13.6
C+	4.4	5.8
B	---	5.8
A	---	---

TABLE NO. 13

First Offenders vs. Recidivists in the Southern States

Percentages

Alpha	First (127)	Recidivists (49)
0-9	34.6	16.3
10-14	15.7	14.2
15-19	12.6	6.1
20-24	9.4	12.2
25-34	9.4	10.2
35-44	8.7	6.1
45-59	5.5	8.1
60-74	1.6	16.2
75-89	1.6	4.0
90-104	---	2.0
105-119	.9	2.0
120-134	.9	2.0
135-149	---	---
150-212	---	---

Letter Grade	Percentages	
	First	Recidivists
E	50.3	30.5
D	22.0	18.3

C—	18.1	16.3
C	7.1	24.3
C+	1.6	6.0
B	1.8	4.0
A	---	---

4. *Recidivism and Concomitant Industrial, Social, Political and Other Factors.*

In this section we exhibit Tables 11, 12 and 13. In the Northern and Western group the recidivists show a slight superiority to first offenders; in the border line states the recidivists show a still greater superiority to the first offenders; while in the Southern states the recidivists are very markedly superior to the first offenders. In the Northern and Western group the numbers of the first offenders and recidivists are about equal; in the border line states the first offenders are approximately twice as numerous as the recidivists; while in the Southern states first offenders are almost three times as numerous as are recidivists.

Tentative Conclusions:

1. Just as in the case of native born white criminals and foreign born white criminals, the negro criminal recidivists consistently show superiority, in ability to make scores in mental tests, to the first offenders, this superiority increasing with degree of recidivism. Certainly feeble-mindedness cannot be a cause of criminal recidivism among negroes any more than it is a cause of criminal recidivism among white criminals.

2. The superiority of the recidivists to the first offenders, though obvious in the case of the negroes born in the Northern and Wesern states, is much greater in the border line states, and is exceedingly marked in the case of those born in the Southern states.

CHAPTER 24

LITERACY

This material was gathered from the Ohio State Penitentiary, the Ohio State Reformatory, the Illinois State Penitentiary at Joliet, the Illinois State Reformatory at Pontiac, the Maryland State Penitentiary, and the New Jersey State Penitentiary. This material concerns the same negro criminals concerning whom other material of varying nature has been published in this book. Literacy will be reported in terms of literacy groups according to the symbols of the following table:

TABLE I

Literacy Group	Years in School
1	0-2
2	3-4
3	5-6
4	7-8
5	9-11
6	12-14
7	15-16

1. *Gross Comparisons with the Army Negroes.*

We have 1,299 cases of negro criminals from the above prisons concerning whom we have definite information concerning literacy. There was no opportunity to give literacy tests to these individuals, so all reports of literacy are made in temporal units. In Volume XV, *Memoirs of the National Academy of Sciences,* 1921, p. 756 and p. 757, Table 297 gives us the literacy distribution of Group 5, Colored Draft North, the sample consisting of 2,850 cases, while Table 299 gives us the literacy distribution of Group 4, Colored Draft South, the sample consisting of 1,481 cases. It seems reasonable to suppose that Tables 297 and 299 may legitimately be used as twin norms in considering the nature of the literacy distribution of our 1,299 cases of negro criminals. At least they are as near being norms as any other material that is available at the present time. Casting the material of these two tables into an identical form with our negro criminals, we get the following table:

Literacy Group	Percentage of Army Negroes (North) 2850 cases	Percentage of Negro Criminals 1299 cases	Percentage of Army Negroes (South) 1481 cases
1	2.0	19.1	6.4
2	15.9	30.7	32.0
3	29.5	25.6	34.1
4	32.8	18.1	20.0
5	12.4	5.1	4.9
6	5.6	.8	3.0
7	2.0	.6	.7

The negro criminals constituting our sample of the negro criminal population are very markedly inferior in literacy to the negroes constituting the samples from the negro populations of the two geographical areas considered in the Army report. However, the major part of that inferiority seems to lie in the very lowest literacy group.

2. *Literacy Distribution in the Various Criminal Type Groups.* "The writer suggests that the seventy-two crimes, for purposes of comparison, be classified into seven groups as follows: (1) Obtaining property through deception and fraud, known legally as forgery, embezzlement, false pretenses, conspiracy, confidence games, receiving stolen property, blackmail, counterfeiting, and uttering of fraudulent checks. (2) Obtaining property through force, known legally as robbery, burglary, assault to rob, breaking and entering, entering to commit felony, burglary and larceny, safe blowing, attempted burglary, kidnapping, child stealing, housebreaking, attempt to rob, and burglary of inhabited dwelling.(3) Obtaining property through common thievery, known legally as larceny, pocket picking, vehicle taking, horse stealing and automobile stealing. (4) Statutory offenses, known legally as unlawful use of motor vehicle, illegal sale of drugs, illegal sale or possession of intoxicating beverages, carrying concealed weapons, unlawful use of explosives, operating motor vehicle without owner's consent, violating automobile law, having burglar tools, concealing weapons to aid escape, escaping prison, and removing railroad property. (5) Crimes of physical injury, known legally as murder, maiming, manslaughter, assault to murder, accessory to murder, cutting, shooting or stabbing to kill or wound; arson, and malicious destruction of property. (6) Crimes of social dereliction, known legally as abandonment, desertion, vagrancy, begging, non-support, neglect of minor child, child abandonment, bigamy, lewdness, seduction, perjury, publishing of obscene writing, abduction, and receiv-

ing earnings of prostitute. (7) Sex crimes, known legally as rape, sodomy, indecent liberty with child, incest, assault to rape, crime against nature, assault to commit crime against nature, crime against child and carnal abuse."[°]

The literacy distribution of the percentages of each type group occuring in each literacy group gives us the following array:

Literacy Group (34 cases)	Fraud	Force (515 cases)	Thievery (245 cases)	Statutory (55 cases)	Physical Injury (375 cases)	Social Dereliction (15 cases)	Sex (60 cases)
1	6.0	17.4	15.5	14.5	25.6	4 cases	16.6
2	23.5	32.4	23.7	34.5	32.8	3 cases	35.0
3	41.2	24.3	29.0	34.5	23.2	5 cases	20.0
4	14.7	19.4	25.3	14.5	12.5	none	21.6
5	6.0	5.6	4.5	2.0	4.5	3 cases	5.0
6	3.0	.6	1.7	none	.3	none	1.6
7	6.0	.2	.4	none	1.0	none	none

Since there were only fifteen cases under Social Dereliction, no attempt was made to give percentages, but the cases were reported in their proper distribution. The literacy distribution in the type groups is very similar to the Alpha test score distribution previously reported.[*]

3. *Some Geographical Concomitants of Negro Criminal Literacy Distribution.*

The following table is wholly the reverse of similar material published on white criminals.[**] The negro criminals incarcerated in their home state seem to be superior, at least in the lower levels of literacy, to the negro criminals incarcerated outside their home state.

Literacy Group	Incarcerated in Home State (384 cases)	Incarcerated outside Home State (915 cases)
1	14.3	21.1
2	28.1	31.8
3	28.0	24.7
4	22.1	16.4
5	6.5	4.5
6	.8	.8
7	.3	.8

[°]*The Journal of Criminal Law and Criminology*, Volume XV, Number 2, August, 1924.

[*]*Types of Crime and Intelligence of Negro Criminals*, The Pedagogical Seminary And Journal of Genetic Psychology, Volume XXXII, No. 2, June, 1925.

[**]*The Journal of Criminal Law and Criminology*, Volume XV, Number 3, November, 1924.

The following seven tables show the literacy distribution and the geographical concomitants of each criminal type group in turn. The Fraud Group, the Statutory Group, and the Social Dereliction Group possess too few cases to be reported in percentages, so are reported only in terms of cases. In the case

Fraud Group

Literacy Group	Incarcerated in Home State (12 cases)	Incarcerated outside Home State (22 cases)
1	2 cases	none
2	3 cases	5 cases
3	5 cases	9 cases
4	none	5 cases
5	1 cases	1 cases
6	1 case	none
7	none	2 cases

Force Group

Literacy Group	Incarcerated in Home State (149 cases)	Incarcerated outside Home State (366 cases)
1	13.4	19.1
2	28.2	34.1
3	24.8	24.0
5	24.1	17.4
5	9.4	4.1
6	none	.8
7	none	.3

Thievery Group

Literacy Group	Incarcerated in Home State (78 cases)	Incarcerated outside Home State (167 cases)
1	12.8	16.7
2	29.5	21.0
3	35.9	25.7
4	21.8	26.9
5	none	6.6
6	none	2.4
7	none	.6

Statutory Group

Literacy Group	Incarcerated in Home State (14 cases)	Incarcerated outside Home State (41 cases)
1	1 case	7 cases
2	4 cases	15 cases
3	5 cases	14 cases
4	3 cases	5 cases
5	1 case	none
6	none	none
7	none	none

Physical Injury Group

Literacy Group	Incarcerated in Home State (107 cases)	Incarcerated outside Home State (268 cases)
1	18.7	28.4
2	26.1	35.4
3	21.5	23.9
4	24.3	7.6
5	7.5	3.4
6	.9	none
7	.9	1.1

Social Dereliction Group

Literacy Group	Incarcerated in Home State (5 cases)	Incarcerated outside Home State (10 cases)
1	1 case	3 cases
2	1 case	2 cases
3	3 cases	2 cases
4	none	none
5	none	3 cases
6	none	none
7	none	none

Sex Group

Literacy Group	Incarcerated in Home State (19 cases)	Incarcerated outside Home State (41 cases)
1	5.2	22.0
2	36.8	34.1
3	31.6	14.6
4	15.8	24.4
5	5.2	4.9
6	5.2	none
7	none	none

of all the groups the literacy of those incarcerated in their home state is consistently superior to the literacy of those incarcerated outside their home state. This would seem to indicate that a psychological or sociological migratory factor functions in quite a contrary way in the case of negro criminals than it does in the case of white criminals. This assumption is greatly weakened, however, when we consider the literacy distribution of negro criminals from the Southern states, from the Borderline states, and from the Northern and Western states. The Southern states will be considered to be Virginia, North Carolina, South Carolina, Georgia, Florida, Alabama, Mississippi, Louisiana, and Tenessee. The Borderline states are the ones that border the Southern states on the north and west, and are Maryland, West Virginia, Kentucky, Arkansas, and Texas, All the other states of the Union are classified as Northern and Western.

Literacy Group	Southern (508 cases)	Borderline (279 cases)	Northern and Western (488 cases)
1	25.2	19.0	12.5
2	36.4	34.1	22.9
3	21.6	27.3	30.3
4	11.4	14.7	25.6
5	3.9	5.0	6.3
6	.6	none	1.4
7	.8	none	.8

The above table indicates that literacy becomes lower and lower as we pass from the Northern and Western states through the borderline states into the Southern states, and that it becomes higher and higher as we pass from the Southern states through the borderline states into the Northern and Western states. It is possible that the psychological and sociological factor resulting in lower literacy on the part of the negroes incarcerated outside their home states may be entirely due to the extremely low literacy of Southern negroes, and the fact that migrating negroes in the Northern and Western states have come from the Southern states.

4. *The Literacy Distribution of Negro Criminal Recidivists.*

The material for this section is confined to 503 cases from the Maryland State Penitentiary, and the New Jersey State Prison. The following table gives the literacy distribution of first offenders, and of second and habitual offenders combined. The 183 cases classified as recidivists are so classified solely on the authority of records existing in the offices of the wardens in the above two prisons.

Literacy Group	First Offenders (320 cases)	Second Offenders (121 cases)	Habitual Offenders (62 cases)	Total Recidivists (183 cases)
1	17.5	16.6	17.7	16.9
2	35.6	32.5	27.4	30.6
3	23.4	28.3	25.8	27.3
4	17.2	18.3	19.3	18.6
5	4.4	4.2	8.0	5.4
6	1.2	none	none	none
7	.6	.8	1.6	1.1

The above table does not indicate that education in terms of years spent in school has any causal relation to the repetition of crime after the first conviction. Such difference as exists seems to indicate that the recidivists are slightly more literate than are the first offenders. This finding is in harmony with results previously published concerning white native born criminals and concerning white foreign born criminals.

Tentative Conclusions:

1.   Negro criminals seem markedly inferior in terms of literacy to the sample taken from the army reports, but the major part of such inferiority seems to lie in the very lowest literacy group.

2.   The literacy distribution in the various criminal type groups seems similar to the Alpha test score distribution in the same types.   That is, crimes of Fraud are committed by men possessing relatively high literacy, while other crime groups show a lower literacy seemingly in proportion to the degree to which they lack deception.

3.   Negro criminals incarcerated in their home state seem to be superior, at least in the lower levels of literacy, to the negro criminals incarcerated outside their home state.   This seems to hold true in the case of all the criminal type groups. The reason for this, however, may possibly lie in the fact that migrating negroes in the states where this material was gathered are chiefly from the Southern states.

4.   Literacy, as indicated by number of years spent in school, seems to have no causal relation to the repetition of crime after the first conviction.   Such difference as exists seems to indicate that the recidivists are slightly more literate than are the first offenders.

CHAPTER 25

RELIGION

The data were obtained from two hundred and fifty cases at the Maryland Penitentiary, and consist of information as to the religious preference of the convict himself, the religious preference of both his parents, place of birth, literacy indicated by the number of years spent in school, type of crime committed, past record, and the score made in the Army Alpha test of intelligence. This enables us to study the intelligence of the denominational groups, type of crime, recidivism, and the relation of intelligence to religious inbreeding and outbreeding.

The size of the racial groups to be compared in this section is nearly the same in each case, there being 253 whites and 250 negroes. As they were confined in the same penitentiary and were convicted in the same part of the country, a comparison should prove interesting.

While negroes are generally considered to be more religious than whites, we find that the percentage of Agnostics is only slightly less than in case of the white, native-born criminals. Ten per cent claimed to be Agnostics, as compared with fourteen and three-tenths per cent of the white group. Seventy-two per cent of the negro group are Protestants as compared with forty-three and five-tenths per cent of the whites, and approximately eighteen per cent are Catholics, against thirty-four per cent of the white group. It is interesting to note that ninety-three per cent of the whole negro group have attended Sunday school.

Most of the cases are distributed in four denominational groups: Catholic, Baptist, Methodist, and Agnostic. Other groups will be disregarded in the statistical treatment on account of the small number of cases.

1. *The Religious Groups*

The following table gives the number of negro criminals in each of the religious groups, the percentage which each is of the entire colored group, and the same information for the corresponding white groups, for comparison.

	No.	Percentage of Negro Group	No.	Percentage of White Group
Baptists	98	39.2	21	8.3
Methodists	78	31.2	41	16.2
Catholics	44	17.6	87	34.4
Agnostics	25	10.0	38	15.0

Christian Sc.	2	.8	6	2.4
Christians	1	.4	6	2.4
Presbyterians	1	.4	8	3.2
Mormons	1	.4	--	
Protestants	181	72.4	108	42.7
Catholics	44	17.6	87	34.4
Agnostics	25	10.0	38	15.0

2. Intelligence of the Religious Groups

First we will compare the three groups, Catholics, Protestants, and Agnostics, as to intelligence as indicated by the Army Alpha test. In the tables the numerical scores have been translated into letter grades.

Table Showing the Percentage of Each Group Making Each Letter Grade

Letter Grade	Negroes			Whites		
	Catholic	Agnostic	Protestant	Catholic	Agnostic	Protestant
E	36.4	40.0	38.2	10.3	2.7	7.3
D	13.6	16.0	17.1	8.0	15.3	10.0
C—	20.4	20.0	25.4	13.8	18.4	19.1
C	13.6	8.0	9.9	32.2	21.0	23.6
C+	9.1	8.0	6.6	24.1	21.0	15.4
B	4.5	8.0	2.2	8.0	21.0	13.6
A	2.3	---	.5	3.4	10.5	9.1

In the Negro group the Catholics demonstrate an ability to make high scores in the Army Alpha test which is considerably superior to that of the Protestants and Agnostics. While the Agnostics have no men in the A group, the percentage making grades above C is greater than the percentage making better than C in the Protestant group. Furthermore the percentage making grades below C is smaller in the Agnostic group than it is in the Protestant group. Thus, the order of intelligence runs; Catholics first, Agnostics second, and Protestants third and last. Now this is an interesting fact indeed, for in the white group it is the Agnostics who make the best showing in ability to make high grades, Protestants coming next in order, while the Catholics stand lowest in the scale. Why should negro Catholics be so superior to the other negroes, while white Catholics are apparently very inferior to whites of other faiths?

3. The Intelligence of the Denominational Groups

Those groups which are large enough to consider in the tables are the Catholics, Baptists, Methodists, and Agnostics.

Table Showing the Percentage of Each Denomination
Making Each Letter Grade

Letter Grade	Negroes				Whites			
	Catholic	Agnostic	Baptist	Methodist	Catholic	Agnostic	Baptist	Methodist
E	36.4	40.0	39.8	34.6	10.3	2.7	4.8	12.2
D	13.6	16.0	13.3	23.1	8.0	5.3	_ _ _	14.6
C—	20.4	20.0	26.6	24.4	13.8	18.4	14.3	22.0
C	13.6	8.0	9.2	10.3	32.2	21.0	52.4	9.7
C+	9.1	8.0	8.1	6.4	24.1	21.0	14.3	22.0
B	4.5	8.0	3.1	_ _ _	8.0	21.0	9.5	14.6
A	2.3	_ _ _	_ _ _	1.3	3.4	10.5	4.8	4.9

The order seems to be, in the case of the negroes, as follows: Catholic, Agnostic, Baptist, Methodist. The order of white denominations is: Agnostic, Methodist, Baptist, Catholic,—so that the Baptists and Methodists change places, while the Catholics occupy the highest place in the negro group and lowest place in the white group. Here the standing of each denomination was determined by the percentage making grades above C and below C.

4. *The Geographical Concomitants of the Four Large Religious Groups*

A glance at the first of the next series of tables will show clearly that the Catholics who were born outside the home state demonstrate a much greater ability to make high scores than do those Catholics who were born in Maryland. None of the home grown Catholics were able to make a grade of A or B, while sixty per cent of the migratory Catholics made grades above the average of the two groups. Furthermore, a smaller percentage of the migratory Catholics made grades below C—. In the white group, the home Catholics seem to be somewhat more intelligent than the migratory ones, seventy per cent of the former and sixty per cent of the latter having made grades above C—,

In the case of the Baptists, the superiority of the migratory group is marked. Here a comparison with the whites cannot be made, as no data are available.

The migratory Methodists place 5.9 per cent of their number in the A group, but their percentage of men making grades above C— is 17.7, as compared with 18.7 per cent of the home grown group. The migratory group, however, has a slightly greater percentage in the D and E class, so that the level intelligence of the home grown Methodists is a little superior to that of the others.   Here, too, as in the case of the Catholics, conditions are reversed, but the difference is in the opposite direction.

With the Agnostics, the same is true of both the negroes and the whites.   The Alpha scores indicate that the home grown Agnostics in both cases are considerably superior in ability to make high scores.

Of the forty-four Catholics, twenty-four were born in the state of Maryland while twenty were born outside the state.

Letter Grade	Percentage of Home Catholics	Percentage Born Away
E	23.3	40.0
D	25.0	---
C—	20.8	20.0
C	16.7	10.0
C+	4.2	15.0
B	---	10.0
A	---	5.0

Of the ninety-eight Baptists, twenty-eight were born in the state of Maryland, sixty-seven were born outside the state, and three gave no place of birth.

Letter Grade	Percentage of Home Baptists	Percentage Born Away
E	39.3	37.3
D	14.3	13.4
C—	35.7	25.4
C	7.1	10.4
C+	---	10.4
B	3.6	3.0
A	---	---

Of the seventy-eight Methodists, fifty-nine were born in the state of Maryland, seventeen were born outside the state, while two did not state place of birth.   These two cases were not considered.

Letter Grade	Percentage of Home Methodists	Percentage Born Away
E	32.2	47.0
D	25.4	11.8
C—	23.8	23.5
C	10.2	11.8
C+	8.5	---
B	---	---
A	---	5.9

Of the twenty-five Agnostics, fourteen were born in the state of Maryland, while eleven were born outside the state.

Letter Grade	Percentage of Home Agnostics	Percentage Born Away
E	35.7	45.5
D	7.1	27.2
C—	21.4	18.2
C	14.3	---
C+	14.3	---
B	7.1	9.1
A	---	---

5. The Literacy of the Denominational Groups

Years in school will be reported according to the following table:

Group	Grade or Years
1	0-2
2	3-4
3	5-6
4	7-8
5	9-11
6	12-14
7	15-16

In the following table is exhibited the percentage of each denominational group that is classified in each literacy group:

	1	2	3	4	5	6	7
Catholic	15.9	29.6	27.3	15.9	4.5	2.3	4.5
Agnostic	36.0	40.0	8.0	8.0	4.0		4.0
Baptist	20.4	38.8	22.4	11.2	5.1	1.0	1.0
Methodist	17.9	34.6	25.6	15.4	5.1	1.3	--

The correlation between literacy and the Alpha scores of the religious denominations is not so striking as in the case of the whites. The order of standing as regards percentage in the two highest groups, groups six and seven, is the same as the order of standing according to Alpha scores. One should especially notice the relatively higher literacy of the Catholics.

6. Religion and Types of Crime

For the purpose of studying the types of crime committed by the different religious denominational groups, the many varieties of crime have been distributed in the seven crime classes previously adopted in these reports. These classes are as follows: fraud, force, thievery, physical injury, social dereliction, and sex.

A study of the accompanying table indicates that the Catholics are inclined toward physical injury, and are least inclined toward fraud and social dereliction. The majority of Baptists commit crimes of force and physical injury, and half of the Methodists are charged with committing crimes of physical injury. The Agnostics seem to incline to thievery, but a fair percentage commit crimes of physical injury.

Table Showing the Percentage of Each Denominational Group Committing Each Type of Crime

	Fraud	Force	Thievery	Physical In.	Derelic	Sex
Catholic	2.3	27.3	22.7	36.4	---	11.4
Agnostic	4.0	20.0	44.0	28.0	---	4.0
Baptist	3.1	35.0	19.6	32.0	3.1	7.2
Methodist	3.8	20.5	21.8	50.0	---	3.8

7. Religion and Recidivism

The following is the distribution of cases of recidivism among the religious groups, and the comparison of the percentage of the total prison population in each religious group with the percentage of the number of recidivists in those groups. The corresponding data for the white group is entered in the tables for the purpose of comparison.

Recidivists

Religious Group	Negroes Number of Cases	Whites Number of Cases
Catholic	7	20
Agnostic	8	10
Baptist	29	6
Methodist	20	9
Presbyterian	1	--
Christian Sc.	1	--
Mormon	1	--

Religious Group	Negroes		Whites	
	Percentage of Total Prison	Percentage of Recidivists	Percentage of Total Prison	Percentage of Recidivists
Catholic	17.6	10.4	34.4	35.1
Agnostic	10.0	11.9	14.3	17.5
Baptist	39.2	43.3	8.3	10.5
Methodist	31.2	29.8	16.2	15.8

In the above tables we get a striking contrast. While the white recidivists are mostly from the Catholic and Agnostic groups, by far the majority of negro recidivists are Baptists and Methodists.

8. The Relation of Intelligence to Religious In-breeding and Out-breeding

It is interesting to compare the intelligence of those negro criminals whose parents were of similar faith with that of those whose parents were of different faiths. We have two hundred and three negroes whose parents were of like faiths, and forty-seven whose parents were of different faiths.

Letter Grade	Negroes		Whites	
	Percentage From Same Religious Sources	Percentage From Different Sources	Percentage From Same Sources	Percentage From Different Sources
E	39.0	36.2	7.9	6.8
D	14.8	21.3	9.5	4.5
C—	24.6	23.4	20.1	6.8
C	8.8	14.9	26.4	27.2
C+	7.4	4.2	19.6	18.2
B	4.4	---	11.1	20.5
A	.1	---	5.3	15.9

Here we find another interesting reversal. With the whites, the products of out-breeding show a decided superiority in ability to make high scores, while the negro products of religious out-breeding are quite inferior to the products of in-breeding.

Tentative Conclusions:

1. The Catholics seem to be more intelligent than the other denominational groups among the negro criminals, in this respect the facts being quite opposed to those concerning white criminals.

2. In the case of all the religious groups, with the exception of the Agnostics, the migratory criminals seem more intelligent than do the home grown ones.

3. In terms of literacy, the negro Catholics seem superior to the other religious or demoninational groups, these facts being quite the opposite of those found in the case of white criminals.

4. Baptists and Methodists supply nearly all the negro recidivists, this being quite contrary to the case of the white criminals, where Catholics and Agnostics supply most of the recidivists.

5. Among negro criminals the products of religious out-breeding seem quite inferior to the products of religious in-breeding, these facts being the opposite of those found in the case of white criminals.

CHAPTER 26

LENGTH OF INCARCERATION

This report deals with 248 cases of negro criminals in the Maryland State Penitentiary.

For convenience it will be well to agree upon time-group symbols, the following list of temporal symbols being the one previously adopted and used in this series of reports on criminal populations.

Time Group	Years of Imprisonment
1	Six months, or less
2	Seven months to one year
3	Thirteen months to two years
4	Twenty-five months to three years
5	Thirty-seven months to five years
6	More than five years

If we now tabulate the percentage of each time group found listed in each Army Alpha letter grade, we will get the following table.

Alpha Letter Grade	Time Groups					
	(1)	(2)	(3)	(4)	(5)	(6)
E	50.0	25.6	35.2	42.3	37.5	26.9
D	24.2	23.0	19.6	7.6	2.5	23.0
C—	15.1	25.6	23.5	26.9	32.5	26.9
C	6.0	15.3	11.7	---	17.5	11.4
C+	6.0	10.2	3.9	11.4	5.0	7.6
B	---	---	3.9	11.4	5.0	3.8
A	1.5	---	1.9	---	---	---
No. of cases	66	39	51	26	40	26

A casual inspection of the above table seems to indicate that it is impossible to assume that ability to make high scores in the Alpha test decreases with length of incarceration,—at least within the limits of this particular prison population. The largest percentage of failures occurs in the first time group, that group that has been incarcerated less than six months.

Perhaps the point can be made clearer if we cast the six time groups into two divisions, those who have been incarcerated two years or less, and those who have been incarcerated more than two years. This gives us the following table.

Alpha Letter	Percentage two years or less (156 cases)	Percentage more than two years (92 cases)
E	39.1	35.8
D	21.1	9.7
C—	20.5	29.3
C	10.2	10.8
C+	6.4	7.6
B	1.2	6.5
A	.6	---

The above table shows a decided superiority on the part of the group that has been imprisoned more than two years. The long term men show 45.5% making a score less than C— in the Alpha test, while the short term men show a percentage of 60.2% making a score less than C—. The long term men show a percentage of 14.1% making a score greater than C, while the short term men show only 8.2% making a score greater than C.

Tentative Conclusions:

1. In the case of negro criminals in the Maryland State Penitentiary, the greatest percentage of failures in the Alpha test are to be found in that time group that has served less than six months in prison.

2. The group that has been incarcerated for more than two years is able to make a decidedly better showing in the Alpha test than the group incarcerated less than two years.

3. On the superficial face of the above data it seems impossible to hold that length of incarceration in the average American prison causes deterioration in ability to make scores in the Alpha test.

4. These results agree completely with similar results found in the case of white criminals incarcerated in the same prison.

Chapter 27

OCCUPATIONAL CONCOMITANTS

The various data for this report were obtained from the negro male population of the Ohio State Penitentiary, the Ohio State Reformatory, the Illinois State Penitentiary at Joliet, the Illinois State Reformatory at Pontiac, the Maryland State Penitentiary, and the New Jersey State Penitentiary. In this report no occupational group will be considered which has fewer than sixteen representatives, while the total number of cases involved is 1,080. The Alpha letter grades will be used in at least one of the tables, it being assumed that all readers are now familiar with these grades.

1. *The Alpha Scores of the Occupational Groups.*

The following table gives the percentage of each occupational group making each letter grade. The occupational groups are arranged in order of ability to make high grades in the Alpha test.

Table I

	E	D	C—	C	C+	B	A	No. of Cases
Mechanics	6.2	---	37.5	25.0	18.7	6.2	6.2	16
Barbers	27.6	6.9	24.2	20.7	3.4	17.2	---	29
Tailors	17.6	20.6	20.6	23.6	11.8	2.9	2.9	34
Chauffeurs	15.8	18.3	23.2	26.8	9.7	4.9	1.2	82
Cooks	28.6	11.7	19.5	27.3	6.5	6.5	---	77
Firemen	36.4	15.2	27.3	9.1	12.1	---	---	33
Porters	19.1	15.9	29.8	23.4	10.6	1.1	---	94
Miners	20.8	8.3	54.3	8.3	4.2	4.2	---	24
Teamsters	12.9	27.4	37.1	14.5	8.1	---	---	62
Waiters	20.0	14.3	28.6	27.2	7.1	1.4	---	70
Masons	31.2	6.2	37.5	18.7	6.2	---	---	16
Farmers	51.0	15.7	17.7	9.8	5.9	---	---	51
Laborers	38.6	19.9	23.6	13.0	3.2	1.6	---	492

The table indicates that the first six occupations in order of intelligence are those which require skill and an apprenticeship, the occupation requiring the longest period of apprenticeship standing at the head of the list. The other seven occupations, with the exception of masons, do not require great skill, or a long period of learning, while the most unskilled group stands at the bottom of the list. It might be of assistance to the reader to learn that there were four negroes among all the cases examined who reported themselves as being clerks. Of these four, two made a letter grade of A, one a letter grade of B, and the fourth a letter grade of C. There was one negro who reported himself as being a draftsman, and he made

a letter grade of A. These facts do not disagree in any way
with similar information concerning the relative intelligence
of individuals engaged in civil occupations, and would seem to
indicate that civil occupations represented among the negro
criminals are represented by the same relative intelligence as in
civil life.

2. *The Relative Chronological Age of Occupational Groups.*
    Chronological age will be reported in groups, the temporal
limits of which have been agreed upon and followed in previous reports. The following table gives the percentage of
each occupational group occuring in each chronological age
group, the number of cases in each occupational group being
identical with the table reported above.

Table II

	15-20	21-25	26-30	31-35	36-40	41-50	50-X
Mechanics	12.5	50.0	6.2	25.0	___	6.2	
Barbers	6.9	6.9	27.6	24.2	24.2	6.9	3.4
Tailors	12.1	24.2	33.4	15.1	9.1	6.1	
Chauffeurs	15.5	44.0	21.4	11.9	4.8	2.4	
Cooks	5.2	24.6	18.2	11.7	18.2	16.9	5.2
Firemen	2.9	32.4	17.7	17.7	11.8	11.8	5.9
Porters	23.2	23.2	20.0	14.7	9.5	8.4	1.1
Miners	8.3	33.4	8.3	16.7	12.5	16.7	4.2
Teamsters	12.9	27.4	14.5	25.8	11.3	6.4	1.6
Waiters	7.0	28.2	15.5	24.0	15.5	9.9	
Masons		6.7	20.0	26.6	26.6	20.0	
Farmers	17.6	23.6	27.4	13.7	2.0	13.7	2.0
Laborers	12.5	24.9	20.2	16.5	11.6	11.0	3.3

An inspection of the table indicates that mechanics, tailors,
and chauffeurs, all three being more skilled occupations, show
an unusually large percentage of very young individuals and
no one over fifty years of age. The less skilled occupations
seem to possess a relatively smaller percentage of young individuals, and a relatively larger percentage of older individuals. Perhaps this point can be made more clear if we report
only two groups, one consisting of the six skilled occupations,
and the other consisting of the seven unskilled occupations.

Table III

	Skilled Group	Unskilled Group
15-20	9.5	13.2
21-25	31.1	25.0
26-30	21.2	19.4
31-35	15.0	17.7
36-40	11.7	11.4
41-50	8.8	10.8
50-x	2.6	2.5

The above arrangement indicates that the unskilled group possesses a relatively larger percentage of the very youngest men, while the skilled group possesses a larger percentage of individuals twenty-five years old or less, but it does not appear that there are any especially significant age concomitants in the above occupation group. Occupational groups are not especially well marked and established among negroes.

3. *Occupational Groups and Types of Crime.*

The percentages of negroes committing crimes against the person and crimes against the property are in the ration of 33 to 67 respectively. If in any occupational group no other influence except the law of probability is acting as a distribution factor, we should expect to find the relative percentages of the two classes of crime in that group to be in the ratio of 33 to 67. The following table shows the actual proportion of each occupational group committing crimes against the person and crimes against the property.

Table IV

	Against Person Chance ratio 33	Against Property Chance ratio 67
Mechanics	6	94
Barbers	38	62
Tailors	21	79
Chauffeurs	27	73
Cooks	31	69
Firemen	44	56
Porters	23	77
Miners	46	54
Teamsters	29	71
Waiters	31	69
Masons	33	67
Farmers	33	67
Laborers	37	63

The above table indicates a tendency of the more skilled occupations to be composed of individuals who are more inclined to commit crimes against property than the law of probability would demand. This is not true in the case of barbers, but barbers come into very intimate contact with the person, which probably explains their case. If we also report the occupational groups once more in two groups only, it will be seen that there is at least a slight tendency of the more skilled occupational groups to commit crimes against property to a greater extent than in the case of unskilled groups.

Table V

	Against Person	Against Property
Skilled group	30	70
Unskilled group	34	66

Tentative Conclusions:

1. The occupations requiring considerable training or apprenticeship have been engaged in by relatively more intelligent criminals, while occupations requiring little training or apprenticeship have been engaged in by relatively less intelligent criminals. This conclusion is in agreement with the well known facts concerning the relative intelligence of occupational groups in civil life.

2. There is a slight tendency on the part of occupations requiring considerable training or apprenticeship to be composed of a relatively larger percentage of individuals twenty-five years old or less.

3. There is a tendency for the more highly trained occupational groups to commit crimes against property in a larger proportion than is the case with the less trained groups.

CHAPTER 28

HEIGHT AND WEIGHT

1. *Height Groups*

This report deals with 248 negro cases in the Maryland State Penitentiary. For convenience we will use the same classification of height groups as used in previous reports.

Height Group	Height in Inches
1	60-61
2	62-63
3	64-65
4	66-67
5	68-69
6	70-71
7	72-X

A percentage distribution of the various crime groups in terms of height groups shows a tendency on the part of sex criminals to be found among the taller groups, but there seems to be very little further relation between type of crime committed and amount of physical stature.

	1	2	3	4	5	6	7
Fraud 7 cases	14.2	_ _ _	14.2	42.8	14.2	14.2	_ _ _
Force 68 cases	5.9	2.9	25.3	35.8	16.4	7.4	5.9
Thievery 57 cases	3.7	9.2	29.6	29.6	20.3	5.7	1.8
Physical injury 98 cases	2.0	10.4	13.5	41.6	23.9	7.2	1.0
Dereliction 3 cases	_ _ _	33.3	_ _ _	33.3	33.3	_ _ _	_ _ _
Sex 15 cases	_ _ _	_ _ _	31.2	25.0	25.0	12.5	6.2

Some of the crime groups show a clear distinction between the home-grown and the migratory individuals in terms of height. For example, in the force group there is a larger percentage of tall individuals and a smaller percentage of short individuals to be found in the migratory group.

Height Group	Percentage of Home-Grown (33 cases)	Percentage of Migratory (34 cases)
1	9.0	2.9
2	6.0	_ _ _
3	24.2	26.4
4	39.0	32.3
5	9.0	23.5
6	9.0	5.8
7	_ _ _	8.8

In the case of the physical injury group none of the very short men and none of the very tall men are to be found in the migratory group.

Height Group	Percentage of Home-Grown (55 cases)	Percentage of Migratory (42 cases)
1	3.4	--
2	13.7	5.2
3	13.7	13.1
4	34.4	52.6
5	29.3	15.7
6	3.4	13.1
7	1.7	--

In the thievery group there is again a tendency for the migratory criminals to be taller on the average than are the home-grown criminals.

Height Group	Percentage of Home-Grown (26 cases)	Percentage of Migratory (31 cases)
1	7.6	--
2	11.5	7.8
3	34.5	25.0
4	23.0	35.7
5	19.2	21.4
6	3.8	7.1
7	--	3.5

A case distribution of the sex group shows a clear tendency for the migratory individuals to be taller than the home-grown ones.

Height Group	Cases of Home-Grown	Cases of Migratory
1	--	--
2	--	--
3	3	2
4	1	3
5	1	3
6	--	2
7	1	--

2. *Weight Groups*

For convenience we will also use the classification of weight groups previously adopted.

Weight Group	Pounds
1	X-120
2	121-130
3	131-140
4	141-150
5	151-160
6	161-170
7	171-X

A percentage distribution of the six crime groups in terms of weight groups indicates a tendency for the crimes of force and of physical injury to be committed by the heavier men, while sex crimes and crimes of thievery are not committed by so large a percentage of heavy men.

	1	2	3	4	5	6	7
Fraud 7 cases	_ _	12.5	37.5	12.5	12.5	_ _	25.0
Force 68 cases	7.4	10.4	23.8	16.4	20.8	8.9	11.9
Thievery 57 cases	1.7	16.0	26.7	26.7	14.2	7.1	7.1
Physical injury 98 cases	5.0	8.7	25.0	18.7	16.2	15.0	11.2
Dereliction 3 cases	_ _	_ _	one	two	_ _	_ _	_ _
Sex 15 cases	16.6	_ _	16.6	33.3	16.6	8.3	8.3

Tentative Conclusions:

1. In terms of the 248 negro cases in the Maryland State Penitentiary there seems to be no outstanding relation between type of crime committed and amount of physical stature, the greater tallness of the sex group being the only seeming exception.

2. In the case of the force group, the thievery group, and the sex group, the migratory individuals show a greater tendency to tallness than do the home-grown criminals, exception to this rule being found only in the physical injury group.

3. Crimes of force and of physical injury show a tendency to be committed by heavier men, while sex crimes and crimes of thievery are not committed by so large a percentage of heavy men.

CHAPTER 29

SEASONAL DISTRIBUTION

This report deals with the criminal population of the Maryland State Penitentiary. A direct comparison of the percentage of negro criminals committing crime during the various months of the year can be made with the white criminals in the same prison.

Name of Month	Percentage of cases among Negro Criminals (248 cases)	Percentage of cases among White criminals (255 cases)
January	8.4	9.0
February	10.4	6.6
March	7.6	9.0
April	7.2	8.2
May	10.4	6.6
June	4.8	8.6
July	6.4	6.6
August	5.6	6.2
September	9.2	9.0
October	6.8	7.5
November	8.0	10.9
December	14.5	11.7

Just as in the case of the whites there seems to be a diminished criminal activity during the warm summer months, but an increased criminal activity during the beginning of the fall and again during the beginning of the winter. These variations are no more significant, however, in the case of the negroes than they are in the case of the whites.

The distribution of cases in terms of Alpha letter grades and the months in which the crimes were committed seems to indicate no very definite relation between criminal mental levels and the season.

	E	D	C—	C	C+	B	A
January	9	_	5	5	1	1	_
February	12	2	8	1	3	_	_
March	6	6	4	1	1	1	_
April	8	4	2	3	1	_	_
May	12	2	5	3	3	1	_
June	5	3	3	1	_	_	_
July	4	2	6	2	1	1	_
August	6	4	1	1	2	_	_
September	6	4	7	2	1	2	1
October	6	2	6	2	1	_	_
November	8	4	6	2	_	_	_
December	12	9	8	3	1	2	1

A distribution of cases in terms of crime type and season does not indicate to any remarkable extent a seasonal influence on any particular type of crime, with two possible exceptions. The cases of fraud are clustered almost entirely in the winter months, while an unusually large number of cases of thievery occur also in the month of December. On account of the small number of cases being considered these two tendencies can merely be referred to.

	Fraud	Force	Thievery	Physical Injury	Dereliction	Sex
January	2	10	4	3	–	2
February	2	8	4	11	–	1
March	1	9	3	5	–	1
April	–	4	6	6	1	1
May	1	4	6	12	–	3
June	–	6	1	5	–	–
July	–	2	2	11	–	1
August	–	5	3	6	–	–
September	–	4	6	10	1	2
October	–	3	7	5	–	2
November	–	6	2	9	1	2
December	1	7	13	15	–	–

Tentative Conclusions:

1. In the case of negro criminals confined in the Maryland State Penitentiary there is a seasonal distribution of criminal activity quite similar to that previously reported for whites, and this seasonal distribution offers very little obvious significance.

2. There is an equal lack of obvious significance in a correlation of season and Alpha letter grades.

3. There is no obvious connection between season and type of crime committed, except in the possible cases of fraud and thievery.

CHAPTER 30

CHRONOLOGICAL AGE

1. *The Gross Distribution of Age Groups*

This report deals with 1254 cases of negro criminals incarcerated in the penitentiaries of Ohio, IIllinois, Maryland, and New Jersey, and also in the state reformatories of Ohio and Illinois. For convenience the following age group classification will be used.

Age Group	Years
1	15-20
2	21-25
3	26-30
4	31-35
5	36-40
6	41-50
7	51-X

A direct comparison of the 1254 negro criminals with 3932 white criminals previously reported makes a good point of departure for this report.

Age Group	Percentage of Total (Negroes) (1254 cases)	Percentage of Total (Whites) (3932 cases)
1	12.9	20.9
2	27.1	26.0
3	18.4	17.7
4	17.1	13.8
5	11.4	9.4
6	10.6	8.6
7	2.5	3.6

The youthfulness of both groups of criminals commands our attention. Approximately 47% of the white criminal population are twenty-five years of age or less, while 40% of the negro criminals fall under the same category. In the case of the latter, there is a progressive gain (over white criminals) in the percentages of the groups composed of men from twenty-five to fifty years of age. The percentages, however, of both groups of young men less than forty years old are approximately the same, as almost 88% of the white criminals and 87% of the negro criminals are included under the forty-year-old age limit. But, on the whole, the negroes as a group are slightly older than the whites.

But geographical concomitants also enter in. Let us consider the home-grown and the migratory groups of negroes. The term "home-grown" will be applied to those individuals who are incarcerated in their native states, while the term "migratory" will be applied to those incarcerated outside their native states. The comparison of the two groups is as follows:

Age Group	Percentage At Home (390 cases)	Percentage Away (961 cases)
1	16.6	11.2
2	30.7	25.0
3	19.0	18.1
4	14.8	18.6
5	6.2	13.1
6	10.1	11.1
7	2.0	2.5

The migratory group shows a less percentage of the more youthful cases and a larger percentage of the older cases.

2. The Age of Type-Groups

In this chapter all crimes will be grouped under seven types: fraud, force, thievery, physical injury, social dereliction, statutory offenses, and sex, according to the classification agreed upon in Chapter 5, Pages 58-59.

Since the distributions of the seven types of crime show marked variations from similar ones of white criminals, a comparison of the two groups will be given in each case. Let us begin with the fraud group.

Age Group	Percentage of Home (Negroes) 12 cases	Percentage Away (Negroes) 23 cases	Percentage of Total (Negroes) 35 cases	Percentage of Home (Whites) 181 cases	Percentage Away (Whites) 150 cases	Percentage of Total (Whites) 331 cases
1	41.6	13.0	22.8	19.1	7.6	13.8
2	16.6	13.0	14.2	24.5	15.2	20.2
3	8.3	13.0	11.4	15.3	17.1	16.1
4	16.6	30.4	25.7	13.7	22.8	17.9
5	- - -	21.7	14.2	10.0	12.7	11.1
6	16.6	8.6	11.4	14.2	15.2	14.7
7	- - -	- - -	- - -	3.3	9.5	6.1

The white group has the larger range of ages, covering the maximum distribution, and this group is composed of older men than the negro group. In the case of the former, one should note the small percentage of migratory individuals in the first age group, and the large percent in the fourth and seventh age groups. In the case of the negroes, one should notice the large percentage of home-grown individuals in the first age group, and also the large percent of migratory men in the fourth group.

Comparing the two groups, we see that the negro fraudulent migratory group is representative of the general distribution of the criminal group (older than the home-grown group), while the white migratory group is quite the opposite. Even the home-grown group contains large percentages in the upper ranges of years.

The white fraud group is composed of more mature men than the negro fraud group. In fact, the former is an older group (considering the general distribution of the white criminals), while the latter is fairly characteristic of the total distribution.

The force group is distributed as follows:

Age Group	Percentage of Home (Negroes) 149 cases	Percentage Away (Negroes) 363 cases	Percentage of Total (Negroes) 512 cases	Percentage of Home (Whites) 960 cases	Percentage Away (Whites) 582 cases	Percentage of Total (Whites) 1542 cases
1	23.4	15.1	17.5	26.7	21.6	24.9
2	35.5	28.3	30.4	29.5	31.6	30.3
3	18.7	17.6	17.9	17.2	18.4	17.6
4	11.4	17.6	15.8	15.2	12.2	14.1
5	3.3	12.6	9.9	6.8	8.1	7.3
6	6.7	6.3	6.4	3.3	5.8	4.2
7	.6	2.2	1.7	1.3	2.2	1.7

Here one sees that both groups are composed largely of younger men those of the former type. More than 55% of the whites are twenty-five years of age or younger, while 50% of the negroes are of the same age. It is also noteworthy that in the case of the negroes, in the lower range of years, the differences in percentages between the migratory and home-grown groups are slight, while, in the case of the whites, the differences are somewhat greater. As for the upper range of years, the differences are slight in both cases. But here, as in many cases, the old men are incarcerated outside their native state.

The thievery group is distributed as follows:

Age Group	Percentage of Home (Negroes) 76 cases	Percentage Away (Negroes) 166 cases	Percentage of Total (Negroes) 242 cases	Percentage of Home (Whites) 572 cases	Percentage Away (Whites) 420 cases	Percentage of Total (Whites) 992 cases
1	13.1	14.4	14.0	30.0	22.4	26.8
2	35.5	33.7	34.2	30.0	26.3	28.5
3	23.6	16.2	18.5	14.5	18.2	16.2
4	11.8	19.8	16.5	11.7	12.1	12.0

5	3.9	6.6	5.7	7.6	10.0	8.7
6	9.2	7.2	7.8	5.0	7.9	6.3
7	2.6	1.8	2.8	1.9	3.0	2.4

The negro group is somewhat older than the white group. The latter is younger than the force group as far as home cases are concerned, but the migration element is not quite so young. The negro thievery group is somewhat older than the force group in regard to home cases, but younger in so far as the migration group is taken into consideration. Also, nearly one-third of the white home cases are twenty years or less, while not one-half that proportion is found in the corresponding age group of negro criminals. It is also significant that the negro **migration** group has a smaller percentage of old men than the home group. On the whole the thievery group is somewhat younger than the criminal group taken as a whole.

The following is the distribution of statutory offenses:

Age Group	Percentage of Home (Negroes) 13 cases	Percentage Away (Negroes) 39 cases	Percentage of Total (Negroes) 52 cases	Percentage of Home (Whites) 110 cases	Percentage Away (Whites) 77 cases	Percentage of Total (Whites) 187 cases
1	15.4	2.5	5.7	34.8	17.1	27.7
2	23.0	35.8	32.6	33.0	42.8	36.6
3	15.4	12.8	13.4	14.7	17.1	15.5
4	30.7	25.6	26.9	7.3	4.3	6.1
5	7.5	12.8	11.5	4.6	8.6	6.1
6	7.5	10.2	9.6	4.6	7.1	5.5
7	---	---	---	1.0	2.8	1.6

As in the case of the fraud group, one notes the greater range of ages in the white group. Over 60% are twenty-five or less. On the other hand, nearly 50% of the negro group are over thirty years of age, while approximately 20% of the white group are above this age, in spite of the fact that the latter has a few of the oldest men (Group 7) to "pull up" the total percentage. The group of negroes seems to be fairly typical of the general distribution. One noteworthy exception is that of the second age group in the migratory division, when the percentage exceeds that of the corresponding group of home cases. Here, too, one discovers that it is the mature man who has ventured from his native state to commit his crime.

Let us now examine the physical injury group.

Age Group	Percentage of Home (Negroes) 112 cases	Percentage Away (Negroes) 269 cases	Percentage of Total (Negroes) 381 cases	Percentage of Home (Whites) 333 cases	Percentage Away (Whites) 187 cases	Percentage of Total (Whites) 520 cases
1	7.1	5.9	6.2	10.0	7.1	9.1
2	25.8	16.7	19.6	14.5	17.0	15.4
3	19.6	20.8	20.4	23.7	21.7	23.1
4	18.7	17.8	18.0	16.3	17.0	16.6
5	9.8	17.4	15.2	14.2	10.6	13.0
6	15.1	18.5	17.5	13.6	16.5	14.6
7	3.5	2.2	2.6	7.4	9.4	8.1

In the above group there is a lack of youth and a preponderance of maturity in years. It is distinctly an older group, influenced somewhat by the fact that older men seem more inclined than younger men to commit such crimes.

The social dereliction group is distributed as follows:

Age Group	Percentage of Home (Negroes) 5 cases	Percentage Away (Negroes) 10 cases	Percentage of Total (Negroes) 15 cases	Percentage of Home (Whites) 53 cases	Percentage Away (Whites) 66 cases	Percentage of Total (Whites) 119 cases
1	---	---	---	9.2	2.9	5.7
2	---	---	---	11.1	14.7	13.1
3	1	2	3	13.0	22.1	18.0
4	1	3	4	14.8	19.1	17.2
5	1	1	2	22.2	17.6	19.7
6	1	2	3	18.5	17.6	18.0
7	1	2	3	11.1	4.9	8.2

The small number of negro cases in this group renders a sound comparison with the white criminals impossible. However, we may note that the negroes are all over twenty-five years of age, while nearly 19% of the whites are twenty-five or less. This table is given for completeness in the study of chronological age.

The following is the distribution of the sex group:

Age Group	Percentage of Home (Negroes) 17 cases	Percentage Away (Negroes) 43 cases	Percentage of Total (Negroes) 60 cases	Percentage of Home (Whites) 170 cases	Percentage Away (Whites) 83 cases	Percentage of Total (Whites) 253 cases
1	29.4	9.3	15.0	12.6	3.4	9.4
2	23.5	16.2	18.3	20.4	11.2	17.2
3	5.8	20.9	16.6	16.2	19.1	17.6
4	17.6	11.6	13.3	8.4	19.1	12.1
5	17.6	11.6	13.3	13.2	12.3	13.3
6	5.8	20.9	16.6	21.6	23.6	22.3
7	---	9.3	6.6	6.6	11.2	8.2

Negroes between twenty-one and twenty-five years of age seem to be more prone to engage in sex crimes, while white men in the prime of life, between forty and fifty, are the ones most likely to commit these crimes. As in the case of physical injury, there are two chief periods of crime behavior, both of which are appropriately illustrated by the above cases. On the whole, the negro group is composed of younger men than the white group. The largest percentage in the whole distribution is claimed by Group 1 of the negro home group. But old men predominate in the migratory group, the differences between the home and migration elements of the negro groups being by far the greater.

3. *The Age of Recidivists and First Offenders*

In this portion of the problem on chronological age, the discussion will be confined to data from the Maryland and New Jersey State Penitentiaries (502 cases). One should keep in mind that the first offender is not necessarily a younger individual than the recidivist. The difference between the two is not one that can be stated in terms of time. It is probably due to an emotional difference, the expression of which will have to await further psychological development.

The distribution of the seven types of crime will not be given because of the small number of cases found in some groups. Instead, the physical injury and sex crimes have been combined into one group known as "crimes against person," and the five remaining groups into one classification known as "crimes against property."

The following is the distribution of crimes against person:

Age Group	Home First (57 cases)	Home Recidivists (20 cases)	Away First (91 cases)	Away Recidivists (22 cases)
1	12.2	15.0	5.4	9.0
2	28.0	15.0	24.1	22.7
3	19.2	10.0	24.1	9.0
4	19.2	15.0	13.1	31.8
5	7.0	15.0	16.4	18.2
6	10.5	30.0	13.1	---
7	3.5	---	3.2	9.0

Here the reader finds that the first offenders predominate the lower age levels, with the home group in the lead, while the recidivists are more numerous in the upper age levels, with approximately equal percentages of men thirty years old or less.

In the home group, the first offenders are more numerous than the recidivists, nearly 60% of the first offenders committing their crimes before the age of thirty. Likewise, in the migratory group over 50% of the first offenders engage in criminal behavior before the age of thirty.

The distribution of the total first offenders and recidivists of the same group is as follows:

Age Group	Percentage First (148 cases)	Percentage Recidivists (42 cases)
1	8.1	11.9
2	25.6	19.0
3	22.2	9.5
4	15.5	23.8
5	12.9	16.6
6	12.1	14.2
7	3.3	4.7

Here we see more clearly the differences between the two groups.

Let us examine the distribution of the crimes against property.

Age Group	Home First (58 cases)	Home Recidivists (53 cases)	Away First (108 cases)	Away Recidivists (86 cases)
1	13.7	5.6	12.0	3.4
2	48.2	32.0	35.1	29.0
3	24.1	30.1	18.5	19.7
4	5.2	24.5	18.5	25.5
5	1.7	3.7	7.4	10.4
6	3.4	1.8	4.6	9.3
7	3.4	1.8	3.7	2.3

At a glance, one sees the clustering in the second age level. Here, too, one finds that the first offenders are largely younger men than the recidivists. The migratory recidivists are the oldest men in the group.

The following is the total distribution of the same group:

Age Group	Percentage First (166 cases)	Percentage Recidivists (139 cases)
1	12.6	4.3
2	39.7	30.2
3	20.4	23.7
4	13.2	25.1
5	5.4	7.9
6	4.2	6.4
7	3.6	2.1

Here the reader may see the differences to better advantage.

It might be desirable to examine the distribution of the total first offenders and recidivists, given as follows:

Age Group	Home First (115 cases)	Home Recidivists (73 cases)	Away First (199 cases)	Away Recidivists (108 cases)
1	15.2	18.2	8.6	4.6
2	37.2	24.3	28.7	27.7
3	21.1	21.9	24.8	17.5
4	11.8	19.5	15.3	26.8
5	4.2	6.0	11.0	12.0
6	6.7	8.5	8.1	7.4
7	3.3	1.2	3.3	3.7

In all cases, Group 2 claims the largest percentage of individuals. The distribution differs more greatly in the lower age levels, approaching proximity in the upper ranges of years. The total distribution of the entire group is as follows·

Age Group	Percentage First (314 cases)	Percentage Recidivists (181 cases)
1	11.0	10.5
2	31.8	26.3
3	23.5	19.4
4	14.0	23.6
5	8.5	9.4
6	7.6	7.8
7	3.3	2.6

The first offenders are not by any means distinctly younger than the recidivists. Such differences as exist are certainly not extremely significant.

4. *The Age of Criminals from the Southern, Borderline, and Northern and Western Groups of States.*

In this discussion, the southern states will include Virginia, Tennessee, North Carolina, South Carolina, Georgia, Florida, Alabama, Mississippi, and Louisiana; the borderline, Maryland, West Virginia, Kentucky, Arkansas, and Texas; the northern and western, the rest of the states. The distribution of approximately 1,300 cases is as follows:

Age Group	Percentage Southern (480 cases)	Percentage Borderline (282 cases)	Percentage Northern & Western (492 cases)
1	12.4	8.8	15.4
2	25.9	28.4	27.0
3	17.0	20.2	19.4
4	19.2	16.3	16.5
5	12.4	12.4	8.6
6	10.1	12.0	10.0
7	2.6	1.4	2.9

The North and West lead in youthful criminals, while the Borderline produces the greater (slightly) number of mature individuals. The Southern criminal group seems to follow very closely the gross distribution. This suggests the influence of the southern negroes in determining the total distribution.

Tentative Conclusions:

1. To the extent that we may make conclusions from the above data, we are justified in assuming that negro prison populations are somewhat older than white prison populations. The marked exceptions occur in the crimes of fraud and sex, in which two cases the negro offenders are markedly younger than the white offenders committing the same crimes.

2. As in the case of whites, negro recidivists are not necessarily older than are first offenders.

3. There is a slight tendency for the northern and western states to produce a larger percentage of very young criminals than is the case of the southern or borderline states. The difference, however, is not large enough to be important.

CHAPTER 31

SOME MARITAL CONCOMITANTS

The various data comprising the basis of this report were gathered from 250 negro men prisoners in the Maryland State Penitentiary.

There were in this group 139 single men, and 99 married men, so that the proportion of single and married men is 60 to 40. If in any crime group the Law of Probability alone determines the relative proportion of single and married men, that proportion should be 60 to 40. If probability is not the sole cause determining proportions, then the proportion of single to married men will be greater or less than 60 to 40.

1. *Gross Comparison of the Intelligence of Single and Married Men.*

The following table gives the percentage of single and married men making each letter grade in the Alpha test, the table also including a comparison with the single and married white criminals in the same prison, the numbers of negroes and whites being approximately the same.

Comparative Intelligence of Single and Married Men

| | Negroes | | Whites | |
	Percentage Of Single	Percentage Of Married	Percentage Of Single	Percentage Of Married
E	38.8	38.4	6.3	8.6
D	12.9	22.2	7.0	7.5
C—	23.0	25.2	18.1	9.7
C	12.9	5.0	29.3	24.7
C+	7.9	5.0	20.3	21.5
B	2.9	4.0	14.0	14.0
A	1.4	---	4.9	14.0

The above table indicates that the married negroes are somewhat less intelligent than the single negroes, while in the case of the whites the opposite is the case.

2. *Migratory Concomitants.*

The following table gives a comparison, both in the case of negroes and whites, of the percentages of both single and married men imprisoned in the home state, or outside the home state, making each letter grade in the Alpha test. There are 69 cases of home grown single negroes, 68 cases of migratory single negroes, 53 cases of home grown married negroes, and 43 cases of migratory married negroes. The percentages in the case of the white criminals are quoted directly from Chapter 15, Page 155.

Comparison of Home Grown and Migratory Types
Negroes

	E	D	C—	C	C+	B	A
Single At Home	33.4	17.4	23.2	15.9	7.2	2.9	---
Single Away	45.6	7.3	22.0	10.3	8.8	2.9	2.9
Married At Home	35.8	24.6	28.3	5.7	3.8	1.9	---
Married Away	37.2	21.0	23.2	4.6	7.0	7.0	---

Whites

	E	D	C—	C	C+	B	A
Single At Home	6.7	9.4	18.9	36.5	17.5	9.4	1.3
Single Away	5.8	4.5	17.3	21.7	23.2	18.8	8.7
Married At Home	11.7	7.8	9.8	25.5	27.4	13.7	3.9
Married Away	4.7	7.1	9.5	23.8	14.3	14.3	26.2

According to the above table the migratory criminals are uniformly more capable of making scores in the Alpha test than are the home grown criminals. But the negroes differ from the whites in that migratory single negroes constitute the superior negro group, while the migratory married white men constitute the superior white group. The sociological factors functioning in the case of negro criminals seem to vary markedly from those functioning in the case of white criminals.

3. *Marital State and Types of Crime.*

"The writer suggests that the seventy-two crimes, for purposes of comparison, be classified into seven groups as follows: (1) Obtaining property through deception and fraud, known legally as forgery, embezzlement, false pretenses, conspiracy, confidence games, receiving stolen property, blackmail, counterfeiting, and uttering of fradulent checks. (2) Obtaining property through force, known legally as robbery, burglary, assault to rob, breaking and entering, entering to commit felony, burglary and larceny, safe blowing, attempted burglary, kidnapping, child stealing, housebreaking, attempt to rob, and burglary of inhabited dwelling. (3) Obtaining property through common thievery, known legally as larceny, pocket picking, vehicle taking, horse stealing and automobile stealing. (4) Statutory offenses, known legally as unlawful use of motor vehicle, illegal sale of drugs, illegal sale or possession of intoxicating beverages, carrying concealed weapons, unlawful use of explosives, operating motor vehicle without owner's consent, violating automobile law, having burglar tools, concealing weapons to aid escape, escaping prison and removing railroad property. (5) Crimes of physical injury, known legally as murder, maiming, manslaughter, assault to murder, accessory to murder, cutting, shooting or stabbing to kill or wound; arson and malicious destruction of property. (6) Crimes of social dereliction, known legally as abandonment, desertion, vagrancy, begging, non-support, neglect of minor child, child abandonment, bigamy, lewdness, seduction, perjury, publishing of obscene writing, abduction, and receiving earnings of prostitute. (7) Sex crimes known legally as rape, sodomy, indecent liberty with child, incest, assault to rape, crime against nature, assault to commit crime against nature, crime against child, adultery, and carnal abuse."*

In this section, however, we will not consider crimes of social dereliction, since such crimes, by classification, would be committed chiefly by married men. Statutory cases will also be omitted since there are too few cases to be considered.

In the remainder of this article we will deal with proportions only. The reader is asked to remember that the proportion determined by probability is 60 to 40, and that variation from proportion indicates the influence of other causal factors.

The following table gives the proportion of single and married men found in each crime group, the proportions of whites being reported from Chapter 15, Page 156, for comparative purposes.

Marital State and Type of Crime

	Negroes		Whites	
	Single Men	Married Men	Single Men	Married Men
Fraud	14	86	35	65
Force	73	27	69	31
Thievery	48	52	69	31
Physical Inj.	61	39	56	44
Sex	50	50	60	40

In the above table the significant variations from probability occur in the Fraud group, both in the case of negroes and whites. In the case of both negroes and whites the single men are more disposed to commit crimes of Force than probability would require. In the case of Thievery, married negroes are more likely than are white criminals to be found in this group. Married negroes are more likely to commit

---

*Journal of Criminal Law and Criminology, Volume XV, Number 2, August, 1924.

sex crimes than are single negroes, while in the case of whites marriage seems to have no causal relation to sex crimes.

4. Marriage and Recidivism.

There are sixty-five cases of recidivism among the cases being considered in this paper. The proportion of single men to married men among the recidivists is exactly 60 to 40, marriage thus seeming to have no bearing on the tendency of criminals to repeat crime.

5. Literacy and Marriage.

The following table gives the proportion of single and married negroes in each literacy group.

Years in school	Number of cases	Proportion of Single	Proportion of Married
0-2	50	69	31
3-4	88	57	43
5-6	57	53	47
7-8	35	58	42
9-11	13	69	31
12-14	3	67	33
15-16	4	67	33

The only significant tendency in the above table is for the higher literacy groups to be composed of larger percentages of single negroes than the Law of Probability would lead us to expect. This is quite the opposite of the facts found in the case of white criminals, where the married men composed a larger proportion than expected of the higher literacy groups. However, the number of cases of negro criminals in the upper literacy groups is too few to give norms that can be taken very seriously.

Tentative Conclusions:

1. On the average, married negro criminals seem somewhat less intelligent than the unmarried, these tendencies being opposite to those of the white criminals in the same prison.

2. Among negro criminals the unmarried migratory men seem to be the superior group, while among white criminals in the same prison the married migratory men are very decidedly the superior group.

3. Crimes of Fraud are decidedly more likely to be committed by married negroes than by unmarried negroes, the tendency in this respect being even greater among negroes than among whites.

4. Crimes of Force are committed by an unusually large

proportion of unmarried negroes, this tendency also being similar to the facts found concerning white criminals.

5.   Among negroes crimes of thievery are committed by an unusually large proportion of unmarried men, while the opposite is the case among the white criminals.

6.   There seems to be no causal relation between the marital state and the commission of crimes of Physical Injury either among the negroes or the whites.

7.   Among negroes sex crimes are committed by a larger proportion of married men than probability would lead us to expect.

8.   There seems to be no causal relationship existing between the marital state and recidivism, as far as negroes are concerned.

9.   Among negro criminals there is a greater tendency for the higher literacy groups to be composed of unmarried men than probability would lead us to expect.

PART V

Women Criminals

CHAPTER 32

SOME WHITE WOMEN CRIMINALS

I have only 85 cases upon which to base the tables of this report, these cases at the time of examination residing in the Ohio Penitentiary for Women in Marysville, Ohio. It is true that 85 cases is a precariously small number upon which to base important tables, but it seems better that these cases be reported in such form that additional data from others parts of the country may be added in the future.

1. *Alpha Test Comparison with Men Criminals.*

There are no norms of women from the general population of Ohio with which to compare these 85 cases. It seems reasonable, however, that a comparison can be made with the 1418 cases of native-born white men criminals tested in the Ohio penitentiaries. A direct comparison gives the following results.

Alpha Scores	Native-born White Women Criminals (85 cases)	Native-born White Men Criminals in Ohio (1418 cases)
0- 9	---	3.4
10- 14	4.7	3.1
15- 19	5.9	2.9
20- 24	5.9	2.9
25- 34	16.4	8.5
35- 44	14.1	9.9
45- 59	14.1	15.0
60- 74	16.4	14.6
75- 89	13.0	12.3
90-104	4.7	10.9
105-119	3.5	7.3
120-134	1.2	4.2
135-149	---	2.8
150-212	---	2.2
Letter Grades		
E	4.7	6.5
D	11.8	6.0
C—	30.5	11.4
C	30.5	29.6
C+	17.7	23.2
B	4.7	11.5
A	---	5.0

If it is valid to compare a distribution of 85 cases with a distribution of 1418 cases, then we must presume, provided women in general are of equal intelligence with men, that the major women criminals in Ohio tend to score lower in the Alpha mental test than do the major men criminals in the same state. The difference seems most significant in the C— groups.

2. Geographical Concomitants.

In order that future additions may make the data more comparable with the more extended data on native-born white men criminals, the following tables give the percentages of the 51 cases born in Ohio and the 30 cases born outside the state of Ohio.

Alpha Scores	Women Criminals Born in Ohio (51 cases)	Women Criminals Born outside State of Ohio (30 cases)
0- 9	---	---
10- 14	2.0	10.1
15- 19	6.0	3.3
20- 24	7.8	3.3
25- 34	13.7	23.3
35- 44	21.6	3.3
45- 59	11.8	20.0
60- 74	17.8	16.6
75- 89	16.8	6.6
90-104	---	6.6
105-119	3.9	3.3
120-134	---	3.3
135-149	---	---
150-212	---	---
Letter Grades		
E	2.0	10.1
D	13.8	6.6
C—	25.3	26.6
C	29.6	36.6
C+	16.8	13.2
B	3.9	6.6
A	---	---

Significant differences in geographical concomitants as indicated by the above tables are not obvious.

3. Types of Crime

One is struck with the very restricted range in types of crime committed by women. A large penitentiary for men will have more than 50 types of crime well represented. These cases of women are distributed as follows: Adultery 5, Bigamy 1, Burglary 5, Child Neglect 11, Cutting or Shooting 1, Delinquency 22, Forgery 1, Fornication 10, Indecent Exposure 2, Larceny 17, Manslaughter 1, Peddling Dope 1, Pocket Picking 2, Robbery 5, Using Obscene Language 1. Approximately all of these 85 cases, however, are confined to child neglect, property crimes, and the common sex crimes. Sex crimes comprise approximately one-half of the total population of the prison. A large penitentiary for men would show little more than five per cent confined for the various sex crimes. This can in no way be construed as a reflection on the sex morality of women. This form of crime has an economic inducement in the case of women which is totally lacking in the case of men. A distribution of Alpha scores in terms of the three chief crimes represented in 85 cases gives the following results.

Alpha Scores	Child Neglect (11 cases)	Property Crimes (30 cases)	Sex Crimes (40 cases)
0- 9	---	---	---
10- 14	9.1	3.3	5.0
15- 19	9.1	3.3	5.0
20- 24	---	6.6	7.5
25- 34	18.2	16.6	17.5
35- 44	9.1	10.0	20.0
45- 59	27.2	20.0	7.5
60- 74	---	23.3	17.5
75- 89	9.1	13.3	12.5
90-104	---	---	5.0
105-119	18.2	---	2.5
120-134	---	3.3	---
135-149	---	---	---
150-212	---	---	---

Letter Grades			
E	9.1	3.3	5.0
D	9.1	9.9	12.5
C—	27.3	26.6	37.5
C	27.2	43.3	25.0
C+	9.1	13.3	17.5
B	18.2	3.3	2.5
A	---	---	---

4. *Comparative Literacy.*

Comparing these 85 cases with the literacy distribution of 3,932 cases of native-born white men criminals gives the following results.

Years in School	White Native-born Women Criminals (85 cases)	White Native-born Men Criminals (3932 cases)
0- 2	2.3	2.9
3- 4	11.8	16.6
5- 6	32.9	27.8
7- 8	40.0	36.4
9-11	11.8	11.6

12-14	1.2	3.8
15-16	---	.8

The group does not markedly vary from the more extensive group of men. It was found that men criminals ranked markedly below army norms in literacy.

5. *Literacy of Crime Groups.*

Years in School	Child Neglect (11 cases)	Property Crimes (30 cases)	Sex Crimes (40 cases)
0- 2	9.1	---	2.5
3- 4	---	23.3	7.5
5- 6	36.3	16.6	45.0
7- 8	54.5	43.3	32.5
9-11	---	16.6	10.0
12-14	---	---	2.5
15-16	---	---	---

The sex crimes are committed throughout nearly the entire literacy range, this being the chief distinction in terms of literacy of the three crime groups.

6. *Chronological Age Comparisons.*

Nothing is more precarious than to attempt to deal scientifically with chronological age reports of women. A direct comparison with 3,942 cases of native-born white men criminals gives the following distribution.

Age Group	White Native born Women Criminals (85 cases)	White Native born Men Criminals (3942 cases)
15-20	31.7	20.9
21-25	38.8	26.0
26-30	10.6	17.7
31-35	12.9	13.8
36-40	---	9.4
41-50	5.9	8.6
51-x	---	3.6

There is a marked clustering of women criminals in the lower ranges of chronological age as compared with men. This may be important and may be entirely the result of the universal desire of women to appear to be as young as possible.

7. *Chronological Age of Crime Groups.*

Age group	Child Neglect (11 cases)	Property Crimes (30 cases)	Sex Crimes (40 cases)
15-20	18.1	40.0	32.5
21-25	27.1	30.0	52.5
26-30	36.3	13.3	---
31-35	9.1	13.3	10.0
36-40	---	---	---

41-50	9.1	3.3	5.0
51-x	---	---	---

The child neglect cases tend to be older than the other crime groups, as would be the biological expectation. The sex crime group is so remarkably young as to merit additional comparison.

8. *Chronological Age Comparison with Native-born White Men Sex Criminals.*

Age Group	White Women Sex Criminals (40 cases)	White Men Sex Criminals (253 cases)
15-20	32.5	9.4
21-25	52.5	17.2
26-30	---	17.6
31-35	10.0	12.1
36-40	---	13.3
41-50	5.0	22.3
51-x	---	8.2

It is seen that 85% of the women sex criminals are only twenty-five years old or less. This is in marked contrast to the much greater chronological age levels of men sex criminals. Of course it is possible that these women lie more magnificently concerning their ages than do women criminals in general. Of that I can not say. Nevertheless it seems obvious that the economic reward for illegal sex behavior is much greater in the case of the lower chronological age levels. This would create a special inducement for criminal behavior at these early ages that would be lacking in the case of property crimes.

Tentative Conclusions:

1. The Alpha score distribution of the 85 cases considered shows lower tendencies as compared with the 1,418 cases of native-born white men criminals in the same state.

2. Geographical concomitants are not obvious.

3. There seems to be a marked restriction in the range of criminal behavior as compared with men, the range seeming to be confined to such crimes as child neglect, larceny, and the common sex crimes.

4. There is not a marked variation from similar men criminals in terms of literacy.

5. There is a distinct tendency for the women criminals to be segregated in the lower chronological age levels, this being especially true of the sex criminals.

6. The outstanding characteristic of the group as compared with similar men criminals is the large percentage of individuals confined for sex offenses.

Chapter 33

SOME NEGRO WOMEN CRIMINALS

I have among my papers data on 41 cases of negro women criminals in the Ohio Penitentiary for Women, Marysville, Ohio. This is a very small number of cases indeed, but they are being reported in order that further additions may be made from time to time.

1. *Alpha Test Comparison with Negro Men Criminals in the Same State.*

Making a direct comparison with 164 cases of negro men criminals in Ohio prisons, these give the following distribution:

Alpha Scores	Ohio Negro Men Criminals (164 cases)	Ohio Negro Women Criminals (41 cases)
0- 9	6.0	12.2
10- 14	9.0	7.3
15- 19	3.6	7.3
20- 24	7.9	12.2
25- 34	11.5	14.6
35- 44	10.9	19.5
45- 59	16.9	12.2
60- 74	14.0	12.2
75- 89	6.6	2.4
90-104	4.9	---
105-119	4.2	---
120-134	1.8	---
135-149	1.2	---
150-x	.6	---
Letter Grades		
E	15.0	19.5
D	11.5	19.5
C—	22.4	34.1
C	30.9	24.4
C+	11.5	2.4
B	6.0	---
A	1.8	---

The distribution shows an inferiority of the negro women criminals as compared with the negro men criminals, this being similar to results found in comparing white women criminals with white men criminals.

2. *Geographical Concomitants.*

Alpha Scores	Born in Ohio (18 cases)	Born outside Ohio (23 cases)
0- 9	16.6	8.7

10- 14	5.5	8.7
15- 19	16.6	---
20- 24	16.6	8.7
25- 34	---	26.1
35- 44	22.2	17.4
45- 59	---	21.7
60- 74	22.2	4.3
75- 89	---	4.3
90-104	---	---
105-119	---	---
120-134	---	---
135-149	---	---
150-x	---	---
Letter Grades		
E	22.1	17.4
D	33.2	8.7
C—	22.2	43.5
C	22.2	26.0
C+	---	4.3
B	---	---
A	---	---

Such differences as can be noted validly would seem to be in favor of assuming superiority on the part of the individuals born outside Ohio as compared with those born in the state of Ohio. This assumption, if made, would be in agreement with previous findings concerning criminals.

3. *Types of Crime.*

The total list of crimes consists of Carrying Concealed Weapons 1, Cutting or Shooting 4, Larceny 7, Manslaughter 6, Murder Second Degree 4, Pocket Picking 8, Robbery 9, Delinquency 2. It will be recalled that this list of crimes is quite different from the list of crimes reported for the 85 cases of white women criminals in the same prison. The very small percentage of sex crimes is especially striking as compared with the high percentage of such crimes among the white criminals. Negro women criminals do not vary very markedly from negro men criminals in kinds of crimes committed, while women criminals do vary very strikingly from white men criminals in types of crime committed. It would be absurd to entertain the idea that negro women as a result are consequently more virtuous than white women. Too many other factors seem more probable. The economic inducement may be almost entirely lacking or there may be a lack of prosecutors or plaintiffs in the case of negro women. Where moral indignation is dormant, plaintiffs are scarce.

Practically all of the above offenses can be listed as crimes against property and as physical injury crimes. These two groups if distributed in terms of Alpha scores give the following results:

Alpha Scores	Property Crimes (24 cases)	Physical Injury Crimes (14 cases)
0- 9	12.5	7.1
10- 14	4.1	7.1
15- 19	8.3	7.1
20- 24	16.6	7.1
25- 34	8.3	28.6
35- 44	20.8	14.3
45- 59	12.5	14.3
60- 74	16.6	7.1
75- 89	---	7.1
90-104	---	---
105-119	---	---
120-134	---	---
135-149	---	---
150-x	---	---
Letter Grades		
E	16.6	14.2
D	24.9	14.2
C—	29.1	42.9
C	29.1	21.4
C+	---	7.1
B	---	---
A	---	---

These two groups do not differ obviously in distribution of Alpha scores more than might be anticipated because of the fewness of the cases.

4. *Comparative Chronological Age.*

These negro women criminals differ markedly from the white women criminals in the same prison in distribution of chronological ages reported.

Age in Years	Negro Women Criminals (41 cases)	White Women Criminals in the Same Prison (85 cases)
15-20	12.2	31.7
21-25	36.6	38.8
26-30	36.6	10.6
31-35	7.3	12.9
36-40	---	---
41-50	4.9	5.9
51-x	2.4	---

The small number of very young cases among the negro women as compared with the white women is especially interesting. This is reasonably explained by the almost complete absence of sex crimes among the negro women.

5. *The Chronological Age of Type Groups.*

Age in Years	Property Group (24 cases)	Physical Injury Group (14 cases)	Total (41 cases)
15-20	12.5	14.3	12.2
21-25	37.5	28.5	36.6
26-30	33.4	43.0	36.6
31-35	8.3	7.1	7.3
36-40	---	---	---
41-50	8.3	---	4.9
51-x	---	7.1	2.4

No obvious difference in chronological age of type groups appears observable.

6. *Literacy.*

Years in School	Property Group (24 cases)	Physical Injury Group (14 cases)	Total (41 cases)	Negro Men Criminals (1299 cases)
0- 2	12.5	14.4	14.6	19.1
3- 4	20.8	14.4	19.5	30.7
5- 6	29.1	43.2	31.6	25.6
7- 8	33.3	21.4	29.2	18.1
9-11	4.2	---	2.4	5.1
12-14	---	7.2	2.4	.8
15-16	---	---	---	.6

Tentative Conclusions:

1. Within the limits of the number of cases involved the negro women criminals show a mental test inferiority as compared with negro men criminals.

2. In types of crimes committed the negro women are more similar to negro men than white women criminals are similar to white men criminals. A very small percentage of negro women criminals are imprisoned for sex offenses, this characteristic showing similarity with men criminals and a wide variation from white women criminals.

3. In chronological age negro women criminals tend to be older than white women criminals, the difference being very marked in the lower age levels.

PART VI

Legal Punishment

CHAPTER 34

THE PREVAILING FALLACY OF MATERNALISM

During recent years the idea has become more and more fixed in the minds of those who are appointed by society to deal with matters relating to criminals that it is in some way unethical to punish severely those criminals who are young, or feeble-minded, or insane; and that it is a sign of great cultural development for the State to use the indeterminate sentence in dealing with offenders. This idea in its various branches has grown concomitantly with an alarming increase in crimes committed, at least here in America. As the crime wave attains more and more fearful proportions, there are many who become agitated with fear that the idea is not being applied generously enough. So indifference to law flourishes in the matrix of this fallacy of maternalism.

Is there any reason why young criminals of college age should not receive the death penalty for murder, or a long sentence in the penitentiary for robbery? Approximately one-fourth of all criminals are of this age. Intelligence, as tested by mental tests, does not increase after this age. The average individual has completed his formal education even before this age. The influence of the home has already passed its maximum. The influence of religion has begun to wane. All the methods of love have been tried for all the years of his young life, and have failed. What earthly logic or sense is there for assuming that such an individual is too young to hang or to be sent to prison? All the facts are against the validity of such an assumption. The maternalistic methods having failed already, the logical procedure is swift, sure, and severe punishment.

This maternalism is frequently the result of a distorted and misinterpreted philosophy of determinism. How frequently we hear the plea that a young criminal has never had a chance, that he has been a victim of circumstances, that his behavior has been determined by his environment! A philosophy of determinism, though valid in science, is sheer nonsense in the province of social control when applied only to the individual offender and not also to the community which contains him. If it has been determined by circumstances that an individual commit crime, let it also be determined by circumstances that a social community will strike back with sure and swift punishment. It is quite likely that such circumstances will alter many cases that now clutter our criminal dockets.

This maternalism is also frequently stimulated by unfounded claims made concerning the health condition of the criminal. It is frequently asserted that criminals are sick men. Such assertions appeal to the sympathies of the members of the community. There could be no objection to criminals being classed as sick men, if such claims were not used as bases for reducing guilt and punishment. Logically, punishment should be all the swifter before the sickness spreads.

One of the most pernicious claims of recent years is that criminals of low intelligence should not be punished as severely as others. The reason given is that these people do not have intelligence enough to know any better. That is all the more reason for swift and sure punishment, since such methods alone are capable of being understood by such people. The entire removal from society of such people certainly cannot be criticised on the basis of any principle of social welfare. A maternalistic attitude towards feeble-minded criminals can be defended only in the light of principles that involve the welfare of the feeble-minded alone, and by definition the feeble-minded can never understand such principles. It would be just as useful to formulate such principles for the protection of flies, mosquitoes, snakes, and disease germs.

But the great and crowning glory in the practice of criminal law is the protection offered to the insane, and the methods made available for facilitating proof of insanity. If a criminal is insane, that is all the more reason for extinguishing him from society. He can never be of any service to the State or to himself.

Practically all the literature of the last fifty years in the fields of criminology and penology has fostered the development of this maternalistic fallacy. It is time to call attention to the fact that criminal data do not support the fallacy. Many crime commissions are now before the public. All of them will make reports, retire, and be forgotten. I do not anticipate a single good suggestion from any one of them, for all of them are political commissions. It is suicidal in politics to admit that established democratic institutions are sheer nonsense. That is why I do not expect that any crime commission now before the public will advocate the abolishment of the jury system. Yet that is the first step that must be taken in any sure stamping out of the criminal gangs that infest the country. The average citizen thinks of the jury system as something venerable and precious. The able criminal lawyer thinks of it as something ridiculous and silly, something to be laughed at and jested about. Consult the best lawyer you know on this point.

The indeterminate sentence should be wiped off all our statute books. It is the legalistic offspring of the maternalistic fallacy. Because of it, hundreds of criminals are pushed out of prison every month,—it being a legal method of making room for more indeterminate prisoners. The figures on recidivism do not reveal any virtue in the indeterminate sentence.

There is a distinct spirit of antagonism between the police and the courts, this spirit being fostered chiefly by the system of release on bond and the system of release on probation. These two systems should be wiped out of existence. If a man were forced to stay in jail till his case were decided by the courts, there would be a great speeding up of court procedure. The crowded condition of the dockets may be explained largely by the prodigious amount of legalistic poppycock that is allowed by the law.

No moral or legal principle would be violated if the third penitentiary conviction carried an automatic death penalty. If it is moral to hang a murderer, it is even more moral to hang the habitual robber or burglar.

There will continue to be much talk concerning the causes of crime, but none of that talk will be of assistance in eliminating the criminal thug from society. As long as there are laws, there will be criminals. Practical and effective methods for removing criminals from our midst are well known and at hand. They are:

1. The abolition of the jury system.
2. Uniform punishment for the insane, the feeble-minded, and the young.
3. The abolition of the system of release on bond.
4. The abolition of the indeterminate sentence.
5. The abolition of the parole system.
6. The application of the deterministic philosophy to the behavior of the State as well as to the behavior of the criminal.
7. The third penitentiary conviction to carry an automatic death penalty.